Fighting Foreclosure

LANDMARK LAW CASES

&

AMERICAN SOCIETY

Peter Charles Hoffer
N. E. H. Hull
Series Editors

JOHN A. FLITER AND
DEREK S. HOFF

Fighting Foreclosure

The *Blaisdell* Case, the Contract Clause,

and the Great Depression

UNIVERSITY PRESS OF KANSAS

Published by the University Press of Kansas (Lawrence, Kansas 66045), which was
organized by the Kansas Board of Regents and is operated and funded by Emporia
State University, Fort Hays State University, Kansas State University, Pittsburg State
University, the University of Kansas, and Wichita State University

Library of Congress Cataloging-in-Publication Data

Fliter, John A., 1959–
Fighting foreclosure : the Blaisdell case, the contract clause, and the Great
Depression / John A. Fliter and Derek S. Hoff.
p. cm. — (Landmark law cases and American society)
Includes bibliographical references and index.
ISBN 978-0-7006-1871-2 (cloth : alk. paper)
ISBN 978-0-7006-1872-9 (pbk. : alk. paper)
1. Blaisdell, John H. — Trials, litigation, etc. 2. Blaisdell, Rosella — Trials, litigation,
etc. 3. United States. Constitution — Contract clause. 4. Foreclosure — United States.
5. Mortgage loans — Law and legislation — United States. I. Hoff, Derek S. II. Title.
KF228.B575F55 2012
346.7304'364 — dc23
2012016539

British Library Cataloguing-in-Publication Data is available.

Printed in the United States of America

10 9 8 7 6 5 4 3 2 1

The paper used in this publication is recycled and contains 30 percent postconsumer
waste. It is acid free and meets the minimum requirements of the American National
Standard for Permanence of Paper for Printed Library Materials Z39.48-1992.

CONTENTS

No case in our common law system is ever truly forgotten. Some are negative reference points, like *Plessy* and *Dred Scott*, reminding us of past injustice, while others are iconic landmarks of decency and principle, like *Brown*. *Home Building and Loan Association v. Blaisdell*, a.k.a. the Minnesota mortgage moratorium case, is one not commonly recognized for what it is: the most important property law case of its time, and now of our own. For the question at the heart of the case was the legality of a state-imposed moratorium on the repayment of home loans. In effect, Minnesota was preventing lienholders, usually the first to be paid the debts of an estate in default, from exercising their power to collect on their investments. In the depths of the Depression, when city folk and farm families were losing their households to foreclosure, a progressive majority in the legislature stepped in to give mortgagors extra time to remedy the default. While equity of redemption was an old English legal concept, the Minnesota statute, and the judicial rulings that upheld it, caused a widespread outcry among conservative legal theorists, as well as banking and certain other moneyed interests. It still does.

No one has told this story as well as Fliter and Hoff. Combining the skills of the political scientist and the historian, these two Kansas State University scholars have dug deeply into the records. They have recovered the intimate details of the lives of the parties, brought the politics of the time to life again, and tracked the convoluted tale from the legislature and the governor's office through the state courts to the United States Supreme Court. The early-Depression Supreme Court has often been regarded as a defender of property interests and the enemy of New Deal state and federal economic policy, but in this case the Court found the statute constitutional.

Fliter and Hoff analyze the opinions on a sharply divided Court, making sense of complex legal issues. They do not hide their own views, but so ably do they disentangle the issues, and so well do they root the case in its particular circumstances, that a fair-minded reader will likely find their exposition persuasive. That is true as well of their concluding pages, in which they trace the impact of the case, and the logic of the Court's majority, out into the world. While some scholars and jurists continue to inveigh against the case as a betrayal of the Constitution and private property, here human needs trumped abstract theory. In these days of massive foreclosures and bankruptcies, no case is more relevant than *Blaisdell* and no account more vital reading than this.

ACKNOWLEDGMENTS

This project began a few years ago, during the early months of what is now known as the Great Recession. As the worst mortgage crisis since the Great Depression unfolded, we observed a very different set of politics, economic ideas, and policy responses than those engendered by the 1930s crisis, during which several states passed bold measures along the lines of Minnesota's 1933 foreclosure moratorium. We thought it would be useful to examine these Depression-era state moratorium laws for their own sake, and we were also quite surprised that no full-length study existed of *Home Building and Loan Association v. Blaisdell*, the landmark Supreme Court decision that upheld them. Soon after delving into our research, we realized that we had very rich social, economic, and constitutional stories to tell, and we are grateful to the University Press of Kansas and its Landmark Law Cases and American Society series for an opportunity to share them. We thank University Press of Kansas editor-in-chief Michael Briggs for his enthusiasm and support of the project from the start. We also thank series editor Peter Charles Hoffer for his detailed and insightful comments on the manuscript; the additional reviewer, who identified several flaws and pointed us toward solutions; our production editor, Larisa Martin; and our marketing manager, Susan Schott. Carol Kennedy skillfully transformed a cowritten draft that uneasily incorporated two sets of style conventions — neither of which included correct number and capitalization usage! — into a coherent manuscript.

Several scholars, friends, and family members generously read portions or even all of *Fighting Foreclosure*. We especially thank William Bahr, Virgil Dean, William Grant, Sara Gregg, John Hoff, Daniel Holt, Doug Hurt, Alton Lee, Bonnie Lynn-Sherow, Charles McCurdy, and Spencer Wood. Although the manuscript benefited enormously from the comments of these individuals, errors of fact and interpretation are ours alone.

This book would not have been possible without the assistance of Kansas State University and the support of our respective academic departments and their heads, Jeff Pickering and Louise Breen. We both received University Research Grants to conduct research at the Library of Congress, Minnesota Historical Society, and Minnesota

Law Library, the staffs of which were tremendously helpful and giving of their time. Grants from KSU's Institute for Military History and 20th Century Studies and departmental travel funds greatly aided our research. Derek would like to thank Justice David Minge (his former U.S. representative) for helping him navigate the state's legal records and David Murphy (his college roommate) and Anne for housing him in St. Paul twice. Everyone in the Twin Cities reminded Derek of why he became such a Minnesota-phile in the first place. Several graduate students helped out meaningfully with the research, including David Vail, Wendy Snyder, Daru Zhang, and Kristi Mendenhall, who also valiantly scrambled at the end to help us pore through piles of microfilm. We appreciate the assistance of Philip Freimann of the Blaisdell Family National Association, who provided a useful genealogy of the family, and of Michael Blaisdell, who shared his recollections of family history.

Coauthoring a book, we discovered, takes more than half the time of writing one alone — time spent away from home and family. John thanks his wife, Leah, and their sons, Eric and David, for their unwavering patience and support. In his enthusiasm to share the Blaisdell story with his family, John sometimes had to be reminded by David to just "give us the short version." That was sound advice to us as writers, to remember our audience. Derek thanks Leah for letting him take over her dining room but takes no blame for John's crazy work hours! Most of all, Derek thanks his wife, Jeanine, for her unyielding patience and encouragement and for putting up with the worst work year of his life. He would be lost without her.

John would like to thank his friend and colleague, Derek, whose historical expertise and editing skills vastly improved the manuscript. Although this book was John and Derek's first collaboration, and at times the two were like the odd couple, their respective talents and personalities blended nicely. And working with Derek provided John a deeper appreciation of the historian's craft. Derek, finally, would like to thank John for inviting him onto the project in the first place, for his skillful research and astute formulation of the narrative, for his patience as Derek's other deadlines loomed, and for enduring several all-day, line-by-line editing sessions. No one ever said coauthoring a book is easy, but this one was at least fun.

Introduction

In the 2005 film *Sweetland*, a young German woman named Inge arrives in southern Minnesota in 1920 to marry Olaf, a farmer she has never met but comes to love. The movie's plot centers on the anti-German bigotry and bureaucratic incompetence that prevent the couple from marrying, but the severe post–World War I downturn in American agriculture provides an important backdrop. Olaf's friend Frandsen is way behind on his mortgage, in part because he over-invested in a fancy new tractor, and Olaf must intervene dramatically to save Frandsen's farm. The stoic Olaf is no socialist, but on several occasions he caustically remarks, "Farming and business don't mix."

Olaf's observation was prescient. After a prosperous period just before and during World War I, the American farmer suffered through the 1920s. The Great Depression, beginning after the stock market crash of October 1929, merely downgraded the agricultural economy from perilous to hopeless. Between 1922 and 1932, farmland values decreased by two-thirds, crop prices plummeted to less than half of pre–World War I levels, the percentage of farms run by tenants rather than owners rose, and mortgages secured during better times became nearly impossible to pay. The Farm Credit Administration later reported that, in 1933, "almost one-half of the mortgaged farms in the United States were potentially subject to foreclosures because of inability of their owners to meet interest and tax payments." The mortgage crisis in America's cities was nearly as dire: by January 1934, about one-half of all urban mortgages were delinquent.

As students of American history know well, Franklin D. Roosevelt's New Deal provided immediate emergency aid to millions of desperate Americans, created numerous job programs, greatly expanded the American welfare state, and launched several regulatory programs designed to tame the vagaries of industrial capitalism and promote stable economic growth. To address the mortgage crisis, Congress created the Home Owners' Loan Corporation (HOLC) during FDR's famous first "Hundred Days" of frenetic policymaking. Over the next three years, the HOLC purchased and refinanced over a million delinquent home loans, but it hardly dented the surface of the crisis, especially on the nation's farms. Over 100,000 farms entered foreclosure every year from 1926 to 1940. Throughout the Depression, farmers and their political allies clamored for direct aid to farmers at both the state and federal levels.

Initially, New Dealers tried to "plan" portions of the economy and stimulate recovery by sanctioning cartels in various industries (through the National Recovery Administration) and stabilizing agricultural prices through production controls (through the Agricultural Adjustment Administration). The Supreme Court initially rejected much of the legislation comprising the New Deal, and specifically struck down the NRA in 1935 and the AAA in 1936, but then, after 1937, sanctioned a much greater role for the state in economic policy making and regulation. Ironically, this legal transformation occurred just as the New Deal, and American liberalism more broadly, were moving toward a strategy of primarily promoting economic growth by bolstering purchasing power and encouraging mass consumption rather than intervening on the production side or directly challenging capitalist arrangements. The New Deal also built a liberal coalition that dominated American politics until the 1980s.

Given the seminal economic, political, and constitutional legacies of the New Deal, most studies of this critical period understandably focus on federal policy making. But state governments did not sit idly by as the nation descended into depression. They responded to public pressure for economic assistance and expanded regulation by enacting untried and wide-reaching reforms, many of which, including moratoriums on mortgages, served as experiments for subsequent federal policy making. This book tells the story of one of those moratorium laws—the Minnesota Mortgage Moratorium Act of 1933—and its subsequent place in the remaking of constitutional law in the United States.

Thanks to novelists, a rich photographic record, and Hollywood, the phrase "Great Depression" tends to conjure images of "Hoovervilles" and "Okie" farmers fleeing the Dust Bowl in dilapi-

2

dated trucks. Behind these images lurked the tragedy of millions of foreclosures. Indeed, as miserable as unemployment, meager food, and limited access to health care were, many Americans feared losing the family home above all. In the early 1930s, slightly more than half of Minnesotans lived on family-run farms. But between 50 and 60 percent of those farms were mortgaged, and crop prices had fallen so dramatically that few farmers could earn enough to pay their taxes and mortgages. In urban areas, skyrocketing unemployment led to a surge of mortgage defaults as well. In Minneapolis, the homeless overwhelmed several missions and the Salvation Army's Industrial Home.

Between February 1933 and July 1934, as banks and credit loan associations foreclosed on both rural and urban properties in record numbers, twenty-seven states passed mortgage-moratorium laws intended to increase homeowners' chances of saving their homes and to arrest the downward spiral of economic activity. As might be expected, banks and other financial institutions opposed mortgage-grace-period measures, arguing that they violated the Contract Clause of the U.S. Constitution, which states, "No state shall . . . pass any . . . Law impairing the Obligation of Contracts" (Article I, Section 10). State moratorium laws directly challenged the central principles underlying the Contract Clause: that private property is a natural right and that governments should not interfere with contractual obligations, even during economic emergencies. Initially, state courts overturned many mortgage-relief laws. The constitutional conflict between the need to protect the validity of contracts on the one hand and efforts to protect homeowners and prevent economic collapse on the other — and more immediate conflicts between lenders and borrowers — were resolved in the landmark 1934 United States Supreme Court case of *Home Building and Loan Association v. Blaisdell*, which upheld Minnesota's mortgage-moratorium law.

The story of *Blaisdell* begins with the 1920s farm crisis. After World War I inflated crop prices and land values, midwestern farmers borrowed heavily to expand their operations. When crop prices fell below prewar values, farmers struggled to pay off their debt. Many survived by taking out new loans, including some issued directly by a handful of new state-run lending agencies, including the Minnesota Rural Credit Bureau, but these agencies ran into serious financial problems during the late 1920s. Farm organizations also lobbied for direct federal relief to the farmer during the 1920s, especially price supports that would guarantee the grower a break-even or "cost of production" price. Yet only modest federal programs — loans to rural banks and programs to help sell the nation's agricultural surplus — emerged. After the October 1929 stock market crash, prices for nearly all agricultural commodities plummeted "faster and further than any period in the history of American agriculture," concluded a leading historian of 1930s rural protest. Large crops in the early 1930s only exacerbated the trend. From 1929 to 1932, annual per capita farm income dropped from $945 to $304. President Herbert Hoover's administration was reluctant to intervene in agricultural markets directly, and the congressional farm caucus, not yet the unified juggernaut that it would become by the mid-1930s, lacked the power to secure relief legislation.

Farmers everywhere were desperate, frustrated, and angry, and many turned to direct economic action. Iowa and Minnesota were particular hotbeds of farm protest. In May 1932, several thousand farmers met at the Des Moines, Iowa, fairgrounds and formed the Farmers' Holiday Association. They selected as their president Milo Reno, a radical leader in the National Farmers Union, a well-established organization. During the next year, thousands of midwestern farmers engaged in sporadic "holidays" — collective refusals to bring crops to market. These boycotts did not seriously threaten urban food supplies or raise prices to the cost of production, but farmers had more success stopping foreclosure sales by intimidating sheriffs and lenders. Violence was uncommon, but the threat of it was very powerful.

The ongoing farm foreclosure crisis reached a breaking point in 1933, when prices hit rock bottom. Citizens and policy makers across the political spectrum supported some form of relief for farmers. Iowa became the first state to enact a strong mortgage-moratorium law, in early February. Within a month, six other states had moved to halt or to slow down farm foreclosures, by either executive order or legislative action.

Events in Minnesota climaxed in early 1933, as well. In 1930, Minnesotans had elected Floyd B. Olson their first governor from the Farmer-Labor Party, a left-leaning third party that rose to prominence just after World War I. After the elections of 1932, the Farmer-Labor

Party enjoyed a working majority of the Minnesota Senate and House. In late January 1933, the Farmers' Holiday Association organized a surge of foreclosure stoppages, with more than a thousand farmers participating in some of them. Concerned about potential violence, but also sympathetic to the farmers who elected him, Governor Olson issued an executive order on February 24 imposing a moratorium on mortgage foreclosures until May 1. A week later, the Minnesota legislature passed a temporary measure legalizing Olson's postponement of foreclosures. These stopgap measures, however, did not stem the tide of protests. On March 22, 1933, as many as 3,000 farmers converged on the state capitol building in St. Paul demanding relief and threatening bloodshed in its absence.

As these protests took place, the Minnesota legislature considered several mortgage-relief bills, and the Minnesota Mortgage Moratorium Act passed by a unanimous vote in both chambers on April 18, the last day of the legislative session. The law permitted real property owners, whether farm or residential, urban or rural, to petition a local court for an extension of time in order to meet their obligations. If granted an extension, the petitioner did not pay the contracted mortgage payment but instead paid a fee to the mortgage holder commensurate with his or her budget. The provisions of the law applied to all mortgages, including those entered into prior to enactment of the law. The moratorium was designed to prevent all homeowners from losing their property when they could not meet their mortgage payments. However, pressure from farmers primarily spurred passage of the legislation, and the debate surrounding it focused on providing mortgage assistance to distressed farm families.

John and Rosella Blaisdell, however, did not fit the profile of the rural homeowners the law primarily targeted. They owned a two-story, fourteen-room house not far from downtown Minneapolis, mortgaged to the Home Building and Loan Association, a nonprofit loan cooperative. In early May 1932 (ironically just as the Farmers' Holiday Association was formed), the Home Building and Loan Association foreclosed on the house. Under existing Minnesota law, the Blaisdells had one year to redeem their property by paying the full amount owed. In the interim, Minnesota enacted the moratorium, and the Blaisdells petitioned for an extension under its terms. A Hennepin County district judge denied the request and declared the law unconstitutional. The Minnesota Supreme Court reversed. When the case returned to the district court, the judge granted the Blaisdells a two-year moratorium on mortgage payments, although during this period they were obligated to pay a monthly fee to the Home Building and Loan Association to be applied to taxes, insurance, interest, and the mortgage principal.

The Home Building and Loan Association opposed the extension and appealed on the grounds that the law impaired contracts in violation of the Contract Clause of the U.S. Constitution. After the Minnesota Supreme Court upheld the law in the summer of 1933, the *Blaisdell* case became the first involving economic recovery legislation, state or federal, to reach the U.S. Supreme Court during the Depression. On January 8, 1934, the Supreme Court upheld the Minnesota Mortgage Moratorium Act by a 5–4 decision, finding that it did not violate the Contract Clause.

Chief Justice Charles Evans Hughes wrote the majority opinion. He stressed the temporary, reasonable, and limited nature of the law and the unusual severity of the emergency, concluding that the law was within the reserved "police powers" of the states to protect the security and fundamental interests of the people. Traceable to medieval British common law, the police powers doctrine maintains that democratic governments possess the right and indeed the obligation to intervene in private market transactions when necessary to protect the public's safety, health, and welfare. In a strongly worded dissenting opinion, Justice George Sutherland and the Court's three other conservatives, including one who hailed from Minnesota, argued for a consistent interpretation of the Constitution regardless of economic exigency.

Today, *Home Building and Loan Association v. Blaisdell* remains vitally important to debates concerning the evolution of American constitutional thought, jurisprudence, and the Supreme Court, as well as those concerning the economic and social effects of state regulation. Since 1934, liberal theorists have employed *Blaisdell* and subsequent New Deal precedents to justify increased state intervention in the economy. Conservatives see in *Blaisdell* nothing less than the Magna Carta of a runaway paternalistic state. For instance, constitutional theorist and NYU law professor Richard Epstein recently argued, *"Blaisdell* trumpeted a false liberation from the constitutional text that has paved the way for massive government intervention that undermines the security of private transactions. Today the police power exception has come to eviscerate the contracts clause."

"Eviscerate" may be an overly strong word, but by greatly expanding the legal grounds for state intervention in contracts, *Blaisdell* indeed marked a critical point in the history of Contract Clause jurisprudence. In addition, the *Blaisdell* decision was — and remains — a crucial moment in the debate between those who believe in the doctrine of a malleable or "living" Constitution that rightly evolves in tandem with shifting economic and social conditions and those who stress judicial reliance upon the often-difficult-to-detect "intent" of the framers.

A close study of *Blaisdell*, finally, sheds light on an important historical debate about the existence and timing of a legal "revolution" by which the Supreme Court came to accept the New Deal's economic interventions. According to the traditional interpretation, the Supreme Court in 1935 and 1936 had rebuffed Roosevelt's programs, which sparked FDR's proposal to increase the number of Supreme Court justices, a failed reform derided as his "court-packing plan." Then, in 1937, in a "switch in time that saves nine," centrist Justice Owen Roberts joined the four liberal-leaning justices in *West Coast Hotel v. Parrish*, which upheld Washington State's minimum-wage law, and *NLRB v. Jones and Laughlin Steel*, which allowed Congress to regulate local labor conditions under its Commerce Clause power. (The Constitution stipulates that Congress may regulate "commerce between the states," more commonly referred to as interstate commerce.) As legal scholar Morton Horwitz put it, for example, these decisions constituted a decisive break with "a structure of legal thought that had crystallized over more than a century since the American Revolution." According to the traditionalists, the Revolution of 1937 was complete after subsequent deaths and retirements allowed FDR to appoint several justices sympathetic to the New Deal.

Although we do not downplay the significance of the 1937 decisions, we do join a growing group of scholars who believe that the Supreme Court lit the fires of revolution well before 1937. Along with another key 1934 decision that followed close on *Blaisdell*'s heels — *Nebbia v. New York*, which upheld a New York State law fixing the price of milk — *Blaisdell* revealed an increasing willingness to uphold state efforts to respond to the Great Depression and augured the Court's complete acceptance of the New Deal in 1937.

This is not to say that *Blaisdell* was intended to be open-ended, to allow the states carte blanche powers over the economy. Chief Justice Hughes upheld the Minnesota Mortgage Moratorium Act because it responded to an economic emergency, was temporary, and left many aspects of the mortgage contract intact. The Hughes Court in fact struck down several debtor-relief laws after *Blaisdell*. Still, these later decisions do not diminish the significance of *Blaisdell* — they simply show that Chief Justice Hughes viewed *Blaisdell* as maintaining some restrictions on state action. By 1941, deference to legislative authority had become the norm on the Court, which, in the context of the states' efforts to combat the Depression, supported economic regulation and weakened the Contract Clause. Thereafter and until the present, notwithstanding a brief revival of Contract Clause jurisprudence in the 1970s, conservative efforts to overturn or limit *Blaisdell* have been unsuccessful.

We hope that this book sheds light on the 1930s agricultural crisis, the evolution of the Contract Clause, and perhaps even the history of Minnesota's fascinating politics. After all, this is the state that elected pro wrestler Jesse "The Body" Ventura governor in 1998 and currently sends to Washington a congressional delegation that includes Keith Ellison, the first Muslim member in the history of the House of Representatives, and Tea Party favorite Michele Bachmann. Above all, we hope to contribute to America's never-ending debate about the appropriate roles that federal and state governments should play in regulating the economy and providing relief to distressed citizens. Several years into the worst housing crisis in the United States since the Great Depression, this debate remains more salient than ever.

CHAPTER I

Origins of the Contract Clause

Constitutional experts have long agreed that the Contract Clause, by protecting contractual obligations and property rights, helped spur the remarkable economic development of antebellum America. In his classic legal treatise *The General Principles of Constitutional Law* (1880), Thomas M. Cooley, chief justice of the Michigan Supreme Court, noted that the Contract Clause had become "one of the most important, as well as one of the most comprehensive, in the Constitution." English political economist Sir Henry Maine wrote of the Contract Clause in 1886 that "there is no more important provision in the whole Constitution" because its principle had "in reality secured full play to the economical forces by which the achievement of cultivating the soil of the North American Continent has been performed." Maine added that the clause "is the bulwark of American individualism against democratic impatience and socialistic fantasy." The clause also was one of the most litigated constitutional provisions in the nineteenth century. In *The Contract Clause of the Constitution* (1938), Benjamin Wright concluded that the clause was the basis for about 40 percent of all cases prior to 1889 that challenged the validity of state economic regulation.

The Contract Clause is part of Article I, Section 10, of the U.S. Constitution, which declares that no state "shall enter into any Treaty, Alliance, or Confederation; grant Letters of Marque and Reprisal; coin Money; emit Bills of Credit; make any Thing but gold and silver Coin a Tender in Payment of Debts; pass any Bill of Attainder, ex post facto Law, or Law impairing the Obligation of Contracts; or grant any Title of Nobility." The phrase "or Law impairing the Obligation of Contracts" is what we refer to as the Contract Clause. A "contract" in the ordinary legal meaning of the term creates a legally binding obligation between two or more parties to do or not to do a particular act. The most basic rule of contract law is that a contract exists when one party makes an offer and the other party accepts it. Most types of contracts can be made either orally or in writing.

The framers of the Constitution recognized that the right to enter into contracts was closely tied to private property rights. Property ownership implies the right to buy, sell, occupy, and lease private property, including land and dwellings. Legally binding contractual relationships are necessary in order for citizens to voluntarily undertake personal and business activities with the confidence that courts will enforce the obligations created thereby. Contract rights are not absolute, however. The state and judges may void contracts that involve fraud, coercion, or duress, and those made by incompetent parties lacking the capacity to carry out the terms of the agreement. Moreover, contracts that involve illegal activities such as gambling or prostitution, or that create a nuisance for a community, may be declared invalid.

Along with prohibitions on ex post facto laws and bills of attainder, which together bar legislatures from declaring an act a crime after the fact or declaring a citizen guilty of a crime without trial and confiscating their property, the Contract Clause was one of several individual-rights-protecting provisions of the Constitution as originally ratified. It was also one of the few provisions that operated directly on the power of the individual states before the adoption of the Fourteenth Amendment in 1868. As we will see later, after adoption of the Fourteenth Amendment, contract law gradually came under the purview of not only the Contract Clause but also that amendment's Due Process Clause, which reads, "nor shall any State deprive any person of life, liberty, or property, without due process of law." Moreover, beginning in 1897, when it forced the states to honor the just-compensation requirement of the Fifth Amendment's Takings Clause ("nor shall private property be taken for public use, without just compensation"), the Supreme Court further pinched the power of the states by applying various provisions of the Bill of Rights to them. (The Bill of Rights, the first ten amendments to the Constitution, adopted in 1791, had applied only to Congress.) This process of "selective incorporation" of the Bill of Rights to the states continues to the present day.

By placing it in Section 10 of Article I, which imposes several restrictions on state authority, the framers clearly intended the Contract Clause to limit the power of a state to interfere with contracts. Combined with the Full Faith and Credit Clause of Article IV, which requires each state to honor the public acts, records, and judicial proceedings of every other state, the Contract Clause provided substantial protection to contract rights. In his *Commentaries on the Constitution* (1833), Supreme Court Justice Joseph Story, a leading conservative legal theorist, described all of the prohibitions on state power found in Article 1, Section 10, as "essential to the establishment of a uniform standard of value in the formation and discharge of contracts." The clause limits the authority of the individual states, not federal authority, and in that sense it helps define the complex system of federalism embodied in the Constitution.

Although the language of the Contract Clause — "No state . . . shall pass any . . . Law impairing the Obligation of Contracts" — suggests a clarity and purpose that would limit interpretive conflict, fractious debate has always surrounded it. Justice Story noted that it would "seem difficult to substitute words more intelligible, or less liable to misconstruction, than these," but he acknowledged that numerous questions surrounding the basic meaning of the clause and the intent of the framers remained unresolved in the decades following ratification of the Constitution. For example, what kind of state action constitutes an "impairment" of contractual obligations? Does the clause apply only to private contracts or also to public ones? Does the prohibition extend solely to retrospective laws impairing the obligation of contracts or to prospective ones as well? Are judicial as well as legislative impairments prohibited by the clause?

Our search for answers to these questions begins with the "Critical Period" of March 1781 to March 1789, the years of the first governing charter of the United States, the Articles of Confederation. In many ways, the Contract Clause and other provisions of Article 1, Section 10, were a reaction to state efforts to help debtors during the economic turmoil of these years. More specifically, several states had enacted debtor-relief legislation and engineered inflation by printing too much money. In *An Economic Interpretation of the Constitution* (1913), historian Charles Beard wrote that "the economic history of the States between the Revolution and the adoption of the Constitution is compressed" in the Constitution's Contract Clause and prohibition on coining money. More specifically, Beard argued that the authors of the Constitution, predominantly elite merchants, landowners, bondholders, and creditors, were motivated primarily by personal financial interests contrary to the interests of farmers and the debtor class. The creation of a stronger national government with limitations on state powers over currency, contracts, and interstate commerce supported the personal financial interests of the framers.

Beard's thesis remains controversial because the framers of the Constitution are often viewed as demigods driven by the ideals of representative democracy, and numerous historians seeking to restore the founders to their pedestal have attacked it. For example, in *We the People: The Economic Origins of the Constitution* (1958), Forrest McDonald identified over three dozen interests represented at the Constitutional Convention—such as those of large states and small states, slaveholders and non-slaveholders, and farmers and merchants. More recently, Robert McGuire's *To Form a More Perfect Union* (2003) applies a multivariate economic model to the roll-call votes of the framers at the convention. McGuire confirms the importance of economic and financial issues in shaping the Constitution but argues that these considerations were not the primary ones motivating the men assembled in Philadelphia in 1787. Other factors, such as the general political philosophy of the delegates, were just as important as economic interests.

Regardless of how one views this debate over the founders' motivations, the economic problems of the Confederation period—and the inability of a weak national government to address them—clearly shaped the subsequent inclusion of the Contract Clause in the U.S. Constitution. The structure of government under the Articles, as the name implies, was a confederation of thirteen sovereign states loosely joined together to form a national government of limited scope and capacity. The federal government consisted of a single branch, the Congress, with equal representation for the states regardless of population. Each state had one vote, and a super majority, nine of thirteen states, was required to pass legislation. No separate executive office or federal judiciary existed. Congress lacked the power to tax and to regulate commerce between the states, and states retained the authority to regulate trade, issue money, and require the use of their currency for payment of debts. Probably the most critical flaw of the

Articles was that amendments required the unanimous consent of all thirteen states — a level of agreement never achieved.

These limitations on federal power contributed to a nationwide economic crisis during the 1780s. Both the national government and the states were burdened with Revolutionary War debt. By the end of the war, Congress had issued about $240 million in Continental currency, known as Continentals, which had depreciated to one-fortieth of their face value as the new government under the Articles of Confederation became effective. Lacking the power to tax under the Articles, Congress had to requisition funds from the states. In the first three years of the Confederation, Congress requested over $10 million, but the states, broke themselves, supplied only $1.5 million. In 1785 and 1786, seven states tried to solve their revenue problems by printing paper money and by allowing debtors to pay their debts with this depreciated paper money and what were often worthless parcels of land.

Rhode Island was the worst offender. In 1786, its government issued over £100,000 in paper money and declared it legal tender for all payment of debts. These actions prompted an exodus of creditors from the state, and many merchants closed their doors to avoid accepting the worthless money. Riotous mobs successfully pressured the legislature to pass a "forcing act" that imposed fines on anyone who refused to accept the currency and even denied alleged violators a trial by jury and right of appeal. The law was challenged by butcher John Weeden, who refused to accept payment in depreciated paper money at face value from a cabinet maker named John Trevett. Weeden's lawyer argued that the legislature could not pass a law "repugnant to the [Rhode Island] Constitution." In *Trevett v. Weeden*, the Rhode Island Superior Court of Judicature did not formally declare the law unconstitutional, claiming it lacked jurisdiction. According to newspaper accounts, however, some of the judges verbally declared the forcing act "to be unconstitutional," and one of them claimed that its phrase "without trial by jury" was "internally repugnant" to the constitution because it was not possible to be tried under the law of the land if denied a trial by jury.

Trevett v. Weeden is an early example of the exercise of judicial review, the power of courts to rule on the constitutionality of legislation and executive actions. In the aftermath, the governor called a special session of the legislature and summoned the justices to explain their reasons for characterizing the act as unconstitutional. Judge David Howell, who spoke for the court, defended judicial review and the independence of the courts. Upset with the exercise of judicial review and attack on legislative supremacy, the legislature considered a motion to unseat the judges, but it failed. The legislature eventually repealed the forcing act, but four of the five judges failed to win reelection to another term on the bench.

Meanwhile, farmers across the nation faced financial hardship during the Critical Period of the 1780s. Many had taken out unmanageably large loans and were burdened with state taxes. Growers demanded governmental assistance, and most states responded by passing a variety of debtor-relief laws that impaired the obligation of private contracts by adjusting the terms of payment. Some of these laws permitted debtors to pay outstanding debts in installments, while "stay" laws authorized moratoriums on debt payments, similar to the moratoriums of the 1930s. The states also passed a variety of bankruptcy laws favoring debtors. Although debtors may have welcomed these relief measures, creditors were outraged over state intrusion into contractual obligations and violation of their property rights. Many historians believe that these state actions were a major factor in calls for a constitutional convention and that the debtor-relief laws weighed on the minds of many delegates assembled in Philadelphia during the summer of 1787.

Indeed, anarchy and mob violence threatened the Confederation. The Commonwealth of Massachusetts exacerbated the financial crisis by imposing high court fees and insisting that citizens pay their taxes with gold and silver, even though there was little such "hard money" in circulation and even less in the hands of farmers. Many farmers lacked the means to pay, while some simply refused, and state judges were quick to confiscate their farms. The stakes were high as farmers and other debtors also faced imprisonment for nonpayment of debts. Dozens of towns across the commonwealth petitioned the legislature for debtor relief and lower court costs. In place of relief, however, the government in Boston urged "patience and frugality."

That response did not sit well with desperate farmers, and political agitation turned violent in August 1786, when Captain Luke Day marched a band of armed debtors to various courthouses to prevent the courts from executing foreclosures. Day and his debtor army succeeded in closing several courts throughout the commonwealth. Over the next few months, Daniel Shays, a former Revolutionary War captain, emerged as the leader of the Massachusetts rebellion. Calling themselves the "Regulators" because they believed it was their duty to regulate (that is, check) tyrannical government, Shays' army of 1,400 men raided a federal arsenal at Springfield in January 1787. Shays' Rebellion was suppressed by the state militia in February, and Daniel Shays fled the state, lost his farm, and never resided again in Massachusetts.

Shays and his men may have lost the battle, but the following year, the Massachusetts legislature passed a moratorium on debts and significantly cut direct taxes. Shays' Rebellion illustrated the economic instability of the times and the weakness of the Confederation Congress. In commenting on the rebellion from his diplomatic post in France, Thomas Jefferson famously remarked that "the tree of liberty must from time to time be refreshed with the blood of patriots and tyrants." Jefferson's response was atypical, however. George Washington expressed the sentiments of most elites when he wrote, "I am mortified beyond expression that in the moment of our acknowledged independence we should by our conduct verify the predictions of our transatlantic foe, and render ourselves ridiculous and contemptible in the eyes of all Europe." Shays' Rebellion convinced many political leaders of the need to call a constitutional convention to amend the Articles of Confederation.

After an initial attempt to assemble state representatives in Annapolis, Maryland, in 1786 failed because only five states sent delegates, a call went out for a meeting in Philadelphia the following summer. Delegates to the Constitutional Convention from twelve states (Rhode Island did not participate) met in Philadelphia in May 1787 to revise the Articles. From the start, however, it was clear the convention would move far beyond mere revision. The delegates first selected George Washington as the presiding officer and decided to meet behind closed doors in order to facilitate fruitful debate. The Virginia delegation, led by James Madison, arrived early and proposed a plan establishing a stronger national government. This "Virginia Plan" became the basis for discussion for the convention's first two months. It included a proposal to give Congress the power "to negative all laws passed by the several States contravening, in the opinion of the national legislature, the articles of union, or any treaties subsisting under the authority of the Union." Delegates initially approved this broad grant of authority to Congress without debate or dissent, but they eliminated it on July 17, and later attempts to include it in the Constitution failed. Instead of a general prohibition on state action, the delegates would ultimately impose more specific constraints on state economic powers in Article 1, Section 10.

As the drafting progressed, Roger Patterson from New Jersey introduced an alternative plan, favored by delegates from smaller, less populated states, allowing the thirteen states to retain much of the sovereignty they enjoyed under the Articles while giving the federal government expanded powers over commerce. The differences between the two plans, especially over the structure of Congress, were eventually resolved by the "Great Compromise," which established the structure of the nation's bicameral legislature.

As we show in a moment, the Contract Clause spurred little debate either when it was first introduced at the Constitutional Convention or during the subsequent state ratifying conventions. The lack of a substantial historical record poses problems for historians and judges alike, especially considering that the opinions in *Home Building and Loan Association v. Blaisdell* refer to the founders' intent and that Justice Sutherland's dissenting opinion argues for a strict adherence to the intent of the framers and fidelity to the original meaning of the clause. The absence of extended discussion over the clause could imply consensus among the framers, but the scant historical record also invites various interpretations over the meaning and scope of the text.

Late in the deliberations, the Constitutional Convention delegates began work on the language that would become Article 1, Section 10. They first adopted a specific prohibition on state power to coin money, issue bills of credit, or accept for legal tender of debts anything other than gold or silver. On August 28, Rufus King of Massachusetts, according to James Madison's notes, "moved to add, in the words used in the Ordinance of Cong[res]s establishing new States, a prohibition on the States to interfere with private contracts." King was referring to Article II of the Northwest Ordinance of 1787, which declared that "no law ought ever to be made or have force in the said territory that shall, in any manner whatever, interfere with or affect private contracts, or engagements bona fide, and without fraud previously performed."

Although King was simply borrowing language from a law recently passed by Congress, two delegates immediately raised objections and complained that the provision too broadly restricted state power. Gouverneur Morris of Pennsylvania claimed that the proposed language regarding contracts "would be going too far" given the presence already of "a thousand laws relating to bringing actions — limitations of actions and which affect contracts." George Mason of Virginia cautioned that some situations would inevitably demand state interference, and he mentioned the existence of statutes of limitations as an example of appropriate state intervention. (Statutes of limitation establish a deadline for filing lawsuits over a contractual obligation.) Mason warned that the proposed prohibition on interference would be "carrying the restraint too far. Cases will happen that can not be forseen, where some kind of interference will be proper, & essential." James Madison admitted that inconveniences might arise from such a prohibition, but he still supported King's provision. Madison believed that a "negative on the State laws," in the form of a congressional veto, was sufficient to secure the desired effect of restricting state violations of property rights. James Wilson, a prominent Pennsylvania attorney and orator, also supported King's motion; he responded to the objections by asserting that only "retrospective interferences will be prohibited." Madison then asked if that was not already done by the prohibition of ex post facto laws, which he believed, incorrectly, applied to both criminal and civil cases.

Madison's views prevailed, and John Rutledge of South Carolina moved to replace King's original motion with one prohibiting the states from passing bills of attainder or retrospective laws. Rutledge's amendment was approved by a vote of seven states to three. The following day, after consulting Blackstone's *Commentaries on the Laws of England*, John Dickinson of Delaware corrected Madison's error about retrospective and ex post facto laws; the prohibition against making something illegal after the fact applied only to criminal cases, and thus Rutledge's provision would not prevent the states from passing retrospective laws in civil cases. Nonetheless, the draft was sent to the Committee of Style on September 8 without any revisions. Near the end of the convention, Elbridge Gerry from Massachusetts moved to extend the ex post facto provision to civil cases, but his motion was defeated.

On September 12, the Committee of Style returned a working draft of the Constitution. It is here, with language that prohibited the states from passing laws "altering or impairing the obligation of contracts," that the Contract Clause makes its first appearance. Notably, the word "private" had been deleted from Rufus King's original motion. Two days later an amendment striking out the word "altering" was passed, and the Contract Clause as we know it entered the text of the proposed Constitution.

Madison's notes from the convention indicate that on September 14, Elbridge Gerry spoke on the importance of public faith and the propriety of putting restraints on states to prevent them from impairing the obligation of contracts. A motion made by Gerry to put Congress under the same restriction was not seconded; the delegates were weary of excessively restricting Congress. To this day, the Contract Clause does not limit congressional power, although the Fifth Amendment's Takings Clause prohibits the federal government from taking private property for public use without just compensation. On September 17, the delegates completed their work, signed the document, presented it to the public, and went to a local tavern to celebrate. Fifty-five delegates were present at various times throughout the months of the convention. At the end, forty-two were present and thirty-nine signed the Constitution. George Mason, Edmund Randolph, and Elbridge Gerry refused to sign.

From the limited discussion at the convention, we may conclude that the framers intended the Contract Clause to apply only to retrospective laws. A ban on retrospective laws prevents the states from changing the terms of existing contracts but does not preclude legislation that affects future contracts. Yet this conclusion does not get us very far in understanding the intent surrounding the clause. Even confirming whether the clause was designed to protect only private contracts is difficult. After all, the word "private" from King's original motion was subsequently deleted. The scope of the clause depends on how one defines contracts, contractual obligations, and impairment. The lack of extended discussion and explanation at the convention promoted the ambiguity and conflicting interpretations surrounding the clause.

The framers made two strategic decisions to enhance the Constitution's prospects for ratification. First, they determined that the document would be sent to state ratifying conventions, newly chosen by voters, rather than to state legislatures. The framers believed that this approach would improve the chances of approval because the legislatures were wary of surrendering power to the proposed new government. Second, and more importantly, they decided that the Constitution would become effective when three-fourths (nine) of the states ratified. The unanimous consent requirement under the Articles had been a fatal flaw because at least one state, usually Rhode Island, objected to any changes. On December 7, 1787, Delaware became the first state to ratify the new Constitution, and by early January 1788, four additional states had approved it.

Opposition began to build in other state conventions, however. The opponents of the Constitution, called Anti-Federalists, favored states' rights, the addition of a Bill of Rights as protection for individual liberty, and "republican," small-scale representative government. (Republicanism was a theory of democracy that harked back to ancient Greece and Rome and deemed a virtuous, public-oriented citizenry a necessity.) Federalist and Anti-Federalist arguments during the ratification debate ("Federalists" here describes supporters of the Constitution; the Federalist Party was a separate entity born in the 1790s), public commentary, and the actions by state legislatures and courts in the years following ratification reveal diverse interpretations of the Contract Clause. Varying opinions were influenced not only by the language of the clause but also by different views on America's mixed federal system of governance and the proper role of the state in protecting property rights.

One interpretation of the Contract Clause prevalent during the ratification discussion linked it closely to the other prohibitive monetary provisions in Article 1, Section 10. This view seems reasonable in light of the unpopular relief measures enacted by the states during the Confederation period. At the North Carolina ratifying convention, delegate William Maclaine connected the clause to the prohibition against states coining money.

Others asked whether the clause applied to contracts made by state governments as well as to private contracts. Public contracts included those entered into with individuals or businesses to provide services and infrastructure, land grants, corporate charters, state-sanctioned monopolies, and licenses. At the Virginia convention, Patrick Henry, a staunch opponent of the Constitution, argued that the clause "includes public contracts, as well as private contracts between individuals." But Governor Edmund Randolph, a participant at both the federal and Virginia conventions, stated that he was "still a warm friend of the prohibition, because it must be promotive of virtue and justice, and preventive of injustice and fraud." He insisted that the clause applied only to "private contracts." James Galloway, a Scottish immigrant and critic of the Constitution, asked at the North Carolina ratifying convention whether the Constitution would force North Carolina to pay off depreciated state-issued securities in hard money at face value. William Davie, a Revolutionary War veteran and lawyer from North Carolina who attended the federal convention, responded that the clause only limited state authority to interfere in "contracts between individuals." He assured Galloway that the general government would not be able to interfere with state securities.

As the ratification debate raged, James Madison, Alexander Hamilton, and John Jay wrote a series of essays for newspapers in New York and Virginia encouraging citizens to vote for pro-Constitution delegates to the state ratifying conventions. Hamilton chose the pen name "Publius" for all of these essays, a reference to Publius Valerius Publicola, a Roman consul and one of the founders of the Roman Republic. Madison and Hamilton penned the bulk of the essays while Jay, who did not attend the federal convention but had served as a diplomat for the Confederation government, wrote just five essays, mostly dealing with foreign relations. These eighty-five essays are collectively known as the *Federalist Papers*, and they provide an excellent description and defense of the proposed government under the Constitution.

The only direct commentary on the Contract Clause in the *Federalist Papers* comes in Madison's *Federalist No. 44*, published January 25, 1788. Here Madison argues that the "sober people" of America were "weary" of state legislative intrusions in "cases affecting personal rights." He singles out for criticism installment laws that allowed debtors to make payments over a period of months rather than all at once. Madison writes that "laws impairing the obligation of contracts, are contrary to the first principles of the social compact and to every principle of sound legislation. . . . Very properly, therefore, have the

Convention added this constitutional bulwark in favor of personal security and private rights." Madison warns that "one legislative interference is but the first link of a long chain of repetitions"; that is, if the Constitution were to give the states an inch in regulating contracts, they would take a mile. Madison's comments provide natural-rights justification for the Contract Clause but do little to explain the scope of the provision. Alexander Hamilton offers the only other reference to contracts in the *Federalist Papers* in *No.* 7. Here he notes that state laws threatening "private contracts" would be a source of tensions between the states, but he does not refer directly to the Contract Clause.

The records of the state ratifying conventions and letters, pamphlets, and speeches offer additional commentary about the clause. In a speech before the Maryland legislature subsequently published as an Anti-Federalist pamphlet, Luther Martin, delegate to the Constitutional Convention, warned that the Constitution threatened Maryland's existing solvency laws. Martin voted against the Contract Clause because he wanted the states to have the power to pass debtor-relief laws in extreme circumstances, and he believed that the clause would prohibit that kind of action. Martin said:

> I considered, Sir, that there might be times of such great public calamities and distress, and of such extreme scarcity of species, as should render it the duty of a government, for the preservation of even the most valuable part of its citizens, in some measure to interfere in their favor by passing laws totally or partially stopping the courts of justice, or authorizing the debtor to pay by installments or by delivering up his property to his creditors at a reasonable and honest valuation. The times have been such as to render regulations of this kind necessary in most or all the States, to prevent the wealthy creditor and the moneyed man from totally destroying the poor though even industrious debtor. Such times may again arrive. I therefore voted against depriving the States of this power, a power which I am decided they ought to possess, but which, I admit, ought only to be exercised on very important and urgent occasions.

Another Anti-Federalist, publishing under the pen name "Deliberator," was all too aware of the scope of the clause. He warned that under the Constitution "no state can give relief to insolvent debtors, however distressing their situation may be; since Congress will have the exclusive right of establishing uniform laws on the subject of bankruptcies throughout the United States; and the particular states are expressly prohibited from passing any law impairing the obligation of contracts."

Other writers enthusiastically supported the Contract Clause. In the *New Hampshire Spy*, one advocate of the Constitution recommended the new form of government to his fellow citizens by calling attention to the provision. This New Hampshirite wrote, "It also expressly prohibits those destructive laws in the several states which alter or impair the obligation of contracts; so that in future anyone may be certain of an exact fulfilment of any contract that may be entered into or the penalty that may be stipulated in case of failure." Another pro-Constitution voice emphasized the protection of existing contracts: "My countrymen, the devil is among you. Make paper as much as you please. Make it a tender in all *future* contracts, or let it rest on its own credit—but remember that *past* contracts are sacred things—and that legislatures have no right to interfere with them—they have no right to say, a debt shall be paid at a discount, or in any manner which the parties never intended." In a letter to the governor of Connecticut, Roger Sherman and Oliver Ellsworth, members of Connecticut's delegation to the Constitutional Convention, wrote that the "restraint on the legislatures of the several states respecting emitting bills of credit, making anything but money a tender for payment of debts, or impairing the obligation of contracts by *ex post facto* laws, was thought necessary as a security to commerce, in which the interests of foreigners, as well as the citizens of the different states may be affected." Speaking before the Pennsylvania state convention, James Wilson, one of the most influential delegates at the Constitutional Convention, insisted that the Constitution proscribed not only debt-installment laws but also "other acts of a similar effect."

At the New York ratifying convention, delegates debated the proposed Constitution paragraph by paragraph. They briefly disputed the definition of "impair" in the Contract Clause. Samuel Jones, a lawyer from Queens County, suggested that the word was of "doubtful signification." Alexander Hamilton noted that "impair" is an English word that means to weaken or injure. Jones conceded the word's

English origins but wondered how far that definition extended. Despite his reservations, Jones ultimately voted in favor of the Constitution.

Although he did not single out the Contract Clause, James Madison defended the need for federal power over state legislation in an October 1787 letter to Thomas Jefferson. Madison explained the importance of the federal courts in connection with the restrictions laid down in the Constitution on laws affecting private rights. He wrote:

> The mutability of the laws of the States is found to be a serious evil. The injustice of them has been so frequent and so flagrant as to alarm the most steadfast friends of Republicanism. I am persuaded I do not err in saying that the evils issuing from these sources contributed more to that uneasiness which produced the Convention, and prepared the public mind for a general reform, than those which accrued to our national character and interest from the inadequacy of the Confederation to its immediate objects. A reform, therefore, which does not make provision for private rights must be materially defective.

The Federalists' pro-Constitution arguments ultimately prevailed. New Hampshire provided the ninth affirmative vote, putting the Constitution into effect on June 21, 1788. Virginia and New York, arguably the two most powerful states, ratified within the next month.

Scholars generally conclude that the Contract Clause represented a victory for the creditor class over debtors. But even in the years following ratification of the Constitution, opinion diverged on its meaning and potential impact. Under the most expansive interpretation, the clause prohibits all state-level impairments of private and public contracts, including any state laws enacted before ratification. Moreover, the federal power to pass bankruptcy laws is exclusive — states have no powers here, and the Constitution gives broad authority to Congress to regulate interstate commerce. The most ardent Federalists argued this position. A contrary interpretation, advocated often by those who favored states' rights, asserted that the clause restricts particular kinds of state intervention in private contracts, such as installment laws, but still allows the states to intervene in economic affairs.

During the ratification debates, some Anti-Federalists acknowledged that the Contract Clause would prohibit debtor-relief laws, but they held that the states could and should pass such legislation before the Constitution became effective. In a 1788 essay, "Tullius" urged the South Carolina legislature to pass a debt-installment law, but no action was taken before ratification. In November 1788, however, the South Carolina legislature did enact a law that made all debts contracted before January 1, 1787, payable in five annual installments beginning in March 1789. Many Federalists believed that this law was strictly prohibited by the Constitution. Those who supported the measure, including a few Federalists, claimed that the Constitution did not limit state authority until the new government was established and that any law passed prior to March 4, 1789, the date the new government became effective under the Constitution, would not be affected by the Contract Clause. This issue was not resolved until 1820, when the Supreme Court decided *Owings v. Speed*, a case involving a Contract Clause challenge to a land grant made by the Virginia legislature in 1788. Here the Court affirmed the constitutionality of laws adopted before the new government took power.

No single interpretation of the Contract Clause dominated during the first twenty-five years under the Constitution. In the 1790s, two lower federal courts used the clause to strike down state laws as impairments of contracts. Reported widely in newspapers in June 1792, *Champion v. Casey* was the first case in which a federal court held a state act an unconstitutional violation of the Contract Clause. Rhode Island merchant Silas Casey had experienced a series of financial hardships in the 1780s, and he petitioned the Rhode Island General Assembly for relief. The assembly passed a stay law, postponing by three years the time for Casey to pay his creditors. Although no official record appears on the docket, newspapers reported that a unanimous circuit court for the district, presided over by U.S. Chief Justice John Jay, ruled that the stay law impaired the obligation of contracts contrary to Article I, Section 10. In another circuit court decision, *Van Horne's Lessee v. Dorrance* (1795), U.S. Justice William Patterson, an influential participant at the Constitutional Convention, declared that a Pennsylvania statute that divested one person of property and vested it with another without compensation violated the Contract Clause. Justice Patterson's words that "the preservation of property . . . is a primary object of the social compact" are often cited by contemporary conservatives and libertarians in their defense of property rights. Besides these cases, federal courts (including the Supreme Court) did not hand down major decisions concerning the clause until the early nineteenth century.

It was the state legislatures that took the lead in giving meaning to the clause. Between 1789 and 1815, eleven of eighteen states had laws impairing the obligation of contracts. Some of these laws had been on the books prior to ratification of the Constitution, while others were enacted following the establishment of the new federal government. Vermont, Rhode Island, Connecticut, New York, Maryland, and South Carolina all had bankruptcy laws on the books during this period, and New Jersey, Pennsylvania, and North Carolina had insolvency laws. Vermont and Virginia had stay laws in effect during the entire twenty-six years, and Rhode Island, Pennsylvania, North Carolina, and Georgia had stay laws in place for at least a few years during this time. South Carolina was the only state to have an installment law on the books from 1789 to 1793. Massachusetts and New Hampshire were the only states among the original thirteen not to have any of the three types of debtor-relief laws in force after ratification of the Constitution. Rather than enacting general bankruptcy laws, a few states preferred to grant bankruptcy by special petition. Maryland tried a general bankruptcy law during the year preceding ratification but switched to bankruptcy by special petition. Between 1789 and 1805, almost 1,500 Maryland debtors had their obligations discharged before the state again adopted a general bankruptcy statute in 1805, and this law continued in force until 1854.

What are we to make of all these state laws in the Early Republic that effectively impaired the obligation of contracts? To begin with, they reflected the failure of Congress to confront economic issues. Congress was given the authority to create a uniform system of bankruptcy laws under Article 1, Section 8, but it did not enact such a law until 1800, and the statute was repealed in 1803. Congress would not enact a bankruptcy law that survived for a meaningful period of time until 1898. In the absence of federal legislation, states filled the void with their own laws, just as they had done under the Articles. Also, state governments during the Early Republic vigorously defended their sovereignty despite — indeed, in part because of — ratification of the

Constitution. Overall, an absolute sanctity of contracts free from state debtor-relief legislation, which many Anti-Federalists had feared and Federalists favored, did not come to fruition during the early years of the republic. Still, state legislatures enacted fewer impairments on contracts than they had during the Confederation period.

Some state debtor-relief laws enacted between 1789 and 1815 were struck down by state and federal courts as violations of the Contract Clause and the intent of the framers. Other state courts upheld the laws by making a distinction between the substantive obligation of a contract, which was protected by the clause, and the remedies available for enforcing the obligation, which the states could regulate. For example, a state could alter the maximum amount of time one had to redeem (pay in full) one's mortgage, or alter the process of foreclosure, as long as it did not change the basic obligation of the debtor to the creditor. This right/remedy distinction buttressed one of the arguments used by Chief Justice Hughes in his first draft of the majority opinion in *Blaisdell*.

This early period of Contract Clause jurisprudence, dominated by state courts and legislatures, ended in the early 1800s. Under Chief Justice John Marshall, the U.S. Supreme Court, exercising its new power of judicial review, would substantially broaden the contractual protections of the Contract Clause.

CHAPTER 2

The Supreme Court and the Contract Clause Prior to *Blaisdell*

Under Chief Justice John Marshall, who led the body from 1801 to 1835, the Supreme Court played a major role in shaping the early prevailing interpretation of the Contract Clause. To borrow a phrase from legal scholar James Ely Jr., the Marshall Court "fashioned the Contract Clause into a muscular restraint on state authority." Chief Justice Marshall was a committed Federalist who promoted the protection of private property and viewed governmental intervention in the marketplace with suspicion. He believed that the federal government should be the primary forum for economic policy making in order to establish a more uniform commercial republic. His decisions favored a broad interpretation of contracts protected under the clause, and this pro-contract doctrine helped fuel the rapid economic development of the United States in the first half of the nineteenth century.

In the first Contract Clause case to reach the Supreme Court, *Fletcher v. Peck* (1810), the Court ruled that a grant of land by a legislature, even though it was tarnished by corruption, was a valid contract. In 1795, the Georgia legislature, induced by bribery, had granted the large Yazoo tract of land, which covered much of present-day Alabama and Mississippi, to four private land companies for a price that amounted to one and one-half cents per acre. With only a single exception, every legislator voting for the measure sold his vote for money or for shares of stock in the companies, and several federal officials also participated in the fraud. Outraged over the spurious land transfer, the citizens of Georgia elected a new legislature, which, in 1796, rescinded the sale.

In the meantime, however, the companies had sold the land at great profit to speculators and settlers. Many of the buyers were from New England and supposedly had no knowledge of the fraud. John Peck, a land speculator from Boston, purchased 600,000 acres of Yazoo land from James Gunn, one of the original buyers. An investor from New Hampshire named Robert Fletcher then purchased 15,000 acres from Peck. Evidence suggests that the two men agreed to test the constitutionality of the Georgia law that repealed the legislature's original land sale, and, consequently, Fletcher sued Peck for recovery of the purchase price. Fletcher argued that Peck could not convey valid title and thus was liable for breach of contract. The Court faced a quandary: if the state legislature were denied the power to rescind the original contract based on an obvious fraud, the public would suffer. If, however, state legislatures were given unlimited power to revoke public grants, the public would lose trust in government contracts.

In *Fletcher v. Peck*, the Court struck down the law rescinding the grant of land by relying on the literal reading of the Contract Clause rather than trying to decipher the intent of the framers. Writing for the Court, Chief Justice Marshall argued that the term "contracts" in the Constitution is not limited to those between private persons but is sufficiently broad to include contracts with the state. The second state law, negating the first, thereby impaired the obligation of contract between the state and the land companies. Marshall wrote:

> But if an act be done under a law, a succeeding legislature cannot undo it. The past cannot be recalled by the most absolute power. . . . Conveyances have been made; those conveyances have vested legal estates. . . . When, then, a law is in its nature a contract, when absolute rights have vested under the contract, a repeal of the law cannot divest those rights. . . . A law annulling conveyances between individuals, and declaring that the grantor should stand seized of their former estates, not withstanding those grants, would be as repugnant to the Constitution as a law discharging the vendors of property from the obligation of executing their contracts by conveyances.

Fletcher v. Peck was one of the earliest Supreme Court decisions that voided a state law on the grounds that it conflicted with a specific constitutional provision. Although he acknowledged that the original transactions were based on bribery and corruption, Marshall concluded that such problems were beyond the power of the Court to rectify because the law was legitimately enacted. Marshall wrote: "[But

if] the title be plainly deduced from a legislative act, which the legislature might constitutionally pass, if the law be clothed with all of the
requisite forms of a law, a court . . . cannot sustain a suit . . . founded
on the allegation that the act is a nullity, in consequence of the impure
motives which influenced certain members of the legislature which
passed the law." According to the Court's holding, the Constitution
prohibits the states from impairing the obligation of any contract,
even those that undermine the public welfare. The decision contributed to the certainty of land titles during a period of rapid west-
ward migration, and it made the Contract Clause an important constitutional provision in protecting property rights during the
nineteenth century.

In *New Jersey v. Wilson* (1812), the Marshall Court reinforced the
principle that the Contract Clause prohibits state legislatures from
repealing laws that establish contractual obligations. In 1758, the colonial legislature of New Jersey settled land claims with the Delaware
Indians by granting the tribe a tract of land. The grant included an
exemption from taxation. When members of the tribe moved to New
York in 1801, they sold their land. Three years later, the New Jersey
legislature imposed state taxes on the property. The new owners of
the land challenged the tax as a violation of the contract in the original 1758 land grant.

Writing for a unanimous Court, Chief Justice John Marshall ruled
in favor of the new landowners, concluding that the repeal of the tax
exemption impaired the original obligation under the 1758 contract.
He noted that the state could have limited the tax exemption to the
period when the land belonged to the Delaware tribe, but because the
state had placed no conditions on the exemption, the tax exemption
passed with title to the land.

The reach of the Contract Clause was further extended in *Dartmouth College v. Woodward* (1819), in which the Marshall Court determined that a corporate charter was a contract that states could not
abrogate. In 1769, Dartmouth College, originally a charity school for
Native Americans, was created as a private corporation by charter of
the colonial governor in the name of King George III. The grant was
made to twelve private trustees, who became Dartmouth's governing
body. Subsequently, the trustees and John Wheelock, the second president of the college, had a falling-out. The trustees fired Wheelock.

The major political parties in New Hampshire became involved in the dispute, with the Federalists backing the trustees and the Democratic-Republicans supporting Wheelock. In 1816, the state legislature, dominated by Democratic-Republicans, passed three laws effectively making Dartmouth a public university. The new administration ousted the old trustees and the faculty who supported them and reinstated Wheelock. The old trustees sued William Woodward, the secretary of the college, to recover their corporate property, and Daniel Webster, the famous orator and future U.S. senator and secretary of state, argued their case before the Supreme Court. Webster's four-hour oration is said to have brought tears to many of those present.

In *Dartmouth College*, the Court ruled that the grant of a corporate charter by the Crown was a valid contract protected by Article I, Section 10, of the Constitution. The contract was made for valuable consideration because the institution was a benefit to the public, and the donors, trustees, and Crown were the original parties. It was a "contract for the security and disposition of property." Although, according to the Court, the contract was not necessarily of the type that the framers had in mind when they wrote the Constitution, it was within the literal meaning of the Contract Clause; therefore, it was to be regarded as within the scope of that clause unless it produced an absurd result, contrary to the spirit of the document. The Court ruled that the 1816 laws taking over the college impaired the obligation of the contract because "the will of the state had been substituted for the will of the donors, in every essential operation of the college."

Dartmouth College was a clear victory for Daniel Webster and the original board of trustees. Moreover, by protecting the sanctity of corporate charters at a time when corporations were still legally fragile, the decision reassured investors in corporate securities, promoted commercial development, and helped stabilize the raucous capitalism of antebellum America. The decision also furthered the Federalist objective of expanding national power at the expense of the states, although Justice Joseph Story's concurring opinion acknowledged that states have the power to include within their charters and contracts provisions reserving the right to amend and repeal them. On that advice, states began inserting reservation clauses in corporate charters, thus weakening the impact of the *Dartmouth College* decision.

The Marshall Court insisted upon a robust Contract Clause in its first decisions regarding bankruptcy law. In *Sturges v. Crowninshield* (1819), the Court determined that a state bankruptcy law was unconstitutional with respect to contracts made prior to its enactment. (*Sturges*, however, is also noteworthy because it recognized a distinction between the obligation of a contract and the remedy given by a legislature to enforce the obligation – the right/remedy distinction later used by those who sought to soften the prohibitions of the clause.) In the same term, *McMillan v. McNeill* invalidated state bankruptcy laws as they applied to future contracts. *Sturges* and *McMillan* effectively denied the states the authority to pass bankruptcy laws.

In its waning years, the Marshall Court treated bankruptcy laws helping debtors more sympathetically, thus chipping away at the Contract Clause's barriers to state regulation. Reversing the *McMillan* precedent, *Ogden v. Saunders* (1827) upheld state bankruptcy interventions as long as they applied to future contracts (those made after the law was enacted). Now the High Court held that once a state passed a bankruptcy law, transactions following enactment of the law could not be challenged under the Contract Clause because the law was part of the existing contractual environment. The majority decision, written by Justice William Johnson, reflected the original understanding of the Contract Clause that it applied only to retrospective obligations.

Chief Justice Marshall opposed this weakening of the Contract Clause. In his first dissenting opinion in twenty-six years on the Court, he wrote that "the power of changing the relative situation of debtor and creditor, of interfering with contracts . . . had been used to such an excess by the State legislatures . . . as to destroy all confidence between man and man." Marshall noted that during the Confederation period, the "mischief had become so great, so alarming, as not only to impair commercial intercourse, and threaten the existence of credit, but to sap the morals of the people, and destroy the sanctity of private faith," and that prevention of this "evil" was one of the "most important benefits expected from a reform of the government."

The death of John Marshall in 1835, and the appointments to the Court made by Democratic president Andrew Jackson, brought significant changes in the interpretation of the Contract Clause. Jackson and his new chief justice, Roger B. Taney, were more sympathetic to policies that favored states' rights and community interests rather than federal power and commercial monopolies. Although the Taney Court maintained a strict application of the Contract Clause with respect to most contract rights, it acknowledged that contracts could be impeded under state police powers in situations where the public welfare demanded action.

The doctrine of state police powers stretches back into medieval England, and, for over two hundred years, American scholars and judges have struggled to define it precisely. The concept of state police powers can be confusing because the phrase is not found in the Constitution, it has little in common with modern notions of a municipal police force, and, in the American context, a "state" police power is often exercised by local governments. The matter is further muddied by the prevalent but incorrect assumption that the national government enjoys a police power! In *Gibbons v. Ogden* (1824), Chief Justice John Marshall referred to the police powers of the states as "that immense mass of legislation, which embraces every thing within the territory of a State, not surrendered to the general government." In the *License Cases* (1847), Chief Justice Roger Taney defined the phrase as "nothing more or less than the powers of government inherent in every sovereignty to the extent of its dominions." At bottom, the phrase "state police power" refers to the long-accepted general authority of a government to regulate for the health, safety, morals, and welfare of its citizens.

Because it is a government with specifically delegated powers, the federal government does not have a general police power. Federal legislation must be based on an enumerated, an implied, or an inherent power. Since the late 1800s, however, Congress often has approximated the police powers by using its control over the postal service, its taxing authority, and especially its power to regulate commerce between the states to address social evils such as lotteries, sexual trafficking, child labor, and racial discrimination. When people and objects cross state lines, they may be regulated as aspects of interstate commerce. For example, under Title II of the Civil Rights Act of 1964, Congress prohibited discrimination based on race, color, religion, or national origin by privately owned businesses that serve the public, such as hotels and restaurants, because such discrimination impedes the flow of commerce between the states.

The individual American states, however, unambiguously possessed general police powers prior to adoption of the federal Constitution. And, under the Constitution, states retain their police powers to pass laws for the general welfare without any specific grant of authority. State police powers are protected by the Tenth Amendment to the Constitution, which reads, "The powers not delegated to the United States by the Constitution, nor prohibited by it to the states, are reserved to the States respectively, or to the people." State legislatures exercise police power by passing laws in such areas as crime, land use, infrastructure, lotteries, discrimination, licensing of professionals, nuisances, schools, and sanitation.

State legislatures delegated police powers to local governments, as well. As described by William Novak in *The People's Welfare: Law and Regulation in Nineteenth-Century America*, municipal ordinances as well as state laws regulated vast areas of daily life during the nation's first century. State and local governments, however, can use the police power to enact laws promoting the general welfare only if the laws do not violate provisions in the U.S. Constitution, including the Contract Clause.

The Taney Court's first opportunity to reconsider the Contract Clause came in the case of *Proprietors of Charles River Bridge v. Proprietors of Warren Bridge* (1837), which narrowed the vested rights protected by a corporate charter and thereby limited the protections of the clause. In 1785, Massachusetts had incorporated the Charles River Bridge Company. The charter allowed the company to charge tolls on its bridge for forty years, later extended to seventy years. As the years passed, bridge traffic exploded, and the legislature responded in 1828 by granting a charter to a new firm, the Warren Bridge Company, to build a state-of-the-art span about 100 yards from the Charles River Bridge. The Warren Bridge would be operated on a toll basis for six years and then be transferred to the state (and made toll-free) when paid for. The owners of the Charles River Bridge sued to stop construction of the new bridge. They claimed that their corporate charter gave them the exclusive right to maintain a bridge in that area of the Charles River and that eventually their income would be destroyed by the new bridge because of its ultimate toll-free status. They never would have built their bridge if they had known that the state would later grant a charter for a nearby toll-free bridge. The plaintiffs maintained that the law authorizing the Warren Bridge violated the Contract Clause.

The Marshall Court had heard the dispute originally in 1831, but the Court divided and was unable to resolve the case before Chief Justice Marshall's death in 1835. The case was reargued in January 1837 with Marshall's successor, Roger Taney, presiding. Ruling in favor of the Warren Bridge Company, Chief Justice Taney's majority opinion cited the principle that when the public makes a grant, "nothing passes by implication." In other words, the original charter contained no implied prohibition against a toll-free bridge. No provision prohibited others from building a bridge nearby, and the state made no specific commitment in this regard. The Court referred to the police power of the state when it observed, "The object and end of all government is to promote the happiness and prosperity of the community by which it is established. . . . A state ought never to be presumed to surrender this power. . . . The continued existence of government would be of no great value, if by implications and presumptions . . . the functions that it was designed to perform were transferred to the hands of privileged corporations." Taney refused to read into the corporate charter an implied limitation on the state's police power. In reviewing the extensive history of state support for internal improvements such as turnpikes, canals, and other infrastructure, the Court noted that the case under review was the first in which an implied contract had been claimed. The absence of any claim suggests individuals and corporations never expected that one could be implied from their charters.

In a dissenting opinion, Justice Story argued that three centuries of law and practice, English and American, favored a broad interpretation of the charter in favor of the Charles River Bridge Company. He located an implied agreement that the state would not grant another bridge so close to the Charles River Bridge in the common law doctrine that "where the thing is given, the incidents, without which it cannot be enjoyed, are also given." If the legislature does not mean to grant any exclusive rights, Story suggested, let it say so expressly in the terms of the charter.

The decision in *Charles River Bridge* established the principle that corporate charters granted by a state were to be construed strictly; powers were not to pass to grantees by implication from terms in the charter. The decision was consistent with the Taney Court's goal of defending the states' police powers and community interests, but its implications for the Contract Clause were ambiguous. Jacksonian Democrats praised the decision for establishing "the great republican principle that a grant is not a monopoly or a vested right" but did not believe that the Court had eroded core contractual rights. Representing the views of Whigs and former Federalists, however, Daniel Webster contended that the decision overturned the Contract Clause and threatened private property (although it is more likely that Taney's opinion promoted innovation and unleashed economic activity). Despondent over the outcome, Justice Story perceived that the "old law" of the Contract Clause, the one forged by the Marshall Court, was slipping away. The Taney justices, however, did not abandon the Marshall Court's insistence on a strong Contract Clause. Instead, the Court struck down state laws that clearly impaired contractual rights.

One constant in the history of the Contract Clause is that each successive period of economic crisis (the panics of 1819 and 1837, the Civil War, the panics of 1873, 1893, and 1907, and the recession immediately following World War I) produced new relief efforts by the states that directly challenged the prohibition on contractual impairments. The states passed every type of debtor-relief law imaginable. But, as University of Minnesota law professor William Prosser noted just after *Blaisdell*, more than two hundred state court decisions and about twenty U.S. Supreme Court decisions revealed that, until the 1930s, the Contract Clause "withstood the attack."

In *Bronson v. Kinzie* (1843), for example, the Taney Court invalidated Illinois laws that expanded the rights of debtors. The facts in *Bronson* presaged those in *Blaisdell*. In response to the Panic of 1837, but without declaring an emergency, the Illinois legislature passed two laws that placed restrictions on mortgage debt and extended the period of time during which owners could repurchase foreclosed properties. These measures were retroactive, applying to mortgages made before the acts were passed. Writing for a 6–1 majority, Chief Justice Taney determined that the attempt to modify the terms of the existing mortgage unconstitutionally impaired the obligation of contracts. Taney acknowledged that a state could alter the remedies available to enforce past as well as future contracts but nonetheless emphasized that such changes could not materially impair the rights of creditors. Taney declared, "Any such modification of a contract by subsequent legislation against the consent of one of the parties, unquestionably impairs its obligation and is prohibited by the Constitution." In broad language, Taney extolled the virtues of the Contract Clause: "It was undoubtedly adopted as a part of the Constitution for a great and useful purpose. It was to maintain the integrity of contracts, and to secure their faithful execution throughout this Union." One year later, in *McCracken v. Hayward* (1844), the Court reviewed the same law with the same result. The rule established in *Bronson* with respect to mortgage-relief legislation would remain in effect for ninety years, until the *Blaisdell* decision.

Every remedy proposed in the Minnesota legislature in 1933 in response to the mortgage crisis of the Great Depression had at one point been held unconstitutional by state or federal courts. Examples included closing the courts, postponing foreclosure sales, requiring a minimum sale price, altering interest rates, and creating various exemptions. In *Gantly's Lessee v. Ewing* (1845), the U.S. Supreme Court invalidated an Indiana statute, as applied to existing mortgages, that stipulated that no real property could be sold on execution (foreclosure sale) for less than half its appraised value. In *Howard v. Bugbee* (1860), the Court overturned an Alabama law authorizing redemption of mortgaged property within two years after the sale. (The typical redemption period was one year or less.) In *Edwards v. Kearzy* (1877), the Court negated a North Carolina statute that increased a debtor's exemptions. The Supreme Court of North Carolina had upheld the law because of the desperate financial situation of the people following the Civil War. In overturning the law, the U.S. Supreme Court ruled that the constitutional prohibition on contractual impairments contained no qualification and that none could be inserted by the courts. Finally, in *Barnitz v. Beverly* (1895), the Court declared unconstitutional a Kansas statute extending the period of redemption for eighteen months and allowing a homeowner to remain in possession and take rents. All of these precedents assumed a forceful Contract Clause, and the Home Building and Loan Association would use them to challenge the Minnesota mortgage moratorium.

Although the courts generally struck down moratoriums both before and after the Civil War, they did, after 1880, move toward an interpretation of the Contract Clause that gave states more authority to exercise their police powers. In *Stone v. Mississippi* (1880), the Supreme Court, citing a state's inalienable police power, upheld a provision of Mississippi's constitution that prohibited lotteries, even though a previous state charter had granted permission to a company to operate a lottery. More specifically, after the Civil War, the provisional state government gave the Mississippi Agricultural, Educational, and Manufacturing Aid Society the authority to operate a lottery in Mississippi for twenty-five years. In return, the society paid an initial sum to the state, yearly payments, plus a tax on receipts. In 1868, a new state constitution explicitly outlawed lotteries. Years later, the state attorney general filed charges against John Stone and other members of the society for operating the lottery. Mississippi admitted that the lottery company was working within the terms of its original charter but claimed that the new constitution and subsequent legislation revoked the grant. Stone responded that he possessed vested property rights under the original charter and that the Contract Clause explicitly prohibited the state from nullifying the provisions of the charter. The Court had to decide if Mississippi bound itself irrevocably by contract to permit a lottery.

In a unanimous decision, the Court found that a legislature cannot bargain away the police power of a state. Writing for the Court, Chief Justice Morrison Waite determined that no legislature can curtail the power of its successors to make such laws as they deem proper in matters of police powers. "The power of governing," he wrote, "is a trust committed by the people to the government, no part of which can be granted away." The police power extends to all matters affecting the public health and morals, and, Waite noted, few would deny that lotteries are the proper subject of this power. The Court concluded by stating that the Constitution protects contracts between private parties, not government contracts. Anyone who accepts a lottery charter does so with the implied understanding that the people, through their sovereign government, may resume it at any time or may rescind the privilege granted. The Court emphasized that the Contract Clause allows states broad authority to regulate civil institutions when the public interest is threatened.

The Supreme Court also made it easier to regulate private contracts—so long as they encroached on the public welfare. In *Manigault v. Springs* (1905), the Court upheld a South Carolina statute that, in authorizing a dam to drain lowlands, abrogated a private contract allowing unimpeded passage up a creek. Alfred Springs had constructed a dam across a creek near the Santee River. Arthur Manigault opposed the dam because it interfered with his right of passage and forced him to raise the levees on his property. After long negotiations, the parties signed a contract whereby the dam was removed. The agreement settled the conflict until 1903, when the state legislature, claiming the necessity of draining the lowlands on the Santee River to protect the public health, authorized the dam. Asserting that a private contract cannot limit the state's control over public waterways, the Court declared that the police power is "paramount to any rights under contracts between individuals."

Other decisions affirmed the primacy of the police powers over contracts. *Hudson County Water Co. v. McCarter* (1908) upheld a New Jersey law that made illegal the performance of a contract to export water from the state. "A state has a constitutional power," the Court argued, "to insist that its natural advantages remain unimpaired by its citizens," and an illegal contract, such as one for diverting water from the state, "is not within the protection of the contract clause of the Constitution." In *Union Dry Goods Co. v. Georgia Public Service Corporation* (1919), the Court upheld the alteration of a rate contract between a power company and consumers. In cases involving both public and private contracts, the Contract Clause was not an impediment to a state's exercise of the police power in the public interest. Of course, deciding whether a law was in the public interest or had a public benefit was often a matter of heated political debate as well as judicial interpretation.

Following the *Stone v. Mississippi* decision and others that limited private contracts under the police powers doctrine, the Supreme Court moved away from a Contract Clause basis for attacking state regulatory laws. As the significance of the Contract Clause diminished, opponents of state economic regulation turned to the Due Process Clause of the Fourteenth Amendment. Originally ratified during Reconstruction to protect the rights of freed slaves, the Fourteenth Amendment's Due Process Clause declares that a state cannot deny any person "life, liberty, or property without due process of law." A similarly worded provision is found in the Fifth Amendment, which applies to the national government. Another important body of law surrounds the Fourteenth Amendment's Equal Protection Clause, which reads that no state shall "deny to any person within its jurisdiction the equal protection of the laws." The Equal Protection Clause entered Contract Clause jurisprudence when property owners claimed that debtor-relief legislation made distinctions among classes of citizens – and therefore violated their equal protection rights.

Prior to the adoption of the Fourteenth Amendment in 1868, judges interpreted the due process guarantees in the Fifth Amendment and in state constitutions as procedural limitations on government power. Due process meant that people were "entitled" to fair and orderly proceedings, especially in criminal cases, where a citizen's life or liberty is at stake. This concept is known as procedural due process. Under procedural due process, a government can deny citizens life, liberty, or property as long as it provides fair and proper procedures.

After the adoption of the Fourteenth Amendment, lawyers representing business interests opposed to growing state regulation began to emphasize substantive due process arguments, which focus on the *reasonableness* of regulatory laws themselves, not on whether proper procedure was used in enacting them. If a court determined that a state regulation of property rights was unreasonable, arbitrary, or "class legislation" that discriminated between citizens, the court could declare a violation of the Fourteenth Amendment. Substantive due process arguments were heavily influenced by an 1868 legal treatise entitled *Constitutional Limitations*, by Thomas Cooley. Cooley emphasized limits on legislative authority in order to protect personal liberty and private property. The protection of liberty, Cooley argued, required a substantive due process interpretation of the Fourteenth Amendment.

Although substantive due process ideas have pre–Civil War roots, a new emphasis on them emerged in the late nineteenth century. State supreme courts were initially more receptive to substantive due process arguments than the Supreme Court, but the latter gradually accepted the doctrine. Most scholars trace the origin of substantive due process in Supreme Court jurisprudence to Justice Stephen Field's dissenting opinion in the *Slaughterhouse Cases* (1873), in which he argued that the Fourteenth Amendment protected "the right to pursue lawful employment in a lawful manner, without other restraint than such as equally affects all persons." In a separate dissenting opinion in the same case, Justice Joseph Bradley wrote, "I hold that the liberty of pursuit — the right to follow any of the ordinary callings of life — is one of the privileges of a citizen of the United States."

The Supreme Court used the substantive due process framework to strike down a state law for the first time in *Allgeyer v. Louisiana* (1897). *Allgeyer* concerned a Louisiana statute that barred its citizens and corporations from doing business with insurance firms in other states. A unanimous Court found that the law unfairly abridged the right to enter into lawful contracts, as guaranteed by the Due Process Clause of the Fourteenth Amendment. Associate Justice Rufus Peckham wrote for the Court:

> The "liberty" mentioned in [the Fourteenth] amendment means not only the right of the citizen to be free from the mere physical restraint of his person, as by incarceration, but the term is deemed to embrace the right of the citizen to be free in the enjoyment of all his faculties, to be free to use them in all lawful ways, to live and work where he will, to earn his livelihood by any lawful calling, to pursue any livelihood or avocation, and for that purpose to enter into all contracts which may be proper, necessary, and essential to his carrying out to a successful conclusion the purposes above mentioned.

Peckham's language announced an important shift. After *Allgeyer*, the Supreme Court increasingly identified a "liberty of contract" residing in the Fourteenth Amendment's Due Process Clause and turned this amendment into a tool for proponents of laissez-faire seeking to protect business interests. A doctrine of substantive *economic* due process emerged that used the notion of a liberty of contract to challenge laws governing the relationship between employer and employee, especially in the arenas of minimum wage, maximum hours, workers' compensation, and unionization. Some regulation of labor would survive the Gilded Age's battles between capital and labor, but state and federal courts used substantive due process to overturn protective labor legislation (laws mandating particular working conditions for women and children) and many other economic regulations.

To a certain degree, the judicial emphasis on protecting private property and preserving the freedom of contract in the late nineteenth century reflected the post–Civil War triumph of corporate capitalism and the concomitant spread of laissez-faire ideology. It also reflected the evolution from procedural to substantive due process. Yet pro-contract philosophies have deep roots in the United States and were hallmarks of classical legal thought, the body of ideas that dominated jurisprudence for much of the nineteenth century. Classical legal thought was based on the conservative worldview that the United States had preserved individual freedom because it relied on a "self-regulating, competitive market economy presided over by a neutral, impartial, and decentralized state." Building on the ideas of Adam Smith, John Stuart Mill, and other "classical economists" of the eighteenth and nineteenth centuries, and shrugging off the substantial role played by the federal and state governments in both subsidizing and regulating the economy, classical legal thought assumed that markets distribute rewards based on one's initiative and that a limited state should protect property rights but not engage in regulation or redistribution. In the classical legal tradition, law and judges should both serve as neutral arbiters in defining private rights and responsibilities. When not guided specifically by constitutions or statutes, a judge is responsible for "finding the law" in existing precedents, traditions, and natural rights such as those to life, liberty, and property. The development of liberty of contract jurisprudence seamlessly emerged from this classical tradition.

As classical legal thought hardened after the Civil War, some legal scholars began questioning it. Increased urbanization, immigration, and industrialization spawned extremes of wealth and poverty and excessive concentration in several industries (and accelerated dramatic changes in social relations, the family, and work under way since the Industrial Revolution). The resulting social and economic conflicts, the starkest of which pitted a burgeoning labor movement against captains of industry, led many theorists to question whether the state and judges could be, as the ideal assumed, objective arbiters of rights. By the early twentieth century, an amorphous but powerful progressive movement had organized to harness the state in the service of social welfare. The progressives' agenda included improving working conditions and limiting work hours.

The progressives also took direct aim at the classical legal tradition. They believed that the law and courts of the era were far from neutral; rather, they promoted a pro-business agenda infused with laissez-faire principles. In particular, progressives argued, the courts had come under the sway of Social Darwinism, an influential doctrine on both sides of the Atlantic in the late nineteenth century that opposed government efforts to protect the weak and saw society as a Darwinian struggle for the "survival of the fittest." Vigilant courts guarding against "class legislation" served only business interests because employers and employees did not bargain from equal positions.

The battle between liberty of contract doctrine and progressive challenges to classical legal thought came to a head in *Lochner v. New York* (1905), one of the most famous and controversial substantive due process cases. In *Lochner*, the U.S. Supreme Court invalidated a provision of the 1895 New York Bakeshop Act, a law passed unanimously. This act contained six provisions. The five that addressed sanitation in bakeries to ensure "unadulterated bread" received little attention; the only controversial section was the one that limited the number of hours that someone could work in a "biscuit, bread or cake bakery" to ten hours a day or sixty hours a week. Before the Supreme Court, New York justified the law by arguing that the police powers gave the state the right to regulate working conditions and to protect workers and consumers from sickness. Joseph Lochner, owner of a tenement bakery, argued that employees and employers have a right to agree on wages and hours and that state regulation of such violates the Fourteenth Amendment. A majority of the justices agreed with Lochner, concluding that the law violated his liberty of contract because it lacked a reasonable relation to public health, safety, or welfare. Wholesome bread, the Court claimed, does not depend on bakers' working hours.

For the past several decades, scholars have debated the extent to which the courts upheld regulatory and protective legislation before and after *Lochner*. They also have debated whether we should see *Lochner* as a culmination of the Gilded Age courts' conservative, pro-contract bent, a decision consistent with pre–Civil War jurisprudence, or a decisive break that set the courts down a new conservative path until the 1930s. Recently, several historians have shown that turn-of-the-century courts were not the uniform tools of big business, as many earlier accounts implied. In addition, the heyday of substantive due process actually came more than a decade after the decision, during the "roaring twenties." From 1920 to 1926, a conservative Supreme Court, led by Chief Justice Howard Taft, overturned more social and economic legislation on due process grounds than it had during the previous fifty years. Nonetheless, there is little question that a powerful strand of pro-contract thought surged through the American political economy as the nation entered the twentieth century.

For our purposes, what is most important about the *Lochner*-era cases is that they increasingly turned on due process and liberty of contract arguments rather than on the Contract Clause. The emphasis in the courts had moved from questions surrounding the enforcement of existing contracts (and state attempts to modify entire categories of contracts, such as through mortgage moratoriums) to questions surrounding the rights of individuals to enter into contracts unrestrained by the state.

Today, Justice Oliver Wendell Holmes's dissent in *Lochner* stands as an iconic critique of classical legal thought and substantive due process liberty of contract doctrine. A Civil War hero, Holmes served on the Supreme Judicial Court of Massachusetts for twenty years before his appointment to the U.S. Supreme Court in 1902. He then served thirty years on the nation's highest court. However, his major work in legal thought occurred before these judicial appointments. In the opening paragraph to his most famous book, *The Common Law* (1881), Holmes challenged prevailing legal thought by declaring: "The life of the law has not been logic, it has been experience. The felt necessities of the time, the prevalent moral and political theories, intuitions of public policy, avowed or unconscious, even the prejudices which judges share with their fellow-men, have had a good deal more to do than the syllogism in determining the rules by which men should be governed." In his *Lochner* dissent, Holmes concluded: "A Constitution is not intended to embody a particular economic theory, whether of paternalism and the organic relation of the citizen to the State, or of *laissez faire*. It is made for people of fundamentally differing views, and the accident of [judges] finding certain opinions natural and familiar or novel and even shocking ought not to conclude our judgment upon the question whether statutes embodying them conflict with the Constitution of the United States."

Holmes's dissent made him a favorite among progressive reformers, and future New Deal liberals would use his rhetoric to defend state intervention in the market. His reputation as a progressive, however, was based on his willingness to allow legislatures to enact laws according to "dominant opinion," without judicial intervention, even if the laws threatened to "take the country to hell." He was actually more of a skeptic than a true believer in progressive reforms. In cases involving economic regulation, Holmes's preference for judicial restraint made him look progressive; in situations where governments restricted civil rights and liberties, however, his method occasionally led to reactionary outcomes. His deferential approach to legislative authority is reflected in his dissent in *Adkins v. Children's Hospital* (1923), in which the Court used substantive due process to strike down a minimum wage law for women in the District of Columbia. Holmes wrote, "When so many intelligent persons, who have studied the matter more than any of us can, have thought that the means are effective and are worth the price, it seems to me impossible to deny that the belief [is held by] reasonable men." Although it is sometimes difficult to characterize legislative debate as rational, Holmes's preference for deference would eventually become accepted doctrine during the 1930s as federal and state legislatures enacted innovative relief measures to fight the Great Depression.

After its period of quiescence in the *Lochner* era, the Contract Clause reemerged in national legal discussion in the 1920s. The most important precedents for the moratorium jurisprudence of the 1930s were those collectively known as the *Rent Cases*. In *Marcus Brown Holding Company v. Feldman* (1921), *Block v. Hirsh* (1921), and *Levy Leasing Co. v. Siegel* (1922), the Supreme Court upheld New York State and Washington, D.C., rent-control laws. Enacted to alleviate a critical housing shortage resulting from increased migration to cities and the return of World War I veterans, these laws deprived landlords of immediate possession of their rental properties upon expiration of a lease, provided the holdover tenants paid a "reasonable" monthly rent. In New York City alone, pending court proceedings could have dispossessed over 100,000 families. In upholding the rent-control laws, Justice Oliver Wendell Holmes stressed the "public health" consideration created by the temporary emergency in housing stemming from the end of World War I. He argued that the laws were a valid exercise of the police power to protect the public interest, and he dismissed the Contract Clause argument against such regulation by insisting that "contracts are made subject to this exercise of the power of the state when otherwise justified."

The *Rent Cases* also solidified a previously vague principle known as the emergency powers doctrine. The emergency powers and police power rationales are closely related defenses of state action to protect the common good. Emergencies often provide a pretext for the exercise of the police power, and lawyers often conflate the emergency and police powers. But the two theories are distinct. The emergency powers doctrine assumes that valid state action is only temporary, lasting the duration of the emergency, whereas the police powers are general and ongoing. In addition, whereas there is no federal police power, emergency powers are assumed for both the federal government and the individual states.

In support of an emergency powers rationale in the *Rent Cases*, Holmes cited *Wilson v. New* (1917), in which the Court sustained hour and wage legislation covering railroad workers. In *Wilson*, the Court emphasized an immediate threat to interstate commerce — thousands of railroad workers had recently struck — and the temporary nature of the legislation. Although the Constitution contains no emergency powers clause, the executive branch has invoked the emergency powers doctrine throughout the nation's history, most famously during the Civil War, when President Lincoln curtailed individual liberty substantially. In the *Wilson v. New* proceedings, the railroads pointed out that Lincoln's declaration of martial law and use of military tribunals to try civilians were declared unconstitutional in *Ex Parte Milligan* (1866). Chief Justice Edward White's majority decision in *Wilson* refused to limit the emergency power. "Although an emergency may not call into life a power which has never lived, nevertheless emergency may afford a reason for the exertion of a living power already enjoyed," White wrote. Holmes applied those arguments to the *Rent Cases*. In his dissent in the *Rent Cases*, however, Justice Joseph McKenna argued that the Contract Clause was "paramount" and should not bend "to some impulse or emergency." The emergency powers exception to the Contract Clause would play a critical role in the majority decision in *Blaisdell*.

By the time *Blaisdell* reached the Supreme Court, therefore, the

Contract Clause had been weakened as a protection against state intervention in contractual obligations. During the 1920s, the courts heard only a fraction of the number of Contract Clause cases they had before 1890. The limitations and exceptions to the clause recognized by the Courts were summarized by U.S. Supreme Court Justice Mahlon Pitney, the great-grandfather of *Superman* actor Christopher Reeve, in *Chicago Alton R.R. v. Tranbarger* (1915):

> It is established by repeated decisions of this court that neither of these provisions [the Contract and Due Process clauses) of the Federal Constitution has the effect of overriding the power of the State to establish all regulations reasonably necessary to secure the health, safety, or general welfare of the community; that this power can neither be abdicated nor bargained away, and is inalienable even by express grant; and that all contract and property rights are held subject to its fair exercise.

Still, Contract Clause jurisprudence was unresolved when the Hughes Court confronted numerous constitutional issues. The courts had recognized various limitations on the Contract Clause but also had stricken many debtor-relief laws. And the maturation of the emergency powers doctrine further complicated the discussion. These tensions converged in 1934, when the Supreme Court was called upon to examine the scope of state police power to alter contracts during an economic catastrophe. More specifically, in *Home Building and Loan Association v. Blaisdell*, the Court was called upon to examine the constitutionality of a moratorium on mortgage foreclosures in Minnesota enacted during the depths of the Depression.

CHAPTER 3

"And We Don't Mean Maybe"

Farmers Demand a Holiday

The Minnesota farmers who responded to the Depression with direct economic action and political lobbying could not have imagined that the mortgage moratorium they secured would alter the nation's constitutional history. Like many policy innovations in the United States, the Minnesota Mortgage Moratorium Act was the product of long-term political and intellectual trends and a short-term crisis that opened a narrow window for decisive reform.

Since the heyday of the Populist Movement in the 1890s, Minnesota had nurtured not only agrarian radicalism but also mainstream, moderate progressivism. After World War I, third parties enjoyed an easier time of breaking the two-party logjam in the upper Midwest than in other regions of the country. In 1918, during a period of rapid growth for the Left, the Non-Partisan League, a political party founded by a socialist organizer in North Dakota, captured control of that state's legislature. Subsequently moving the center of politics leftward in neighboring states, the Non-Partisan League had national aspirations and was anything but nonpartisan! In Minnesota, Charles Lindbergh Sr. ran unsuccessfully as the Non-Partisan League's candidate in the 1918 Republican gubernatorial primary. In an effort to bridge a historic divide within the Left, Lindbergh emphasized that he was the candidate of both workers and farmers. Soon thereafter, Minnesota's Farmer-Labor Party was born as a spin-off of the Non-Partisan League.

Until 1944, when it merged with the state's Democratic Party and ceased to exist, the Minnesota Farmer-Labor Party was never less than the second strongest party in Minnesota, but its fortunes were waning in the late 1920s. In 1930, however, Minnesotans elected the self-described "radical" Floyd B. Olson their first Farmer-Labor governor. At this point, conservative Republicans dominated the state legislature (which was still technically elected through nonpartisan races, in which party affiliations did not appear on the ballot), but in 1932, Farmer-Laborites easily reelected Olson, captured a working (if unofficial) majority of the state house and senate, and elected a majority of Minnesota's delegation to the U.S. Congress. The moratorium law was one of several major liberal reforms enacted by the Farmer-Labor Party during the spring 1933 legislative session.

The root cause of the moratorium was the farm crisis that began in the 1920s and worsened during the early years of the Great Depression. Crop prices decreased steadily during the 1920s, in large measure because a short-lived agricultural boom just before and during World War I had induced overinvestment in new land and machines. Farm income in the United States fell by two-thirds from 1920 through 1933.

The long-running agricultural depression hit the corn-and-hog and dairy areas of the upper Midwest especially hard. These areas contained a disproportionally high percentage of the total farm mortgages in the United States, and much of the land was exhausted. Minnesota also suffered because the timber industry had decimated its northeastern "cut-over" lands. Among thousands like him, the father of future U.S. vice president Walter Mondale lost his farm in Minnesota during the 1920s. After the 1929 stock market crash, the bottom fell out. In Minnesota, paying the average debt on a mortgaged farm had required 116 bushels of wheat in 1919 and 173 bushels in 1925; in 1933, it required 743 bushels. With corn bottoming out at 8 to 10 cents a bushel (down from 80 cents in 1929), but costing 92 cents a bushel to produce, some Minnesotans preferred burning it in their stoves to selling it. Cattle garnered as little as 3 cents per pound. The value of all farmland in the state, minus mortgage debt, was nearly $2.3 billion in 1924 but only $900 million in 1933, and farm tenancy increased 30 percent during this period. Net cash income per Minnesota farm fell from $1,640 in 1918 to a low of $87 in 1932.

About half of Minnesota's farms were mortgaged, and, according to the U.S. Census Bureau, the typical farm in Minnesota had mortgage debt of $4,734. The typical interest rate was 5½ percent, leading to an average annual interest payment of $260. Paying loans in nominal dollars as their incomes plummeted, Minnesota farms were foreclosed in 1931, 1932, and 1933 at the rate of thirty-one, forty-two, and sixty-one per thousand respectively. For those who needed it most, new credit was nearly impossible to secure. Minnesota, like many rural states, barely supported its too numerous small-town banks. Moreover, following a trend toward national consolidation, larger Minnesota banks headquartered in the Twin Cities of Minneapolis and St. Paul had pushed into smaller markets during the Great War. By the time of the Depression, rural bank profits were squeezed and credit had dried up. One Minnesota state lawmaker later recalled simply, "There was no money to lend."

The magnitude of this financial crisis spurred fear of social upheaval or even revolution. One constituent wrote Governor Olson in early 1932:

Conditions in St. Paul are just as bad as the Communists describe them. . . . One evening . . . I heard a little child a crying in an alley. Upon investigating the little fellow was laying [sic] up against a brick wall just a crying his heart out because he had to turn his papers in not having sold a one. He had a nice mother and two little sisters 9 and 12. The father was out of work. . . . This family originally came from the farm to the city and got caught when the industrial activity passed out. Conditions in Minneapolis are just as bad, the bunch hanging around bridge square are just dying from slow starvation and keeping pepped up by the art of draining the wood alcohol out of the radiators and drinking it.

After winning reelection in the fall of 1932, Governor Olson said in his second inaugural address:

We are assembled during the most crucial period in the history of the nation and of our state. An army of unemployed; some 200,000 homeless and wandering boys; thousands of abandoned farms; an ever-increasing number of mortgage foreclosures; and thousands of people in want and poverty are evidences not only of an economic depression but of the failure of government and our social system to function in the interests of the common happiness of the people. Just beyond the horizon of these scenes is rampant lawlessness and possible revolution. Only remedial legislation, national and state, can prevent its appearance.

The nation had debated such remedial legislation for more than a decade. During the 1920s, the overriding goal of the farm lobby was to return farm incomes to the level enjoyed during the prosperous but not yet overheated period from 1909 to 1914. Proposed state mechanisms to boost farm income included price controls that would guarantee the farmer the cost of production; mechanisms that would induce artificial scarcity, for example payments to farmers to take land out of rotation and reduce livestock; and programs to sell the surplus abroad.

Although large-scale agricultural subsidies did not emerge prior to the New Deal, federal agricultural loan policy started much earlier, emerging from efforts during prosperous times to modernize the farm sector and lower food costs for American consumers. In 1909, President Theodore Roosevelt's Country Life Commission proposed a credit system for the American farmer modeled on Germany's state-sponsored nonprofit cooperative system, and the three main parties in the election of 1912 each supported some form of federal support for increasing access to rural credits. The 1916 Farm Loan Act created and funded twelve regional federal land banks (backed by the U.S. Treasury and regulated by the Federal Farm Loan Board) that were empowered to loan money to cooperatives of farmers. Hence, the act also provided the mechanism for farmers to form farmer-owned national farm loan associations, essentially loan cooperatives. The Farm Loan Act worked modestly well in normalizing the agricultural market, and in particular promoting the spread of long-term, amortized farm mortgages. By 1932, farmers had borrowed more than $1.6 billion under it.

Nonetheless, as the agricultural crisis deepened in the 1920s, farmers would have preferred direct aid from the government, and the land banks did little to improve aggregate conditions in the sector. Neither did the Agricultural Credits Act of 1923, which, to increase short-term credit, added a layer of intermediate credit banks to the land bank system that lent to agricultural cooperatives and other institutions. President Coolidge ignored the farm lobby in vetoing a plan to market crop surpluses in 1926 and again in 1927. By the stock market crash of October 1929, fewer than 17,000 Americans possessed outstanding loans from the land banks.

New credit agencies created after the Great Depression began generated bureaucratic chaos but also modest relief. The Reconstruction Finance Corporation, President Hoover's primary initiative to combat the economic crisis, established federally backed regional agricultural credit corporations, which bought up loans to allow more lending. Between October 1932 and March 1934, the key time period for our story, the regional corporation serving the upper Midwest, headquartered in Minneapolis, issued 49,800 loans for over $43 million. The 1929 Agricultural Marketing Act provided for additional federal loans to agricultural cooperatives and also created the Federal Farm Board to help store the crop surplus. Although designed to help create cooperatives, the board turned, unsuccessfully, to trying to prop up prices by buying surpluses directly. By 1933, half of the national farm loan associations affiliated with the land banks were failing.

The individual states also intervened to help farmers. Before the stock market crash, at least ten had passed modest measures to improve farmers' access to credit. Commonly, legislatures authorized state investment boards or other agencies to invest in farm mortgages. But three states established more formal state-run and -financed rural-credit systems, capitalizing them through general appropriations and new bond issuances. At the behest of Governor, later U.S. Senator, Peter Norbeck, South Dakota established a rural-credit system in 1917. Most South Dakota newspapers and farm journals supported the law, deeming it progressive rather than radical. Looking back a few years later, the Sioux Falls *Daily Argus Leader* declared that only a few "lone souls" had opposed the rural-credit program or doubted that it would help South Dakotans. During the anticommunist Red Scare immediately following World War I, Governor Norbeck beat back the Non-Partisan League by tagging the group as disloyal while co-opting much of its statist program.

North Dakota enacted a rural-credit law in 1919, soon after the Non-Partisan League had seized control of the state. North Dakota's state rural-credit system was a key part of a brief but remarkable socialist experiment that included a constitutional amendment explicitly giving the state new powers to develop enterprises, such as a state cement factory. To fund these initiatives, the state legislature created the Bank of North Dakota, today the only state-owned bank in the nation.

In 1921, the Minnesota legislature passed a proposed amendment to the state constitution authorizing the state to make agricultural loans. Minnesota voters approved the amendment, and the legislature then enacted a rural-credit law in 1923. Minnesota's state-run rural-credit system was designed to promote farm ownership through cheap, subsidized state loans, set at no more than three-fourths of a percentage point above the interest rate that the state paid to borrow. The Minnesota Rural Credit Bureau could issue loans for up to 60 percent of the appraised value of land and up to 33⅓ percent of the value of improvements. The system was modeled on the federal Farm Loan Act, but, as the chief economist of the federal Farm Credit Administration later noted, "Minnesota thought the Federal Farm Loan Act was too conservative."

These state rural-credit programs provided thousands of loans. But they failed fiscally and thus politically, and frustration with them helped motivate the drive for mortgage moratoriums. Although the severe agricultural crisis of 1920 to 1923 eased slightly in the middle of the decade, most prices never recovered, which stunted the ability of farmers to pay their debts. Overoptimistic assessors served as local boosters more than market analysts and kept assessments and thus taxes too high. By 1926, South Dakota's system had $15 million in delinquent debt, was mired in scandal, and had taken on the burden of managing thousands of foreclosed farm properties. The South Dakota legislature forbade the rural-credit agency from issuing new loans. North Dakota's program suffered a similar fate, losing about half of its $40 million investment, and was burdened with more foreclosed land than it could sell until 1946. Minnesota farmers would have been very aware of the malfunction of these programs in the Dakotas, especially considering that the Non-Partisan League had moved its national headquarters to St. Paul.

Minnesotans primarily turned against their state's Rural Credit Bureau, however, because it had tightened the screws significantly toward the end of the 1920s after defaults far exceeded initial estimates. The bureau made 13,500 loans between 1923 and 1933, but 8,400 of these were made just from 1924 to 1926. In 1928, A. G. Black, of the University of Minnesota and later the U.S. Bureau of Agricultural Economics, noted, "The Minnesota department also made many ill-advised loans during its early history. The present administration is conservative, however, and if current policies are continued, there seems to be slight ground for concern as to the ultimate success of the department." Black erred on the side of optimism. By 1934, the severe agricultural depression left the Rural Credit Bureau almost $7 million in the hole, although the agency's finances were always in question due to its accounting practices. A battle ensued over the Credit Bureau's habit of keeping itself alive by selling rural-credit bonds to the state's Investment Board. Before Olson was elected in 1930, the Investment Board had purchased over $26 million worth of rural-credit bonds, and another $3.2 million from 1930 to 1932, but thereafter the board bristled and refused to continue these purchases, despite pleading by Olson.

Indeed, the Rural Credit Bureau had few allies outside of Governor Olson's office. After the agency instituted stricter loan standards, Minnesota farmers vilified it as much as the mortgage companies, insurance agencies, and banks to which it had originally been designed as an alternative. One farmer wrote the governor, "I put in my application to the Rural Credit Bureau for a loan on my farm, and expected to get the money last fall, and they are holding me off from time to time." Asking the governor about other potential sources for state funds, this farmer concluded, "I want to know at once, so I know if I have to apply to some other place for the money. I don't want to be fooled any longer." Members of the financial community who competed with the bureau found plenty to dislike, as well. The president of a small-town bank wrote Governor Olson in January 1931:

In my forty years experience . . . business has never been in as bad condition except for about six months in 1893 and 1894. . . . In this part of the state nearly all loan companies have discontinued business. The Federal Land Bank takes a loan once in a while, and the Department of Rural Credit makes a loan occasionally. As a result, fully 50% of our farmers cannot borrow one dollar on their farms except from local people. In the past, no doubt, a goodly portion of the troubles of the Department can be laid to the fact that the men in charge have not had proper schooling in that kind of business. As a result, loans have been made which eventually cause trouble for the Department in the form of foreclosures; but this should be no reason why the Department should not take the good loans now. The time is now ripe for this department to step in and do something of great value to the state by taking the good loans that are offered.

In a 1932 pep talk to the department, Governor Olson also disparaged its pre–Olson administration leadership and hinted at corruption. After conceding that the "Rural Credit system was conceived by progressive minded men and women," he lamented, "Unfortunately, the administration of the law was placed in the hands of persons who were not only unsympathetic but who also used it as a means for cleaning up the bad loans of private banks and private lenders. Their flagrant misconduct has contributed materially to placing the Bureau at its present financial disadvantage."

Rural Credit Bureau loans never accounted for more than a small minority of the total loans in the state. In 1935, when Minnesota had 185,000 farms (195,000 if tracts smaller than 5 acres are included), and thus about 95,000 mortgaged farms, a state senator obtained estimates tallying a total of 7,945 outstanding bureau loans. Nonetheless, the state of Minnesota found itself a substantial player in the farming business due to defaulted loans. By 1931, farms that had come under the state's possession numbered 1,785, and it was actively overseeing the planting and harvesting of many it could not rent. Complaints poured in to the governor's office about the mismanagement of these state farms.

Minnesota tried to sell off its farms but of course found this a difficult, if not impossible, task during the Depression. Like many voices, the *Minnesota Tribune* supported eating a smaller loss in the short term rather than a larger loss later. It editorialized that the state's "opportunities for success in the business of state farming are about equal to those of the inexperienced sailor, plumber, or barber or circus performer who invests his money in a business he knows nothing about. So the state hopes to balance the books by taking its loss as gracefully as possible while returning lands it has acquired through defaulted loans, made at a time when values were for the most part inflated, to the tax rolls." Other individuals criticized Governor Olson for trying to sell state-run lands too cheaply. And finally, farmers resented that foreclosed farms were not subject to taxes, according to a Minnesota Supreme Court decision.

As they bemoaned the failure of state-level policies, Minnesota farmers joined a burgeoning chorus of rural Americans who sought a revolution in federal farm policy. The main fault line was between those who wanted to guarantee the farmer the cost of production (essentially the price that allowed farmers to break even, sometimes plus 5 percent profit) and those who wanted to raise prices through production controls, that is, payments to farmers to plant less and raise fewer animals. A majority of farmers sought direct price guarantees, but President Roosevelt and many in his "Brain Trust" believed that this approach entailed excessive intervention in the market. The New Deal's signature agricultural legislation, the Agricultural Adjustment Act of 1933, erected a system of production controls that in large measure still prevails today. The New Deal also initiated several programs designed to help farmers gain access to credit and, as we will see, a partial national moratorium on rural foreclosures in 1935. Although we can never know what would have happened in the absence of federal (and state-level) intervention, most economic historians agree that New Deal farm programs substantially increased farm incomes and saved over 200,000 farms during the 1930s.

Of course, the New Deal and recovery in the farm sector still lay in the future during the crucial period from the stock market crash of 1929 to the spring of 1933, when the Minnesota legislature passed the mortgage moratorium. And regardless, as the Depression deepened, many Minnesota farmers had little patience for traditional policy debates. Emboldened by the success of the Farmer-Labor Party, many determined that, with a sympathetic government on their side, they could push the boundaries of what constituted legal activities on behalf of their cause. They turned to direct economic action to save the family farm.

The primary vehicle of this direct action was a national organization called the Farmers' Holiday Association, formed at the Iowa state fairgrounds in early May 1932 as the unofficial direct-action wing of the National Farmers Union, the most left-leaning and small-grower-oriented of the three largest farm organizations in the country. The driving force and first president of the Farmers' Holiday Association was Milo Reno, the dominant force in the Iowa Farmers Union. Descended from a family of Greenbackers (a nineteenth-century farm protest movement that anticipated the Populists), the "evangelical," "eccentric," and "shaggy-haired" Reno claimed inspiration from Edward Bellamy's famous utopian novel, *Looking Backward*.

Dutch-born Minnesotan John Bosch, previously leader of the Farmers Union in his west-central home county of Kandiyohi, was the first vice president of the National Farmers' Holiday Association. He was elected president of the Minnesota association when it formed in late July 1932 in a high-school gym in the central Minnesota city of St. Cloud. Bosch's devotion and personal sacrifice to the cause prompted one fellow organizer to comment that Bosch lived on "fried snowballs." In the tradition of radical Populists, Bosch advocated direct grassroots political action over traditional interest-group lobbying. "Economic revolt rather than political revolt," Bosch told two individuals from a Chicago-based group called the League for Justice to Agriculture, "offers more hope to the farmer because, when he withholds production, he has something over which he has control. He cannot control a state legislature. . . . Motor cops may police the highway but motor cops won't milk cows." Of course, the farm protest movement also sought new public policies, and Bosch profited from a personal friendship with Governor Olson. The Holiday hoped that withholding goods from the marketplace would force processors to close and ultimately spur the federal government to impose cost-of-production legislation.

During its heyday, the National Farmers' Holiday Association claimed 90,000 members, although it is hard to agree on a precise figure because (as with most grassroots organizations) only a small minority of supporters paid formal dues—in this case, 50 cents. The Minnesota association grew quickly. During the fall of 1932, Bosch canvassed the state, and branches formed in fifty-eight out of Minnesota's eighty-seven counties. Each county would elect a president, and then each township would elect a chair responsible for recruiting members. The Holiday Association's strongholds were in west-central and southwestern Minnesota, the state's wheat belt, where foreclosure rates were highest. For example, 1,400 of Kandiyohi County's 2,500 landowners and renters joined the association.

The Farmers' Holiday Association acted independently but logically tapped into the networks of more established organizations, in the process building an umbrella group that encompassed growers with diverse political views and incomes. In Douglas County, for example, the Holiday worked closely with the Non-Partisan League, the national left-wing organization formed in North Dakota, and with the Farmer-Labor Association, an unofficial arm of the Farmer-Labor Party that served as a bridge between farmer-activists and Minnesota's more mainstream (if still quite liberal) political establishment. Most members of the Holiday Association owned their land—they were not tenants—but they tended to be less prosperous than average. The League for Justice to Agriculture's researchers met with members of the faculty and the dean of the College of Agriculture at the University of Minnesota, who reportedly agreed that "only the poor and inefficient farmers have joined the Farmers' Holiday Movement and it cannot be taken seriously." The Holiday's core constituency was undoubtedly small growers, but many had done relatively well until the Depression; the researchers' comments reflected a bias commonly seen among middle-class, efficiency-obsessed reformers of the era who correctly (and happily) predicted that "bigness" would define the future of American agriculture.

Lawmakers, on the other hand, certainly took the Holiday seriously. In the period immediately after the organization's founding in the summer of 1932, many legislators anticipated that it would fundamentally change the American political economy, even allowing for the anticipated resistance from lenders and large, well-established property owners. The Farmer-Labor Party and Governor Olson immediately expressed support for the Holiday Association. Governor Olson's agricultural commissioner stated, "Surely, if the farmers unite for their common interest, they could control the food of the nation and assure themselves a reasonable profit. . . . Such an organization would become the most powerful in the world—for people must eat." Olson wrote one constituent, "I consider this Association a splendid, militant organization that is doing, and promises to do, considerable to relieve the distress of agriculture." In a letter to Milo Reno, the governor praised the Holiday for doing "a great deal to make the farmer realize the necessity for organization in order to combat the forces which are gradually grinding him down into a condition of serfdom." Olson also proposed combining the thousands of agricultural cooperatives in Minnesota into a state agency, the marketing power of which, in his words, would "assure the success of the farm holiday." Lieutenant Governor Konrad Solberg admonished a group of farmers to "steal one of your mortgaged pigs and sell it" if they did not have 50 cents for membership in the Farmers' Holiday Association. Such high-level support afforded the Holiday necessary breathing room to succeed and may have tipped the scales toward support among many local elites.

A closer look at the declaration of principles from one local Minnesota branch — that in Grant County, a sparsely populated west-central county — provides a window onto the Holiday's amalgamated political economy. Harking back to the previous century's "free labor" and "republican" agrarian ideologies, which emphasized the necessity of owning the fruits of one's own labor, the Grant County group declared, "We believe also that when a group of pioneering people have developed a Country . . . they should be the owners of at least the greatest part of their developments, and the wealth thus created." In proto-Keynesian terms — the consumption-based economics of British economist John Maynard Keynes would not be accepted widely in the United States until the late 1930s — the organization suggested that the Depression was caused by a lack of "buying power caused by the unequal distribution of the wealth and earning power of the people of the country." Hence the group favored price controls rather than production controls (as the New Deal would implement) because "our problem is under-consumption, not over-production." Echoing the late-nineteenth-century Social Gospel movement, the group claimed that "the centralization of wealth in the hands of a few to the detriment of the many, is caused by the Usury system which was condemned by the Great Teacher over 1900 years ago . . . when he drove the Money Changers out of the temple, and was finally crucified; not for his religious teachings alone, but for His denunciation of the money system of those times, and thereby abolishing the Interest system for about 160 years thereafter." And, of course, the Grant County Holiday "condemn[ed] the present system which tolerates the high rates of interest, which is causing farmers and home owners to lose their homes, even though, in many cases, the purchasers and builders . . . have paid for them several times over." Accordingly, the group resolved, "We will pay no interest bearing debts until we obtain cost of production."

Like all local Holidays, the Grant County chapter demanded "an immediate executive Moratorium on Mortgages until same can be refinanced, or otherwise disposed of." Many farmers noted that President Hoover had recently granted Germany a moratorium on its World War I debts and thus asked, as the *Farmer-Labor Leader* reported, "why they, too, should not enjoy a year's recess. The idea has become contagious and Mr. Hoover and American money lenders will have a busy time explaining why millions of farmers and small business men are not entitled to as much as international debtors." Farmer-activists generally saw a moratorium as a concomitant of state-regulated price guarantees that would boost farmers' incomes. The Minnesota Farmer-Labor Party supported this cost-of-production approach, although Governor Olson adopted a more pragmatic and less rigid position than the Farmers' Holiday Association regarding national farm policy. In advance of a September 1932 meeting of midwestern governors to discuss these issues, Olson said, "I would be willing to join with the governors of the other agricultural states in any plan, however arbitrary, which would tend to raise the prices of farm commodities."

Although it lobbied vigorously for public subsidies for the farmer, the Farmers' Holiday movement was and is most famous for its aggressive direct-action activities, which peaked in the winter and spring of 1932–1933. More specifically, the movement urged farmers to conduct boycotts — to collectively withhold goods from the marketplace (hence the euphemistic term "holiday") until prices at least equaled the cost of production. "Restore the farmers' purchasing power and you have re-established an endless chain of prosperity and happiness in this country," Milo Reno claimed. Reno and Bosch had long advocated boycotts, and immediately after it formed, the national association called for a thirty-day national withholding strike. In August 1932, thousands of farmers, especially in Iowa but also in ten other midwestern states, launched a strike "against the low prices paid to them by Big Business middleman," as the newsletter of the National Farmers Union put it.

The strike quickly radicalized. Although Milo Reno had not envisioned anything more drastic than a selling holiday, farmers spontaneously turned to forcibly blocking the transport of agricultural products. Outside of Sioux City, Iowa, a major early battleground, "the picket line of nail-studded belts, iron cables, ropes, rocks and muscles, proved its effectiveness, and prevented all but about 12 of the usual daily caravan of milk trucks, from going through," the national *Farm News Letter* reported. Picketers also dumped milk on the road. According to one historian, "1,500 farmers stationed over five highways virtually blocked all shipments" of agricultural products to Sioux City. Although this strike did increase modestly the prices paid by some middlemen, especially milk dealers, it was not widely popular. The Iowa press tolerated it for a while. Henry A. Wallace, the wealthy editor of a major Iowa-based farm journal who later became Roosevelt's secretary of agriculture and vice president, compared the strike's galvanizing power to the Boston Tea Party, even as he correctly noted that it was largely irrelevant economically and doomed to fail. But mainstream national farm groups, including the Grange and the Farm Bureau, opposed it — the president of the former called for his membership to "back up law and order" and "put an end to the hysteria," and the president of the latter claimed that the strike was "sponsored by a limited group of misguided farmers." Pitched battles between strikers and "wrecking crews" of men organized by sheriffs to clear roads scared average midwesterners. In Cherokee, Iowa, armed strikebreakers fired into a picket line and injured 14 people, and tear gas was used to break up a picket line of 300 farmers near Council Bluffs. In Omaha, the U.S. Attorney General's Office threatened armed federal action on the grounds that farmers were interfering with interstate commerce.

In early September, midwestern governors convened a conference on farm relief in Des Moines that revealed the still-wide chasm between farm protestors and political realities. Unlike Governor Olson, who said unambiguously, "I am in sympathy with the strikers," many of the governors were outspoken critics of radical farm protests. Testifying to the governors, Milo Reno proposed a four-point program for farm relief that began with state mortgage moratoriums. Reno had called for a cessation of the strike pending the outcome of this conference, but the most radical farmers, fed up with the perceived moderation of the Holiday's leadership, persisted with picketing and withholding goods from the market. A group of Iowa farmers even convened a "Rank and File Farmers Meeting" in Sioux City on the same day as the governors' conference. The first demand issued by this meeting was for a "moratorium on all debts, rents, mortgages, and taxes." According to historian John Shover, "The upshot of the governors' conference . . . was a series of tame resolutions to President Hoover including such time-worn panaceas as tariff protection for farmers, currency expansion, and a request that federal and private agencies desist from foreclosures. On the one proposal where the governors might have taken an initiative, state mortgage moratoriums, their memorial was silent."

The center of militant action then turned to Minnesota. In part due to president John Bosch's emphasis on nonviolence and "moral suasion"—one pamphlet from Minnesota farmer-protestors advised passive resistance based on the methods of Mahatma Gandhi!—Minnesota's more peaceful but hardly less radical Farmers' Holiday Association enjoyed greater success than its Iowa counterpart. Able to organize even in counties dominated by the Farm Bureau, it launched a major withholding strike in mid-September that was reasonably well tolerated if not supported by the general populace. During this strike, the Minnesota Holiday successfully blocked the roads leading into several county seats and into the Twin Cities, although the latter campaign was short-lived and more of a symbolic gesture than a true threat to the food supply of the state's major population center. "The general attitude of newspaper editorials," writes one historian, "was that the strike, although not likely to succeed, was a worthy effort and deserved the support of all farmers and those dependent upon the farmer for their existence." Olson remained a steadfast supporter of the Holiday movement. One scholar writes, "All of these actions posed a law-and-order problem for the Farmer Labor party, especially in an election year. Yet Olson resisted calls for use of state militia and insisted that law and order was a local responsibility." Even some local chambers of commerce expressed support for the Farmers' Holiday movement.

Still, the honeymoon in Minnesota was over by early October, when confrontations broke out between farmers and truckers carrying food to market. Some local authorities warned strikers that authorities would side with livestock haulers and other food processors. One picketing farmer was shot and killed in the town of Canby in the west-central county of Yellow Medicine, and a riot broke out in the hamlet of Howard Lake between 500 strikers and 300 non-strikers. In an effort to embarrass Olson, writes one political scientist, "the Republican attorney general of Minnesota authorized the state highway patrol, whose chief was running against Olson for governor, to assist county sheriffs in disbanding picket lines thrown up by angry farmers." The state leadership of the association then agreed to a peaceful end to the strike in late October. Of course, such collective action was likely to fail even with the continued support of non-farmers. As with any cartel, the temptation was simply too great for an individual grower to break the agreement and sell his or her goods.

The Minnesota Farmers' Holiday Association enjoyed its greatest grassroots success preventing the sale of foreclosed farms at auction. When a sheriff announced an auction, the local Holiday first would try to convince him to postpone the sale. If this plea did not work, the Holiday would summon farmers in droves to descend on and disrupt the public sale. "Sometimes thousands were on hand," observed a history of Minnesota written just a couple of years after these events, "crowding into the courthouse and surrounding the sheriff so closely that he could not get to the front door during the appointed hour." Women actively participated in these protests. Although actual violence was rare — but not unheard of; one Kansas City realtor was found murdered a week after he foreclosed on a property — the threat of violence to the seller and potential buyers was real, and an effective technique. Often, with the seller and sheriff effectively chastened by a looming crowd of farmers, association members would engage in the "penny sale" technique: the dispossessed farmer or friends would provide a couple of miniscule, ceremonial bids on a property, and then the crowd would go silent. When the farcical auction had concluded without a real bid, the property would remain with the owner. (Courts sometimes responded by stipulating a minimum price, called an "upset price," below which a foreclosed property could not be sold at auction.) Farmers also engaged in "Sears-Roebuck sales" of personal property. A tractor might "sell" for 25 cents, or a cow for 10 cents, before reverting to the owner.

The first Holiday movement stoppage in Minnesota occurred in January 1933 in Willmar, the Kandiyohi county seat, when 800 farmers gathered to prevent the sale of a farm owned by a "70-year-old pioneer settler" named Soren Hanson. The owner of the mortgage refused to negotiate, and "in what quickly became a battle of principle, the sale was stopped six times in succeeding weeks despite the death of Mr. Hanson in the interim." A few days later, crowds of up to 900 farmers stopped half a dozen sales in three counties. In Montevideo, 400 farmers stood by as an anxious sheriff, "pinned in a chair," according to newspaper accounts as far away as Atlanta, waited forty-five minutes without receiving a single bid on a foreclosed property. Although most stoppages ended less dramatically, more than a hundred of these showdowns likely occurred in Minnesota in 1932 and 1933. And the threat of such action must have quietly changed the dynamics of countless less publicized transactions in favor of the farmer.

How deeply communism penetrated the Farmers' Holiday Association is a matter of some debate. Before 1936, when liberals and communists joined forces in an international "Popular Front" against fascism and communist activists became an important force within the Farmer-Labor Party, Minnesota's communists (who never numbered more than 1,000) opposed the reformist politics of the Farmer-Labor Party and Holiday, even though these politics were often avowedly anticapitalist. Still, two communist-led groups, the United Farmers' League and the Farmers' National Committee for Action, engaged in direct-action campaigns similar to those conducted by the Farmers' Holiday Association, and at times, writes historian Lowell Dyson, the Holiday and these communist organizations "worked together on the local level and oftentimes were indistinguishable." Yet, Dyson continues, "The Communist leadership . . . always pressed for ideological distinctions from the other organizations." The communists certainly did not consider Holiday leadership fellow travelers. Dyson asserts that "if no stronger organization [than the communists'] had entered the field, they [the communists] might have won great popularity in wide areas during this time of troubles. To the Communists' chagrin, however, Milo Reno and his Minnesota and North Dakota lieutenants, John Bosch and Usher Burdick, had stolen at least half a step on them." Most members of the Holiday were capitalist farmers who simply wanted to return to perceived norms of stable profitability.

The Farmers' Holiday Association was also less strident behind the scenes than newspaper headlines suggested. Historian William Nass writes, "The Holiday preferred to work privately through arbitration and was sensitive to possibly damaging criticism of their interruption of the sacred creditor-debtor relationship and as such . . . [stressed] . . . they were only trying to save good farmers done in by circumstances beyond their control." Before the federal Farm Credit Administration established a more formal system of arbitration boards late in 1933, the Holiday had established their own. Dyson writes that by the fall of 1932, the Farmers' Holiday Association "had perfected its instrument, the local council of defense, made up of from five to eleven members, almost always all farmers." These councils "acted as quasi-judicial bodies," mediating disputes between lenders and creditors and between owners and renters. The communists rejected them for insufficient class-warfare rhetoric. It is difficult to gauge how institutionalized the councils were, as farmers seem to have created such bodies spontaneously. Reporting on a spur-of-the-moment meeting of 600 farmers who had filled an opera house to prevent a sale, the *Minneapolis Tribune* wrote, "Farm mortgage foreclosures in Lac qui Parle county hereafter will be referred to a board of arbitration composed of three farmers in an attempt to forestall sales in 'justifiable' cases."

Peace generally prevailed at foreclosure stoppages, especially as the association targeted sales involving particularly sad cases likely to elicit public sympathy. "No force will be used in stopping sales unless all other methods fail," one of the three members of Lac qui Parle's new board reported. It is also important to remember that, due to the overall economic crisis, many lenders were not eager to foreclose distressed properties on which they would receive zero income and which they likely could not sell. Determining an exact percentage of agriculture loans that were renegotiated or given grace periods seems beyond the historical record, but, importantly, in January and February of 1933, several major national insurance companies, including Prudential Insurance (purportedly the largest farm lender in the nation) and the New York Life Insurance Company, suspended foreclosures. The president of Metropolitan Life said that his company was foreclosing only in cases "where the farmer is unwilling to carry on or try to do his part toward working out his problem."

Farmers skillfully bypassed traditional political channels, but we should not obscure the fact that they often got what they wanted through intimidation. And mob psychology sometimes catapulted events beyond the control of Holiday leaders. Even farmers who *wished* to be foreclosed saw sales on their property forcibly stopped;

one lender who thought he was attending a routine sale — the farmer wanted to sell his goods and retire — was held hostage by activist farmers and "forced to flee . . . minus his pants and on four flat tires." In the end, even Milo Reno conceded that farmers' threats — "ropes under their coats," as he put it — stopped thousands more foreclosures than did arbitration. Perhaps what is most remarkable, and revealing of both the collective political power of distressed farmers and the localized power of a mob of them, is that lenders were willing to negotiate with "boards of arbitration" composed of only farmers!

We do not know the precise percentage of loans held by the various lending agencies, which included local, state, and national banks; the federal land banks; other federal entities; the Minnesota Rural Credit Bureau; and, according to *Time* magazine, at least fifty-two life insurance companies. We do know that the land banks were increasingly important and that at the end of 1936 they held "over 37 percent of the farm mortgage debt of the country," according to the Farm Credit Administration. Regardless, most farmers detested the whole lot. Private lenders were deemed the worst, as they held "no regard for human welfare," according to one farmer's petition. But nonprofit lenders hardly fared better in the court of public opinion. One grower wrote Governor Olson to declare the federal farm land bank system "a flop," lamenting high interest rates and the fees and commissions a loan recipient was required to pay. (This letter was certainly heavy-handed given that land bank interest rates were capped at 5 percent at the time.) And as we have seen, Minnesota farmers especially detested their state's Rural Credit Bureau, which, despite tightening its lending practices, was sitting on a mountain of delinquent farms and foreclosed properties.

True, such opposition was not universal. One Minnesotan wrote the governor:

> I see by the newspapers that there is a great deal of agitation toward liquidating the Rural Credit Department. [Such a move is] certainly not opportune at this time, due to the ridiculous and scandalous [sic] low prices of farm produce, and coupled with high taxes there is no demand for land. . . . The Rural Credit Department of the State should not be blamed for the ungodly deflation in farm produce on farm lands. I know hundreds of individuals who loaned

money on farm lands in this state. They too are taking their loss as well as the state.

Another petitioner praised the bureau for offering lower interest rates and operating expenses lower than private lenders. Still, the more typical sentiment of both competing lenders and farmers was captured in a letter to the governor from a local agent of the Equitable Life Insurance Company. While conceding that "the sentiments expressed" in the formation of the agency were "noble and deserving," he called the Rural Credit Bureau "the most diabolical thing ever foisted upon the tax-payers of Minnesota."

The only state office Minnesota farmers seemed to have faith in was the governor's. John Mollerstrom, owner of the "Variety Store" in Lake Park, appealed directly to the governor for a "long term loan of $2000." "I will come to the point at once, I am hard up," Mollerstrom told the governor. "I would pay $20 a month and if things pick up I would pay more. . . . I have cut down all expenses, we do our own work, and get along as cheap as possible."

As the tough winter of 1932–1933 descended on the northern plains, and the Great Depression neared its absolute bottom, Minnesota farmers turned their attention to the upcoming legislative session, the first since 1931. Few, it is safe to say, cared much about protecting the sanctity of the Contract Clause. Many would have preferred that the state eradicate all lending agencies or at least directly intervene in credit markets to lower interest rates. Arthur Lueders, the secretary of the Carver County Farmer-Labor Association, asked the governor to "liquidate the Rural Credits [Bureau] and other farm mortgages and mortgage companies." Some hoped Congress would lower interest rates or even ban state-level lending. One farmer wrote to Governor Olson calling for federal legislation that would authorize $5 billion to loan to farmers at 2 percent (a couple of points below prevailing interest). Another constituent penned, "We wish some of you down there in the legislature would work for us if you's [sic] could have got down the interest to one half then probly [sic] some of us could be able to pay and keep our farms . . . but if they force everything away from us the state will have to support us and our families."

Many of these proposals were unrealistic, but the idea of offering debtors breathing room enjoyed widespread support, and lobbying for a moratorium represented what one historian termed the "respectable counterpart to penny and Sears-Roebuck sales." "The farmers sure cannot help this depression and price deflation," one farmer exhorted the governor. "But the mortgage companies have the long lever and are heartless, and it is with them pay or get off. . . . These conditions have reached the limit and you must act, and quick."

CHAPTER 4

Passing the Minnesota Mortgage
Moratorium Act

The Minnesota legislature convened for the forty-eighth time during the winter and spring of 1933, the nadir of the Depression. At this time, notes historian R. Douglas Hurt, "farmers were experiencing the lowest agricultural prices and income since the late nineteenth century," and had less than half the purchasing power they did during the golden years of 1909 to 1914. Minnesota farmer-protestors continued to engage in foreclosure stoppages, set up informal mortgage arbitration "committees," and remind urban consumers of the looming specter of boycotts. And of course the farm protest movement in Minnesota did not operate in a vacuum. Close to two dozen other states would pass mortgage-relief legislation during the first half of 1933.

Immediately upon its creation in the summer of 1932, the Minnesota Farmers' Holiday Association had demanded (as had the national Holiday) a state mortgage moratorium until prices equaled the cost of production, and now petitions poured into lawmakers' offices. In an action mirrored dozens of times across the state, the Redwood County Farmers' Holiday met on February 4 to issue its legislative demands. "Resolved," the resultant document began, "that Honorable Floyd B. Olson . . . and the legislature of the State of Minnesota . . . be requested to immediately declare and/or enact orders or laws suspending the foreclosure of all farm mortgages in the State of Minnesota for a period of two years." The Redwood Holiday also admonished the legislature to increase the existing maximum period for redemption on a foreclosure from one to three years, and it proposed the creation of formal state-run arbitration committees. As the 1933 legislative session began, however, Governor Olson seemed to vacillate on the legality and wisdom of a moratorium. After meeting in early February with large mortgage holders in search of what he called a "gentleman's agreement," he declared that "not even the President of the United States, except through establishment of martial law, could suspend the collection of debts." Nonetheless, "a flood of bills poured in upon both houses" designed to aid the farmer.

A communist-sponsored organization tried to bridge the historic gap on the Left between farmers and urban workers, a gap seen in the statement of the Farmers' Holiday Association during the previous fall's strikes that growers should not elicit the support of urban workers in blocking roads. The State Committee of Action, composed of between 250 and 400 "elected delegates of organized farmers and workers," met in St. Paul on February 19 and presented its demands to the legislature. "UNITED WE WILL WIN," the group proclaimed in a letter summarizing this meeting addressed to the Farmers' Holiday Association. The Committee of Action demanded not only the "stopping of all evictions, foreclosures and sheriff sales, and the repeal of all legislation which authorizes foreclosures and evictions," but also a "moratorium on all debts, rents and mortgages for small farmers for the period of the crisis." The group was radical but also called for bread-and-butter progressive reforms, including the "right to organize, strike, and picket," unemployment insurance, and a graduated state income tax. (Minnesota had no income tax of any kind at this time.)

Activists also continued to hurl vitriol at the Rural Credit Bureau, although they seemed to hold back from calling for its outright elimination. The Committee of Action demanded that the department's funds "be used for long term loans to those farmers actually in need, who cannot furnish collateral, and to be administered by representative elected committees of farmers." Governor Olson, too, tried to keep the fledging lending agency alive, stating in his second inaugural address, in January 1933, "The bureau has been the means of keeping down the rate of interest charged on farm mortgages; is extremely necessary to the farmer in this time of need; and its operation should be continued without any impediment."

A legislative campaign, however, had emerged to kill the unpopular agency. State Representative R. W. Hitchcock from the Iron Range city of Hibbing introduced a bill to eliminate the Rural Credit Bureau, claiming that it had cost Minnesota $20 million without "having provided any genuine benefits to the farmers for which it was created." Hitchcock estimated the department's total current indebtedness at $64 million. Republicans in the state senate introduced a resolution, unanimously approved, calling for a legislative investigation of the bureau. A senate committee investigated the unit and by late February was leaking to the press rumors of corruption, collusion between state officials and private lenders, and solicitation of bribes. Something of the chaos of the Rural Credit Bureau was revealed when a whistle blower, a former assistant attorney general working out of the bureau, reported that he had been ousted but refused to leave his office. According to the *Minneapolis Star*, his replacement obtained possession of the office "only by having a door lock changed and sleeping in the office all night."

Sometime in February, meanwhile, Governor Olson backed off from his comment about the impossibility of suspending debt payment and embraced a moratorium. His papers provide few clues that might explain this about-face. Given the overwhelming public pressure for mortgage relief, the governor may have sensed that his political life was at stake. Perhaps the heart-wrenching personal appeals that continued to trickle into his office had some effect. One woman from Montevideo hoping to win a car in a Barbasol shaving cream slogan-writing contest asked Olson to sign his name on a can and mail it to her, which would demonstrate the power of her slogan. She wrote, "I'm a mother with four small children [and] a crippled, unemployed husband [and] no means of Support or place to stay. Now if I could win this car in this Contest, I would sell it, [and] get something for clothing [and] home for my children." Finally, the governor and his political allies were quite aware of the actions of other state legislatures. Iowa's newly elected governor, Clyde Herring (only the second Democratic governor in that state since the Civil War), signed Iowa's mortgage moratorium into law on February 17, 1933. Neighboring South Dakota, Wisconsin, and Nebraska also each delayed foreclosures or gave courts the right to extend redemption periods.

On February 24, Governor Olson issued an executive proclamation, ordering "that each and every sheriff, and each and every constable and police officer of the state of Minnesota refrain and desist until May 1, 1933, or until further order from foreclosing or attempting to foreclose any mortgage." The order applied to farms, farm machinery, and residential real estate. Olson justified this extraordinary measure by invoking the state's traditional police power authority to protect the safety of the populace. In a remarkably blunt accompanying message, he declared that the order was "not based on a moratorium but . . . upon the necessity for preserving order within the boundaries of this state. I have refrained heretofore . . . because I did not believe that I had legal authority . . . until an acute situation developed in the State. Such an acute situation has now developed." Olson did not blame the farmers for this acute situation or identify a dangerous precedent of caving in to threats of violence. The governor also called on the legislature to create a statewide debt commission to handle disputes.

Olson's order was well received. Rather than denouncing it, at least publicly, most business leaders were content to suggest that it was merely unnecessary. The secretary of the Minneapolis Mortgage Bankers Association told the press, "Governor Olson's moratorium comes as a complete surprise . . . recent reports from mortgage loan companies indicate the utmost leniency has been accorded homeowners." Many observers, even sympathetic ones, doubted the constitutionality of Olson's executive order. "I doubt its legality," said the vice president of the First Minneapolis Trust Company, "but considering the emergency of the case, it may be a wise move." A year later, William Prosser, a law professor at the University of Minnesota who consulted with the state House Judiciary Committee on the drafting of the moratorium legislation, called the proclamation "quite unconstitutional" in a law review article. In his correspondence, Olson answered charges that his decree violated the Contract Clause of the U.S. Constitution by suggesting that—in a time of emergency—he had simply postponed the fulfillment of the contracts (the lender's remedy) but had not abrogated property rights. Some historians have speculated that he issued the order because he wanted to trigger legislative action; according to this view, the emergency decree was a clever device designed to make a legislative moratorium seem less radical and intrusive by comparison. The *Minneapolis Tribune* wrote that the order "is of general importance only insofar as it anticipates legislation."

In early March, the Minnesota legislature passed a law codifying the governor's order, which gave sheriffs discretion whether to postpone a foreclosure sale for a period of ninety days (or to follow through on it). The purpose of this law, Governor Olson reported in a telegram to "every sheriff in Minnesota," was to remove any possible liability for sheriffs who complied with his executive order. Later, the Minnesota Supreme Court would strike down Olson's emergency order, but this meant little, as it had been superseded by the moratorium act.

As the legislative session progressed, momentum toward a general moratorium seemed to stall, even though the legislature had already sustained Olson's emergency order and the governor had announced his strong support for formal legislative action. All of Minnesota's major daily newspapers supported a moratorium — which speaks to the perceived moderation of the reform — and, although the legislature was elected on a nonpartisan basis, the Farmer-Labor Party had done well enough in the fall 1932 elections to declare an unofficial working majority. However, concerns about the constitutionality of a moratorium were widespread, and conservatives in the senate sought to delay passage. In addition, the legislature convened a series of public hearings on the matter, some attended by as many as 500 citizens. At one hearing, according to a newspaper account, the House Judiciary Committee learned that the "machinery for establishing mortgage moratoriums would not be nearly as simple as the average debtor has been led to believe, nor would the results be so generally beneficial." Republican Oscar Hallam, a former state supreme court justice, testified that a moratorium would unleash a torrent of costly and delaying lawsuits that "would be expensive to the debtor as well as the mortgagee." The ultimate result, Hallam warned, "would be higher interest rates, smaller loans on given values, and greater difficulty in finding capital." The president of the Minnesota Mutual Life Insurance Company claimed that the proposed law would unfairly force responsible debtors to carry the burden of irresponsible ones.

Grassroots direct action by farmers seems to have tipped the scales. On March 22, 1933 (less than three weeks after FDR was sworn in as president), "a caravan of two to three thousand farmers descended upon St. Paul from southern Minnesota, in an astonishing array of antediluvian automobiles, and swarmed over the capitol, making demands and threats and uttering dire predictions." Three weeks later, with just a few days left in the legislative session, a "more uproarious" delegation of farmers and workers descended on the capitol on April 15 demanding moratoriums not only on mortgages but also on taxes and rent. With dramatic flair, Governor Olson greeted the crowd from the balcony in the rotunda. According to the *Minneapolis Tribune*, Olson, in his most overtly radical statement yet, told the assembled crowd:

> I want to say to the people of Minnesota that if the legislature — the Senate in particular — does not make ample provision for the sufferers in this State . . . I shall invoke the power that I hold. I shall declare martial law. A lot of people who are now fighting the measures because they happen to possess considerable wealth will be brought in by provost guards. They will be obliged to give up more than they are giving up now.

The governor also declared that the Farmers' Holiday movement was "awakening the people of the United States."

The rally on the capitol seems to have galvanized lawmakers, and, on April 18, the last day of the session, both the house and the senate passed the moratorium unanimously. The details of the final legislative negotiations are sketchy, but the final version of the law clearly reflected a compromise tilted in favor of large lenders. Although he praised the law, Minnesota attorney general Harry H. Peterson, a prominent Farmer-Labor leader, wrote in a public statement, "The original mortgage foreclosure moratorium bill which was drawn in the Attorney General's office and which was introduced in the legislature, and also the bill as it passed in the House of Representatives was more liberal to debtors than the law in the form in which it was finally enacted." We know that some lawmakers voted for the legislation expecting the Minnesota courts to nullify it. When the Senate Judiciary Committee recommended passage on April 10, it did so "with obvious misgivings" about its constitutionality, according to the *Minneapolis Star*. Later, after the Minnesota Supreme Court upheld the law, some members of the legislature "received the report of the decision with visible and vocal consternation . . . [and] one or two of them went so far as to reproach the judges of the court for not declaring it invalid." The law's eleventh-hour passage, finally, suggests that some lawmakers voted for it with clenched teeth and a sour taste in their mouth. Nonetheless, the remarkable unanimity of the vote in both chambers obviously revealed a deep reservoir of support. Governor Olson signed Minnesota's mortgage-moratorium law the same day. Citing the prospect of violence, he also issued a new order postponing foreclosure sales for sixty days.

Like Olson, many historians have emphasized the galvanizing specter of violence when accounting for the emergence of Minnesota's moratorium. It is worth mentioning, however, that several states with much less violent rhetoric and far fewer threatening foreclosure stoppages also passed moratoria. Economic historians have proposed that the degree of economic distress on the farm, not pressure tactics, was the key predictor in whether a particular state enacted a moratorium. Not surprisingly, states with the highest rates of farm foreclosures were the most likely to impose moratoriums, and Minnesota ranked very high in terms of farm failures. Yet New York, for example, a state with a low level of farm foreclosures, also enacted a broad moratorium. Apparently, pressure by commercial real estate interests was the key factor in New York. Also, the more federal loans a state had, the less likely it was to pass a moratorium. Preexisting ideological divisions regarding the proper role of the state were insignificant in predicting legislative outcomes.

The Minnesota Mortgage Moratorium Act, often referred to as Chapter 339, provided property owners with two primary remedies when facing foreclosure. First, a party could petition a Minnesota district court to stop foreclosure proceedings by advertisement and to force foreclosure proceedings to continue under court protection. The court then had the power to strike down any sale, especially a sale for an amount it deemed too low. This provision sought to prevent speculators and lenders from swooping in and purchasing properties at bargain-basement prices. It also sought to avoid "deficiency judgments," court orders making a borrower financially liable — even after he or she has lost his or her property — for the difference between the amount of the loan still due and the (depressed) price garnered at the foreclosure sale.

The second remedy allowed a property owner to ask the court for an extension of the redemption period of their mortgages — but not beyond May 1, 1935, when the law was set to expire. During the extension, the homeowners would not have to make their normal mortgage payment but would, in the attorney general's words, "pay such amounts and perform such conditions at such times and in such manner as the court shall deem just under the circumstances." As we will see in the specific case of John and Rosella Blaisdell, the court-nego-tiated fee often was not much lower than the existing mortgage pay-ment. But the debtor got to stay on the property and secured valuable time to improve his or her finances and perhaps renegotiate the terms of the loan. Importantly, the law applied only to those fighting fore-closure. In addition, it merely provided for a potential extension of the redemption period — it did not reverse foreclosures. And by no means did it provide a general moratorium on mortgage payments for the large swath of Minnesotans who were overburdened with debt but not yet facing foreclosure. The provisions of the law applied to all mortgages, including those entered into prior to the enactment of the law. The authors of the Minnesota Mortgage Moratorium Act explic-itly justified the legislation on the grounds of emergency. They chron-icled the dire condition of the state's economy in a series of introduc-tory "whereas" clauses.

Just as the moratorium bill neared passage, Governor Olson and the chairman of the Senate Finance Committee worked out a deal to liquidate the Rural Credit Bureau. Olson stated that he acquiesced in the agency's demise because he hoped that federal policy makers would expand the federal loan apparatus. Late in the session, the house committee investigating the bureau delivered its report. The com-mittee called the bureau a "tragic failure" that had mismanaged many of its 59,000 loans (about 6,500 of which were "seriously delinquent," according to a later report). In a supplementary statement, one sena-tor pointed to the "staggering cost to our State." Just before the ses-sion ended, the Minnesota legislature formally dissolved the Rural Credit Bureau, transferred its assets to a new Department of Rural Credit, and established a conservator to liquidate the department by selling off its nearly 750,000 acres of farmland. With the state unable to sell many farms, the process of divestment remained a fiasco for several years to come.

Satisfied with the demise of the Rural Credit Bureau, Minnesotans tried to make sense of the new mortgage moratorium in the spring and summer of 1933. Reactions were mixed. Olson admitted to a con-stituent that the act was "rather complicated and somewhat difficult for the average person to fully understand." He asked Attorney General Harry Peterson to prepare a memo clarifying the law. "This office is receiving a great many inquiries from distressed farmers and home owners concerning the terms and provisions of the recent Moratorium Act," Olson wrote Peterson. "There seems to be a great deal of misapprehension and misunderstanding." Many average Minnesotans, to be sure, were thrilled. Zillah Wilson of Luverne informed the governor, "I cannot resist the impulse to write and thank you for the inexpressible aid you have given to the legions of aged, impoverished and indigent home owners. Those who profit by your most strenuous effort resulting in this Moratorium Bill will owe you an everlasting debt of gratitude." Many farmer-activists were less pleased, however. The secretary of the Rock County Farmers' Holiday Association wrote Olson, "We have had our first experience with the new Minn. Mortgage Law and I want to say emphatically that we are not enthusiastic over the action nor satisfied with the results." In particular, this individual complained that a county judge had postponed an adjustment trial multiple times. "This delay is annoying and costly for our farmers who have not very much money anyhow. It looks like the law will prove a big thing for the legal fraternity instead of any relief for the farmers."

It is important to remember that average farmers saw the mortgage moratorium as merely a stepping-stone toward a complete federal rescue and then overhaul of American agriculture, including reconfiguration of the lending market. As the *Farmer-Labor Leader* put it, "The Farm Holiday movement arose solely because of the desperate plight of the farmer, and the unwillingness of the federal government to do anything about it." Above all, farmers sought cost-of-production legislation from the federal government, and they wanted a far-reaching federal mortgage moratorium. They vilified the mishmash of state and federal loan programs, and many hoped the federal government would become the sole agricultural lender. The *Minneapolis Star* editorialized:

Moratoria are well enough in the immediate crisis, but unless there is a more fundamental adjustment in price levels they are nothing more than a postponement. As far as it is possible to meet the problems of agriculture in terms of credit, the need of the farmer is long term paper at low interest rates. State rural credit bureaus in Minnesota and South Dakota, federal land banks and intermediate credit banks were all attempts to meet that need. That even they have not proven adequate is now obvious and the pressure to extend the services of the government further in this field is inescapable.

The Farmers' Holiday Association did like the moratorium law well enough that it called for its extension just weeks after passage. On April 29, however, with the *Blaisdell* case already in the Minnesota courts, Governor Olson cabled the secretary of the Lincoln County Association, "Inadvisable to extend moratorium until legal status determined by [Minnesota] supreme court." As the next chapter details, Minnesota's high court would quickly uphold the law.

Grassroots pressure cooled off somewhat in late April and early May as farmers waited to see what kind of federal farm bill would emerge as one of the main planks of the frenzied first "Hundred Days" of the New Deal. Led by Secretary of Agriculture Henry A. Wallace, the camp that favored production controls prevailed over the camp that favored cost-of-production price guarantees. The Agricultural Adjustment Act, passed on May 12, 1933, created the Agricultural Adjustment Administration, which sought to increase prices by paying farmers to produce less of seven primary commodities. A new tax on agricultural processors funded these payments.

The Farmers' Holiday, like most groups across the nation supporting small growers, opposed the structure of AAA farm relief, and local Minnesota chapters petitioned for the removal of agricultural secretary Wallace. Across the nation, AAA programs came under constant fire for artificially trying to induce scarcity, for example by paying farmers to slaughter no more than 6 million hogs, when millions of Americans were hungry. In addition, by filtering payments for acreage reductions through landowners, the AAA tragically drove thousands of tenant farmers and sharecroppers off the land, especially African Americans in the cotton-growing regions of the South, and sped up the corporate consolidation of American agriculture. But commodity prices rose, and thousands of farms were saved. The AAA was the linchpin of New Deal agricultural policy, and although the Supreme Court declared the tax on processors unconstitutional in 1935, the 1936 Soil Conservation and Domestic Allotment Act and the 1938 Agricultural Adjustment Act substituted variations on the acreage reduction program, permitting many crop-payment programs to survive to this day as the controversial subsidy payments that dominate American agricultural policy.

At the same time, Congress continued to improve the credit situation. As discussed in the previous chapter, the federal government had taken several steps in the 1920s to increase farmers' access to credit, but the resulting jumble of programs and agencies could not solve the chronic shortage of rural credit. To bring some measure of order to federal lending policy, President Roosevelt created the Farm Credit Administration by executive order in late March 1933. Title II of the Agricultural Adjustment Act addressed the lending crisis, too; known as the Emergency Farm Mortgage Act, it injected an additional $200 million into the land banks for immediate "rescue" loans and authorized bond issuances of up to $2 billion, made it easier for farmers to reschedule land bank–backed loans, and directly purchased and refinanced private mortgages. Upon signing the law, Roosevelt urged lenders to delay foreclosures, but he did not declare a mortgage moratorium, as many on the Left counseled. In June, Congress affirmed FDR's creation of the Farm Credit Administration.

The New Deal's first credit-policy reforms helped irrigate the dried-up stream of farm credit. These programs were substantial; the land banks, for example, lent more than $2.5 billion between 1933 and 1939. But, at least initially, they hardly placated farm radicalism or rejuvenated the agricultural sector. Minnesota farmers considered the state's mortgage moratorium a short-term fix, believed that the Agricultural Adjustment Act pursued the wrong path toward higher prices, and deemed the new federal loan initiatives woefully inadequate. On the very day in May 1933 that Roosevelt signed the Agricultural Adjustment Act, Governor Olson wrote to Milo Reno, president of the National Farmers' Holiday Association, urging him to call off a planned national farm strike scheduled to begin the next day. "The contemplated farmers' strike at best may cause a slight and temporary increase in prices paid for certain commodities by the middleman to the farmer," Olson wrote, "but its lack of executive organization throughout a large area dooms it to failure." Olson conceded that Secretary of Agriculture Wallace had opposed the cost-of-production approach, but the governor assured Reno that Wallace saw the merits in the Holiday's push for it. Olson also suggested to Reno that Congress would pass a national moratorium. A couple of days later, Reno indeed called off the strike, "giving the excuse," one historian wrote, "that he had received assurances from Olson that a national mortgage moratorium would pass Congress." Reno was also placated by a recent statement by President Roosevelt that urged creditors to work with existing farm credit programs and to "abstain from bringing foreclosure proceedings and making any effort to dispossess farmers who are in debt to them."

Grassroots action such as penny sales continued through the summer and into the fall of 1933, and the Holiday continued to thrive. In June, with a headline reading "Farm Strike Talk Revived," the *Minneapolis Tribune* reported that at a meeting in Kandiyohi County, "Speakers claimed that the refinancing portion of the farm-relief measure [the Emergency Farm Mortgage Act] is so limited in its application and the rate of interest comparatively so much higher than the rate charged industries that the farmers feel great resentment that the Frazier [national moratorium] bill was not enacted."

October 1933 brought an additional burst of federal reforms. Roosevelt and his primary relief administrator, Harry Hopkins, set up the Federal Surplus Relief Corporation to buy crops (and other commodities, such as coal) for relief efforts. Roosevelt also established by executive order the Commodity Credit Corporation, which, under the auspices of the Reconstruction Finance Corporation, established storage programs and lent money ($900 million by 1939) to banks and other agricultural corporations to help farmers more effectively market their crops. Building on a hodgepodge of local and state efforts, the Farm Credit Administration asked governors to form voluntary debt-adjustment committees, usually composed of local leaders from both the farm and business communities, to work on adjusting claims. A year later, President Roosevelt praised these committees in a letter to the head of the Farm Credit Administration, noting the "many thousands of farmers whose homes have been saved through the local groups of public spirited men and women." According to the head of the Farm Credit Administration, over 2,600 such state committees existed by 1935.

But farmer-activists saw these measures as small potatoes and bemoaned the fact that federal credit programs primarily lent money to existing banks and mortgage companies. In November 1933, the

Minnesota Farmers' Holiday Association voted for another withholding strike, this time to be part of a coordinated national effort. Coming after a harvest (unlike in the spring), this strike threatened to have real teeth. Milo Reno supported it enthusiastically, telling farmers, "We have been patient and long-suffering. We have been made a political football for jingo politicians, who are controlled by the money-Lords of Wall Street. . . . We were promised a new deal. . . . Instead, we have received the same old stacked deck and so far as the Agricultural Act is concerned, the same dealers." But the proposed national strike fizzled, and this moment would prove to be the highwater mark of the Holiday's power. In Douglas County, Minnesota, for example, the strike was crippled when turkey growers failed to withhold from the market (Thanksgiving was just around the corner!) and creameries refused to stop accepting dairy products. The dairy farmers feared that consumers would turn to margarine substitutes if they did not provide milk, and they pulled out, too. At the national level, Secretary Wallace helped end the strike by announcing a new corn program that paid farmers above-market prices. "Within three days the strike was essentially stopped," one historian wrote, "and within a month farmers were receiving their first checks from Washington."

Why did the agrarian protest movement fizzle so suddenly at the end of 1933? The economic and psychological relief afforded by state foreclosure legislation, federal support for the farmer through the Agricultural Adjustment Administration (notwithstanding widespread opposition to its production-control approach), emergency aid payments, new loan programs, and improving macroeconomic conditions all helped take the sting out of what turned out to be a fierce but temporary movement. One sees in the historical record an increasing number of letters against the Holiday Association by the fall of 1933. A lawyer from Appleton, Minnesota, told Governor Olson that he saw no "honest reason for permitting the Holiday Association to continue their unlawful tactics by preventing foreclosures by force." He claimed, "The people in this community have become pretty disgusted with this sort of thing," although he also observed that the Swift County Holiday had tapered off and had "ceased to function in the way of obstructing sales." Perhaps the Farmers' Holiday Association was a victim of its own success in securing moratoriums. Agricultural historian John Shover observed, "The passage of moratorium laws reflected upon the Farmers' Holiday Association more than any other single farm organization, giving it an illusion of strength greater than it possessed."

In 1934, a year of terrible drought in all of the Midwest and the Dust Bowl on the southern plains, Congress and Roosevelt continued to aid American farmers, in the process turning them away from the Republican Party and into the New Deal coalition. The Farm Mortgage Refinancing Act injected yet more funds into the system and created the Federal Farm Mortgage Corporation. Soon thereafter, the Crop Loan Act of 1934 authorized short-term loans for farmers to tide them over until harvest. In March, Congress appropriated $40 million for direct emergency loans to farmers. From 1934 to 1935, the federal government increased its share of the total outstanding mortgage debt by 16 percent.

In the spring of 1934, the farm lobby failed in its last-ditch effort to secure cost-of-production legislation. Midwestern governors, including Floyd Olson, met in Des Moines once again to urge the federal government to enact a "code" for agriculture under the National Recovery Act—one similar to the codes regulating production, wage, and price levels that had been negotiated by business and labor in hundreds of industries under the guidance of the federal government. (The farm lobby recognized that NRA codes generally increased prices in the industry covered.) But Roosevelt still balked at the out-and-out price fixing of farm products. Knowing that his administration had already offered unprecedented levels of aid to the farmer, Roosevelt saw no need to move even further to the left on farm policy. Conservatives detested direct price controls. Responding to Governor Olson's invitation to attend the governors' conference, Alf Landon, governor of Kansas and soon to be the 1936 Republican nominee for president, told his Minnesota counterpart, "I will not attend, as the sentiment of my state at this time seems to be almost unanimously opposed to the contemplated program."

For the present study, the most significant federal legislation to emerge in 1934 was the Frazier-Lemke Farm Bankruptcy Act, signed by Roosevelt in late June, which allowed a mortgagor to negotiate with his or her creditors for up to a ten-year extension on foreclosure proceedings. A majority of the creditors had to agree to the extension for it to become valid. If no such agreement was reached, the property owner could appeal in federal court for a three-year moratorium and a permanent scaling down of debt commensurate with assets. To adjudicate these claims, the federal district court appointed a conciliation commissioner for every county with more than 500 farmers. The law contained many loopholes favoring lenders, and even many of its supporters noted that it was poorly written. Not enough time passed for Frazier-Lemke to exert a major impact before the U.S. Supreme Court struck it down in 1935 in *Louisville Joint Stock Land Bank v. Radford* for abrogating the due process property rights of mortgage holders (see chapter 9). Congress then passed a modified version of Frazier-Lemke, which limited the maximum stay to three years. The Supreme Court upheld it in *Wright v. Vinton Branch of Mountain Trust Bank of Roanoke* (1937). Amended and renewed multiple times, some version of the federal Frazier-Lemke bankruptcy law survived until 1949.

Although he consistently reassured constituents struggling with their foreclosure proceedings that Congress was also working on mortgage relief, Governor Olson was actually lukewarm about a national mortgage moratorium. In the summer of 1934, soon after passage of Frazier-Lemke, a representative from the National Farmers' Holiday Association wrote Olson, "Some sixty days ago Mr. Reno, John Bosch [head of the Minnesota Holiday], myself, and two other men called at your office and during this conversation you agreed to telephone President Roosevelt and to ask him if he would agree to a farm mortgage moratorium until such time as cost of production for farm products could be determined and applied. . . . Mr. Reno has never heard from you since that time, and he naturally assumed that you became disinterested in the movement."

Olson may indeed have made a political calculation to distance himself from the Holiday as it petered out in 1934. Despite widespread national support for the moratoriums in his and other states, Olson was coming under attack in the national press for his administration's wide-ranging left-wing reforms and was losing support among Minnesotans. A couple of months earlier, the *New York Times* ran the headline "Farmer-Laborites Now Openly 'Red.'" On the other hand, Olson in fact did urge Roosevelt to declare a national moratorium.

Olson assured Reno, "I was advised [by Roosevelt] that he could not properly declare a moratorium, and it was intimated that the refinancing program of the federal government would take care of the situation."

We need more research into the effects of Frazier-Lemke, but on balance the evidence suggests that the law helped America's farmers. For example, 20,000 farms were foreclosed on across the United States between March 1935 and March 1936, whereas 39,000 suffered that fate in the spring of 1933 alone. Then again, it is hard to disaggregate the effects of Frazier-Lemke from the state-level moratoriums, the general effects of an improving national economy, and, after the emergence of Agricultural Adjustment policies and the multitude of other federal actions, significantly improving farm incomes. In addition, the early-decade wave of foreclosures reduced the total number of farms in the United States, thereby diminishing the pool of farms that could be foreclosed later.

Economists, who tend to look upon state interventions in economic activity less favorably than do historians, have generally criticized the farm-relief policies of the 1930s. Randal Rucker and Lee Alston conducted an empirical study of federal farm policy in this period that yielded findings "consistent with the hypothesis that government programs successfully alleviated farm distress during the 1930s." The authors estimated that various agricultural relief programs and moratoriums saved between 146,000 and 277,000 farms during the decade. Rucker and Alston, however, could not "determine whether government relief programs of the Great Depression corrected a 'market failure' or interfered with properly functioning market processes." They identified significant costs as well, including the ultimate bill to the taxpayer of interest rates kept artificially low by the government. These researchers also concluded that the costs derived from AAA subsidies far surpassed those from the various mortgage moratoriums.

Several scholars have concluded that state moratoriums were largely unneeded. According to this argument, lenders were already quite lenient during the Depression. Moreover, moratoriums may have increased the cost of private lending — and scared off prospective new farmers — as lenders ate the costs of loans they could not foreclose. Other research by Rucker suggests that state farm-relief legislation, although lowering failure rates significantly, "resulted in significant reductions in the supply of loans from certain types of private lenders." The share of private loans versus federal ones decreased more substantially in states with moratoriums than in those without. Rucker also deemed the federal credit programs a net loss, suggesting that they "crowded out" private lending by offering artificially low interest rates and "actually reduced the demand for farm credit because of increased uncertainty to borrowers concerning the sanctity of future private loan agreements."

Of course, such academic debates meant little to an individual who simply wanted to keep farming. Minnesota's moratorium was sufficiently popular that the legislature renewed it for two years in 1935 and then subsequently renewed it on several occasions so that it finally expired in 1942. And the law remained a source of pride for the Farmer-Labor Party. Just before he died in office from cancer in August 1936, Governor Floyd Olson listed the major accomplishments of his administration at the party's 1936 convention. He said:

> Time does not permit in view of the necessity for the discussion of national questions that I review in its entirety the record of the Farmer-Labor party in its administration of state government. I must content myself with citing a few examples of our progress and our record, examples which are significant in character which tend to show the fundamental principles for which we stand and so I cite you the fact among others that the Farmer-Labor Party of Minnesota [secured] the passage of a Mortgage Moratorium Act designed to protect the farmer, particularly of the State of Minnesota.

At this late stage of his governorship, Olson was trying to avoid being called a radical, and thus it is not surprising that he listed first among his accomplishments the moratorium. As will be shown in coming chapters, the courts generally considered the Minnesota Mortgage Moratorium Act a moderate measure that was born of a dire emergency and did not violate the Contract Clause.

The courts' tendency to judge the law as moderate makes sense in light of the attitudes of the farmers who drove passage of Chapter 339. Although the farm protest movement employed militant direct-action techniques, and a smattering of communists used the farm crisis to try to build their party, most supporters of agricultural reform, even the true "family farmers" of our imagination, were non-ideological commercial growers with substantial investments in land and equipment. To be sure, some of the Holidays espoused anticapitalistic rhetoric that harked back to the Populists. One letter to Governor Olson said, "We the farmer laborites of Norman County . . . want to let you know that we are with you and will sustain you in everything you do toward opposing capitalism." But farmers in Minnesota and across the United States actually sought in conservative terms to hold on to an agrarian, capitalistic way of life that they believed — correctly — was disappearing from the nation. Like Olaf from the film *Sweetland*, many farmers lamented that farming and business did not mix, and they felt that industrialists too easily earned high returns whereas they had to struggle mightily to break even. In the tradition of the agrarian, progressive wing of the Republican Party, they supported building state capacity to create a level playing field against large financial firms and food processors. Ultimately, however, rural Americans simply desired higher prices, not a radical restructuring of American capitalism. Exasperated that they had become second-class citizens in a nation that purported to respect its agrarian tradition, they sought to rebalance the political economy through a massive national loan refinancing. After the agricultural crisis passed, they would return to a conservative posture and emerge as one of the key blocs in the modern Republican Party.

But these developments take us ahead of our story. In 1933, Minnesota farmers resolutely supported the state's Farmer-Labor Party and its statist agenda. They resolutely approved of the developments we next chronicle — the successful defense of the Minnesota Mortgage Moratorium Act in state courts and then in the highest court in the land.

The Minnesota Mortgage Moratorium Act in State Court

After Governor Olson signed the Minnesota Mortgage Moratorium Act (Chapter 339) into law, its fate rested with the courts. To survive, this relief legislation would have to run a gauntlet not only of state law governing mortgage foreclosure proceedings but also of legal tests under the Contract and Due Process Clauses of the U.S. Constitution.

The courts faced three key questions. First, and above all, was the Minnesota law—and especially the two-year redemption extension—a justified use of state police power? Despite the language of the Contract Clause, which seems to impose an absolute prohibition on contract impairments, state and federal courts had long recognized that governments, in limited situations, could impair contractual obligations by using their police power to protect public health, safety, welfare, and morals. They could interfere with contracts, however, only if the business or industry regulated was "clothed with a public interest," to use the Supreme Court's phrasing in *Munn v. Illinois* (1877), or presented a nuisance or danger to the community. Put another way, the courts had to decide whether the moratorium law provided a public benefit to the community at large or merely bestowed a private benefit. It was well settled that laws favoring a certain class of citizens (in this case, debtors) were constitutionally suspect. The distinction between private and public benefit was often subjective, however, and the question of how to draw this distinction became a major point of contention in the *Blaisdell* litigation.

The second and related question was whether the foreclosure crisis constituted a general emergency—and whether such an emergency was needed before the state could regulate mortgages under the police power. Third and finally, the courts had to determine whether the Minnesota Mortgage Moratorium Act impaired the vested rights of creditors or simply modified the remedies used to enforce a mortgage foreclosure. Judges long had rejected laws that impaired the substantive rights of contractual obligations but also had recognized the power of a state to alter the remedies available for a contractual violation. The lawyers arguing *Blaisdell* debated due process and equal protection arguments, but these would not be central to the court's decision.

Conflicting lines of precedents provided ammunition for both sides in the legal wrangling over the Minnesota law. Several nineteenth-century Supreme Court decisions struck down debtor-relief laws, including mortgage moratoriums, enacted during economic depressions and panics, and thus it appeared the weight of legal precedent worked against Chapter 339. In the 1920s *Rent Cases*, however, the Court expanded state police power by upholding rent-control laws passed in response to the World War I housing shortage.

Before the wrangling could begin, of course, Minnesotans would have to invoke the protections of the law. John and Rosella Blaisdell of Minneapolis were not the typical rural homeowners the Minnesota Mortgage Moratorium Act was designed to help. Still, the protections of the law were not limited to farm families, and although their financial burdens were different from those faced by farmers, the Blaisdells were like millions of other working-class families struggling to meet the financial challenges of the Great Depression.

John Hoyt Blaisdell was born on May 30, 1888, in Fairmont, Minnesota, and his future wife, Rosella Whelan, was born on November 14, 1886, in Bancroft, Minnesota. The couple married on May 19, 1908, in Albert Lea, a southern Minnesota city where Interstates 90 and 35 now meet. According to his World War I draft registration card, John was a man of medium height and weight with brown eyes and dark brown hair. There is no record that he served on active duty during the Great War. John worked as a farmer in North Dakota for a number of years before the couple returned to Minnesota.

In August 1928, the Blaisdells purchased a two-story, fourteen-room house not far from downtown Minneapolis, mortgaged to the Home Building and Loan Association, a not-for-profit loan cooperative, for $3,800. The original mortgage contract set the monthly payment at $41.80, although on the 1930 census form, the Blaisdells listed their mortgage payment as $50 per month. Court documents describe the Blaisdells' neighborhood as a "closely built section" of Minneapo-

lis. Only a few feet separated the house from the neighbors. The Blaisdells used their home as a boardinghouse; they lived in three rooms
and rented the remaining eleven as apartments. With three children,
the couple must have been a little cramped. The oldest child, Joseph,
was sixteen years old in 1933, Emily was six, and young James was five.

When the Blaisdells purchased the house, John worked as a switchman for the Great Northern Railroad at a salary of $209 per month.
(A switchman operates railroad track switches, couples or uncouples
rolling stock, and signals engineers.) We do not know exactly when
and why John Blaisdell stopped working for the Great Northern, but
railroad employment peaked in the 1920s and declined significantly
even before the Depression, so it is not hard to imagine that he lost
his job near the end of the decade. By 1933, John was employed on the
Minneapolis police force at a salary of $162.80 a month. (His death
certificate suggests that he remained a police officer for the remainder of his career.) Rosella worked at home, caring for the children and
managing the rental units.

The drop in John's income and the general financial climate of the
Depression made it difficult for the Blaisdells to make ends meet.
Before the 1929 stock market crash, the Blaisdells grossed about $2,340
per year in rental income. Expenses for maintenance, insurance, and
taxes averaged more than $960 a year, leaving them with a net monthly
rental income of $115. Their rental income plunged during the Depres-
sion, however, averaging just $37 a month between May 1, 1932, and
May 1, 1933. Struggling to make their house payments and several years
delinquent on their taxes, they faced foreclosure.

Mortgage foreclosure proceedings were well defined by state
statutes and common law doctrine. A mortgage is a financial claim
against property. When people purchase homes, they sign a document
giving that claim (a lien) to the lender, and in return the bank or credit
union loans the purchaser money. The lender takes the mortgage and
holds it until the debt is paid off. When a lender (mortgagee) loans
money to a borrower (mortgagor), a "security interest" is created in
the underlying property, intended to secure repayment of the debt. In
most cases, failure to meet mortgage payments entitles the holder of
the security interest to seize and sell the property and to discharge the
debt that the security interest secures.

This is where foreclosure proceedings enter the equation. Two methods exist for foreclosing a real estate mortgage: foreclosure by advertisement and foreclosure by action. Foreclosure by advertisement is the more common because it is faster, simpler, and less expensive. With this procedure, the creditor prepares a notice of a mortgage foreclosure sale, the contents of which are determined by state law. Once the notice is prepared, it is published in a qualified newspaper, usually for six weeks. Interested parties may attend the sale and bid on the property. Foreclosure by action, also known as foreclosure by judicial sale, requires the creditor to bring an action in court to determine his or her right to foreclose prior to any sale. It is therefore more costly and time-consuming. At the time of the *Blaisdell* litigation, twenty-eight states provided for foreclosure action in court. Fifteen states used either a regulated or unregulated power of sale by advertisement, while the remaining states employed various other procedures.

The mortgage on John and Rosella's home was foreclosed on by the Home Building and Loan Association on May 2, 1932. Holding the security interest on the property but not owning it outright, the Association purchased the property at the foreclosure sale for $3,700. Yet even in the depressed market, the assessed value had risen to $6,000 (in part due to improvements the Blaisdells made), suggesting that the Association was primed to make a healthy profit. According to city records, the Blaisdell mortgage was one of 1,500 foreclosed in Hennepin County, Minneapolis, in 1932. Under existing Minnesota law, the Blaisdells had one year to redeem their property by paying the amount owed to the Association, which, with back taxes and interest, amounted to about $4,000.

Mortgage redemption laws have ancient origins. For example, the Old Testament (Leviticus 25:29–30) describes a grace period on house sales. Modern redemption periods in property foreclosures originated in the 1600s under English common law and chancery courts. When citizens could not find justice in common law courts, they petitioned the king, begging him to follow his conscience, rather than the rigid procedures and doctrines of the courts. Kings generally had little time or patience for such matters, so they referred petitions to the chancellor, a combination of chief of staff and executive secretary. Eventually, petitioners went directly to the chancellor, the keeper of the king's conscience. From this practice came the chancery courts or equity courts. While the common law had been associated with the formal, nondiscretionary application of rules, equity was always more flexible. Equity embodies a concern for fairness.

Before the invention of the redemption period, strict rules governed the due date for mortgage payments. Debtors who could not make payments by sunset of the appointed day, known as law day, forfeited their land and any opportunity to win it back. Mortgagors obviously hated this practice and demanded that restrictions be imposed on mortgagees. At some point, one or more English lord chancellors developed the doctrine of "equity of redemption," which permitted the mortgagor to seek the protection of the courts and pay the debt within a specified period after default, and thus have a chance to regain the land that had passed to the creditor.

This common law practice was adopted in the United States. Over time, the equity of redemption was extended by a statutorily defined period of redemption requiring that a certain time elapse between the commencement of foreclosure proceedings and the sale of the property. By the 1930s, twenty-eight states had redemption laws, and each state developed its own rules governing the nature and scope of the redemption period. For example, the Minnesota Supreme Court ruled in *Orr v. Bennett* (1917) that during the redemption period, the mortgagor's right to possession also included the rents and profits from the property. That ruling allowed the Blaisdells to continue living in their home during the redemption period and to collect rent on their apartments.

The Blaisdells could not raise the necessary funds to redeem their property, however, and they seemed certain to lose their home as their May 2, 1933, deadline loomed. Miraculously for them, Governor Olson signed the mortgage-moratorium law on April 18. To review: the law authorized district courts to determine whether an extension of the redemption period was justified; if so, the court was to determine a monthly fee that the borrower would pay, based largely on the "just and equitable" rental value of the property. Almost immediately after the ink dried on the law, and with two weeks left in their redemption period, the Blaisdells petitioned the district court of Hennepin County for an extension. The Blaisdells retained George C. Stiles, a Minneapolis attorney and counsel for an organization called the Minneapolis Apartment Owners Association, to represent them in the proceedings. Stiles had played an active role in supporting passage of the moratorium law, testifying at the public hearings, and he is pictured next to Governor Olson at the legislation signing.

The Blaisdells sought to extend their redemption period until May 1, 1935, with payment of a reasonable monthly fee for the property as determined by the court. (This end date reflected a request for the maximum extension allowed by the law.) If successful, they would secure two years to improve their financial situation in order to keep their home. The Blaisdells' case was among a select few that, at least initially, made it to trial. In the months following passage of the moratorium law, the Legal Aid Society of Minneapolis, founded in 1913 to provide legal services to low-income residents of Hennepin County, reported that about 200 individuals had applied for legal assistance from the society to secure mortgage relief. Of those, thirty cases were taken to court, and only eight were tried. In the remaining cases, some of the mortgagors were unable or unwilling to make any rental payment on the property, and others were settled before the case reached a judge. Some could not even pay the $4 filing fee.

The trial began on May 11, 1933, with Judge Arthur A. Selover presiding. Judge Selover would become dean of the Minnesota College of Law in 1934 and had been acting mayor of Minneapolis in the early 1920s. Karl H. Covell, of the Minneapolis firm Strong, Myers, and Covell, represented the Home Building and Loan Association. At the start of the trial, John Blaisdell was sworn in and took the witness stand on behalf of the petitioners. His lawyer, George Stiles, asked, "What is your name?" Before Mr. Blaisdell could answer even this opening question, Karl Covell objected to the introduction of any evidence on the grounds the moratorium act violated the United States and Minnesota constitutions. He made a motion to dismiss.

Judge Selover sustained the motion and dismissed the case. John Blaisdell was denied an opportunity to testify, and no evidence was admitted. In his brief order to dismiss, Judge Selover held that Chapter 339 violated the Contract Clause of the U.S. Constitution and a similar provision of the state constitution. He also claimed that the moratorium law violated the Fourteenth Amendment by depriving lenders of their property without due process of law. He characterized Chapter 339 as a "special law and not a general law" and argued that it was preferential "class legislation" because, in his view, it discriminated against other debtors in favor of those who had given security for real property. Finally, Judge Selover asserted that the law was not warranted as an exercise of police power because it served a private rather than a public purpose.

Stiles, the Blaisdells' attorney, filed for a new trial. Judge Selover denied the motion, and he attached to his order a memorandum providing a detailed explanation for his rationale in declaring the moratorium act unconstitutional. Selover wrote that it was "almost too plain for argument" that the act impaired the obligation of a mortgage contract. He cited two Minnesota cases, *Heyward v. Judd* (1860) and *Goenen v. Schroeder* (1863), in which the Minnesota Supreme Court struck down statutes altering the period of redemption on previously existing mortgages. During the initial court proceedings, Stiles had emphasized two of the U.S. Supreme Court's *Rent Cases — Block v. Hirsch* and *Marcus Brown Holding Company v. Feldman* — but Judge Selover distinguished those precedents from the case at hand. He asserted that the High Court sustained rent-control laws in the *Rent Cases* because they promoted the health and safety of the people in their respective communities and were therefore a valid exercise of the police power. In contrast, the Minnesota Mortgage Moratorium Act did not benefit or protect the general public — it helped only a limited class of debtors who take out mortgages on real property. By favoring this one type of debtor, the law discriminated against all other debtors, say, those buying an expensive boat on installment rather than a house. "For every mortgagor who, oppressed by the burden of the mortgage debt, prays the court under the provisions of this Act that both federal and state constitutions be annulled or suspended for his benefit," Selover wrote, "there is a mortgagee equally oppressed by his debts who in order that he may pay them prays as fervently that the protections of these Constitutions be not removed from him." Judge Selover in fact suggested that a law establishing a general moratorium on all debts would pass constitutional muster more easily.

Next, the judge contended that even if one allowed for the existence of an emergency as described by the preamble "whereas" clauses of Chapter 339, the law would still lack justification. "If a legislature can destroy a private real estate mortgage contract under the guise of the police power of the state," he warned, "it can so destroy all other contracts." Apparently, Stiles had intimated to Judge Selover that a ruling striking down the moratorium law might result in protests and possible violence, as had already occurred in several states. The judge, however, was not moved by the warning. "If such disturbances do arise," he wrote, "let the responsibility for them rest where it belongs, upon those who, by initiating and fostering this legislation, have created in the minds of a special and limited class of debtors a false hope that both the Constitutions of the United States and of the state of Minnesota may be annulled or temporarily set aside for their special benefit, rather than upon judicial officers." With the motion for a new trial denied in all aspects, the Blaisdells appealed, and the case moved to the Minnesota Supreme Court.

At this juncture, the Home Building and Loan Association must have been confident of its chances of winning the case before the state's highest court. After all, a number of U.S. Supreme Court Contract Clause precedents, including *Bronson v. Kinzie* (1843), *Howard v. Bugbee* (1860), and *Barnitz v. Beverly* (1896), discussed in chapter 2, supported the Association's position. Moreover, within a month of Judge Selover's decision, several other state supreme courts would overturn moratorium laws enacted in response to the Depression. In June 1933, the North Dakota Supreme Court, in *State ex rel. Cleveringa v. Klein*, struck down a two-year extension on the period of redemption nearly identical to the Minnesota law. One week later, the Arkansas Supreme Court, in *Adams v. Spillyards*, declared invalid a law abolishing deficiency judgments by the courts. Also that month, the Texas Court of Civil Appeals (that state's supreme court) declared unconstitutional a 180-day stay of foreclosure sales in *Life Insurance Co. of Virginia v. Sanders*. The tide of legal opinion in state courts seemed to be working against debtor-relief laws.

Meanwhile, the case elicited significant attention in the Minnesota legal community. Five briefs were filed in the case, four in support of the moratorium act and one in opposition. George Stiles continued to represent the Blaisdells and filed a brief on the merits for the petitioners. Karl Covell continued to represent the Home Building and Loan Association and submitted a brief on behalf of the respondents. The Minnesota attorney general's office joined the litigation and submitted an amicus curiae brief in defense of the constitutionality of the law. (An amicus curiae, or "friend of the court," brief is one filed by a person or organization not directly involved in a case.) Once it became involved, the attorney general's office played a prominent role in the case. William Ervin, assistant attorney general, co-argued the case before the court. A private St. Paul attorney, Bryce Lehmann, filed a second amicus brief in defense of Chapter 339, and State Representative Leonard Eriksson, a member of the Judiciary Committee of the Minnesota House, filed a third. An attorney from Fergus Falls, Eriksson had just been elected to the house in the nonpartisan elections that then prevailed. All of the legal and policy arguments made in these respective briefs would be repeated when the case reached the U.S. Supreme Court, so it is worth reviewing them.

George Stiles and the Blaisdells argued that Chapter 339 was purely temporary emergency legislation. Stiles conceded that in "normal times and under ordinary economic circumstances, [the] act would clearly be unconstitutional." But the times were not normal. For the past two years, he put forward, Minnesota and the rest of the nation had experienced the "most acute and devastating depression and financial panic" in the country's history. Stiles estimated that over 1,750 homes in Hennepin County alone had been foreclosed in the past year, most of them residential homes, resulting in the "imminent dispossession of perhaps ten thousand people." He claimed that there had been "no competitive cash bidding" in any of the foreclosures throughout the state for the past two years. Consequently, mortgagees (lenders) had bid on foreclosed properties at "grossly unreasonable and unfair prices," resulting in a saturated market. These properties in turn were selling at "ruinous and ridiculously low prices," depressing the value of real estate everywhere. It was a vicious cycle.

The Blaisdells' brief invoked the presence of social unrest, mainly in rural areas, and Governor Olson's proclamation initially suspending foreclosure sales until the legislature could provide relief. No one could deny that a serious emergency existed, and even if this were a debatable question, the legislature should be the sole judge on the matter. The brief cited *Sproles v. Binford* (1932), in which the U.S. Supreme Court asserted, "When the subject lies within the police power of the state, debatable questions as to reasonableness are not for the courts but for the legislature, which is entitled to form its own judgment." A court must presume the constitutionality of a law and strike it down only if it believes that it is arbitrary, oppressive, or unreasonable. But laws that are merely bad or unnecessary are not prima facie unconstitutional.

The Contract and Due Process Clauses of the U.S. Constitution, Stiles further argued, do not restrict in any degree a "reasonable exercise of the police power of the state." Nor by adopting those amendments did the states surrender their sovereign right to exercise that power. He acknowledged that early decisions of the federal courts limited the exercise of police power to matters affecting public health, morals, and safety, but he claimed that federal and state courts had abandoned that interpretation in the previous fifty years. Many courts at both levels had expanded their interpretation of state police power to "meet the requirements of changed and changing economic and industrial conditions and the growth of the states and the nation."

The last section of the Blaisdells' brief argued that the moratorium law was a general rather than a special law — that is, it was not class legislation. Stiles cited numerous public benefits of the relief legislation. For example, the extended redemption period would "prevent or minimize the wholesale dumping of thousands of properties on an already stagnant and flooded market." The law would deter wholesale evictions and divestment of title in foreclosure proceedings until Congress could enact more effective national relief. Stiles also suggested that the law exerted a powerful psychological effect by "encouraging and building ambition, hope and courage in the hearts and minds of men." The brief referenced President Roosevelt's observation in his 1933 inaugural address that, as Stiles summarized it, "genuine public confidence is among the first and chief essentials to a return of prosperity." Moreover, the act would help "lessen or prevent outbreaks and serious breaches of the peace," for it was "designed and intended to create bread-winners, not bread lines." For all these reasons, the Blaisdells' brief concluded, the moratorium law was a reasonable exercise of the state police power designed to promote the public welfare. The police power of the state, the reserved power of self-preservation, "is subservient to no law and to no constitution."

Karl Covell's brief made three main arguments on behalf of his client, the Home Building and Loan Association. First, it claimed that the abolition of the remedy of foreclosure by advertisement and the extension of the time to redeem a foreclosure sale were impairments of contracts, which under normal circumstances do not fall within the police power of the state. Covell cited three Minnesota Supreme Court cases, *Heyward v. Judd* (1860), *Goenen v. Schroder* (1863), and

O'Brien v. Krenz (1886), along with the U.S. Supreme Court decision in *Barnitz v. Beverly* (1896), as support for his assertion that abolishing the remedy of foreclosure by advertisement and extending the redemption period are not within the police power of the state under ordinary circumstances. Second, Covell conceded that a state may take property or impair the obligation of a contract, but only for the public welfare — a scenario almost always triggered by an emergency. He cited additional Minnesota and federal cases holding that a state could take property or impair contracts provided the action promotes the public welfare and impairment is only incidental. But, Covell insisted, the moratorium law was not directed at the public welfare because it benefited only a limited class of debtors — and did not occur during a true emergency.

Thus, picking up on an argument Judge Selover made in his memorandum, Covell distinguished the *Rent Cases* from *Blaisdell* by arguing that the relief at issue in the former cases promoted the public welfare. "When a large portion of citizens have no place to live — no shelter — it is a concern of government," he argued, "and their health is a matter of public interest." Whereas the *Rent Cases* concerned a shortage of housing, a "necessary of life," it was not a matter of public concern whether the title to a mortgage was held by one group of citizens rather than another group. In fact, Covell argued somewhat dubiously, the current down market actually offered an abundance of available housing! Finally, Covell contended that once society crosses the point at which a taking of property may be justified, it has entered the field of eminent domain. (Under eminent domain, a government may take private property for a public use provided it offers just compensation to the property owner.) Covell concluded that Chapter 339 was "no more a valid exercise of the police power than it is of the power of eminent domain."

In his brief in support of Chapter 339, Minnesota attorney general Harry Peterson emphasized that the times and conditions were abnormal, if not extreme. "A great emergency," he claimed, forced Minnesota to enact the moratorium law in order to promote and protect the public health, safety, and general welfare of the people. Peterson then detailed the plight of the one-half of Minnesotans who lived on farms. When the moratorium law was passed, "prices of farm products had fallen to a point where most of the persons engaged in farming could not realize enough from their products to support their families, and pay taxes and interest on the mortgages of their homes." More than half of the farmers in Minnesota "have lost or are about to lose their homes by tax sales or mortgage foreclosures," and the plight of homeowners in cities was just as bad. "They cannot find employment; their small reserves are exhausted; the banks that held the savings of many of them are closed and in addition there is the ever present menacing danger of wide-spread rioting and lawlessness by people otherwise peaceful and law abiding about to be rendered homeless and shelterless." The possibility of violence should the moratorium law be overturned was contested throughout the litigation. To bolster their argument that an emergency existed, supporters of the moratorium law stressed the real possibility of violence. Opponents of the law tended to downplay the existence or threat of violent protests and to argue that the courts should not be swayed by a mob.

Attorney General Peterson devoted most of his brief to arguing that the *Rent Cases* buttressed the legality of the moratorium law. He claimed that the New York rent-control laws upheld in these cases did more to interfere with contracts than the moratorium law before the court. In the former, he explained, "a tenant's right of occupancy continued for a period of two years after the passage of the law as a matter of right, notwithstanding the expiration of his lease." In contrast, under Chapter 339 the owner of a mortgaged property was not entitled to an extension of the year of redemption—and could obtain such an extension only at the court's discretion. Moreover, the post–World War I housing emergency paled in comparison to the severe 1930s Depression.

Separately, Peterson insisted that it was solely the legislature's duty and responsibility to determine when "an emergency exists and how it will be met," and he urged the court to show deference to that legislative judgment unless the law has no real or substantial relation to the emergency. He reminded the court that the Minnesota legislature passed the moratorium law without a single dissenting vote. "When members of a great legislative body . . . entertaining widely different economic and political views on practically every public question," he wrote, "all arrive at the same conclusion and declare that an emergency exists . . . the court should not attempt to say that every member of our legislative body was wrong."

In his capacity on the Judiciary Committee, State Representative Leonard Eriksson had invited William Prosser, a professor at the University of Minnesota Law School, to outline a constitutional theory in support of the moratorium law. Professor Prosser advised that the proposed law follow the pattern of the New York Emergency Housing Acts upheld in the *Rent Cases*. In turn, Eriksson's amicus brief concluded that the "whereas" clauses of Chapter 339 sufficiently proved the existence of a public emergency, and that commonsense observations "conclusively demonstrate its existence in such dreadful proportions as to threaten the safety, health, and morals of our people, as well as the peace, well-being and order of the state." Minnesota's urban mortgage debt was approximately $1.2 billion, Eriksson's brief noted, and its farm debt was "approximately five hundred million dollars. . . . From August, 1929, to March, 1932, the retail prices of food fell thirty-six percent, and prices paid to farmers for the same food fell fifty-seven percent." Eriksson estimated that the net cash income of the average Minnesota farm had plunged from $888 in 1920 to $141 in 1932 (and his estimates were not the lowest). But of course these were averages; many of those trying to make a living producing America's food were actually losing money, thousands were at risk of eviction, and rural communities were approaching a boiling point. "People, out of natural despair, because of a situation over which they had no control," this amicus brief stated, "openly rebelled and prevented, not alone in this state but in other states, foreclosure sales by the constituted authorities." Indeed, the crisis had turned many people against capitalists. Urban developers were once hailed as men who helped improve their communities but now were "referred to as undeserving speculators."

Eriksson's brief concluded that citizens were closely watching the actions of the legislature and were "ready to pronounce the sentence of death on sham relief, just as they pronounce now the sentence of death on sham arguments." The moratorium was a policy necessity during a time of emergency. Moreover, the legislature had soberly considered a variety of relief proposals, carefully weighing the economic conditions and principles of law. The legislature "recognized that law is neither static nor an exact science" and that courts keep step with the progress of society. The Preamble to the Constitution itself, Eriksson noted, was "ordained to 'establish justice, insure domestic

{ *Chapter 5* }

tranquility (and to) promote the general welfare.'" The Minnesota legislature also recognized that relief for the debtor could not come at the expense of the creditor. A proper balance had to be found to protect the interests of both. But the courts – "man's best and safest friend" – could be relied upon to find this balance.

The amicus brief by Bryce Lehmann, the private attorney, relied more on precedent than on descriptions of the current crisis. First, it argued that "every law is presumed to be constitutional unless its violation of the constitution is proved beyond all reasonable doubt." Lehmann admitted that a number of debtor-relief laws had been declared unconstitutional under the Contract Clause, but he noted precedents upholding a change in remedy for contractual obligations that did not violate constitutional provisions. Second, his brief asserted that creditors were not "substantially affected" by the moratorium law because they still owned their properties and received at least partial payments. When the public interest in protecting a class of individuals and providing it with relief becomes more important than protecting vested contract rights, a partial change in the contractual rights of individuals is justified. Without relief, large numbers of Minnesotans were likely to become public charges, and homeownership, real estate values, and state property-tax income would all decline further. Citing case law as far back as a moratorium Wisconsin enacted during the Panic of 1857, Lehmann's third (and by now quite familiar) argument was that Chapter 339 did not violate the Due Process Clause but rather legitimately exercised the police power. Fourth and finally, Lehmann's brief argued that the law was a legitimate regulation of an equitable jurisdiction already possessed by the courts: "The title of the act, the preamble, and the provisions of section 4, indicate that the law simply imposes the requirement of fairness upon the mortgagor and mortgagee in their dealings with each other during this economic emergency." Under the provisions of the moratorium law, the proper role of the courts is to ensure fairness and equity.

In *Blaisdell v. Home Building and Loan Association*, the Minnesota Supreme Court upheld the moratorium law in a 6–1 decision announced on July 7, 1933. The majority opinion was written by Associate Justice Andrew Holt, the most senior member of the court. Holt had been appointed in 1911 and elected one year later. Although he never actively sought votes, Justice Holt was reelected five times, each time by increasingly larger majorities. A memorial by the Minnesota State Bar Association upon his death in 1948 described his opinions as intellectually honest in their treatment of precedent, unbiased, and restrained. Holt was not known as a judge who felt that it was his duty to revise the common law or judicially alter statutes or the state constitution. Yet he was also described as one who recognized that law is neither rigid nor inflexible but amenable to gradual evolution in order to keep pace with a changing society.

Writing for the court, Holt acknowledged that the law impaired the obligation of contracts but concluded that the Contract Clause did not bar the state from protecting public health, safety, morals, and welfare during an economic emergency. The law did not go beyond what was reasonable in a temporary crisis. "Although emergency cannot become the source of power," Holt wrote in a line that U.S. Chief Justice Hughes would lean on, "an emergency may afford a reason for putting forth a latent governmental power already enjoyed but not previously exercised." Justice Holt relied on the *Rent Cases* for the proposition that, in a public emergency, "statutes may be enacted which impair temporarily the obligations of contract, provided they be such as the emergency reasonably demands and the impairment be no more than is just and equitable."

Holt rejected the Home Building and Loan Association's assertion that the so-called emergency addressed by the legislation was merely a private one between mortgagors and mortgagees. Comparing the mortgage crisis in Minnesota to the housing shortage following World War I, he insisted that "whether numerous owners of homes and lands — providing the necessary shelter and means of livelihood — must lose them because a temporary, unforeseen economic depression prevents a redemption within the time the law or contract permits" was entirely a matter of "public concern."

Justice Holt further stressed the moderate nature of the law. Although the right to foreclose by advertisement would be withheld up to May 1, 1935, the right to foreclose by action remained intact. The district courts could extend the period of redemption, and during that period the mortgagor had to make payments toward taxes, insurance, and the mortgage. Holt also distinguished the Minnesota moratorium from a similar statute struck down by the North Dakota Supreme

Court a few weeks earlier in *State ex rel. Cleveringa v. Klein.* The broad North Dakota moratorium had set no maximum time period for redemption, whereas the Minnesota law required the mortgagor to pay the reasonable rental value of the property for a limited redemption period.

Chief Justice Samuel B. Wilson and Justice Ingerval Olsen wrote separate concurring opinions. Wilson agreed completely with Justice Holt's majority opinion. In addition, he noted that the law merely transferred statutory foreclosure by advertisement into foreclosure by action, that is, through the courts. Minnesota's chief justice further noted that as "time marched on," the U.S. Supreme Court, especially in the *Rent Cases*, had established a "modern judicial doctrine" that allowed the courts to meet new and changing conditions. He deemed the Minnesota moratorium a reasonable exercise of the police power of the state because it protected the interests of both the mortgagor and the mortgagee during hard times. He next asserted that "mortgagees have little to fear from this particular statute." While the law temporarily shielded the mortgagor from loss of property and a deficiency judgment, Wilson wrote, it took "so little away from the mortgagee that it cannot be said to invoke an unreasonable application of the police power." When police powers are exercised by the state, all parties must make sacrifices. For the chief justice, the law was not a violation of the constitution but a "vindication of our form of constitutional government."

Justice Olsen focused his concurring opinion on the nature of emergencies and how they lowered the threshold for justifiable police-power interventions. He, too, assured skeptics of state intervention that Chapter 339 was not "drastic or dangerous," as the dissenting opinion (discussed below) would suggest. He also rejected the dissenting argument that financial crises cannot authorize emergency powers simply because they are recurring events that can be anticipated, unlike natural disasters. "The present nation-wide and world-wide business and financial crisis has the same results as if it were caused by a flood, earthquake, or disturbance in nature," he averred, "and to say that economic crises are to be anticipated is no good ground for making any distinction." According to Olsen, the test of an emergency is not its causes but the resulting "want, suffering, and danger." Citing the rent-control cases as precedent, Olsen concluded that an economic emergency existed and that the law was a reasonable exercise of the police powers.

The lone dissenter, Justice Royal A. Stone, insisted that the moratorium law violated the Due Process and Equal Protection Clauses of the federal and state constitutions. He claimed that it "made no attempt" to define standards or establish rules for what shall be "just and equitable." In his view, judges were left with too much discretion to fashion substitute contracts. Stone acknowledged that constitutions must change from time to time but insisted that such change "should be brought about openly and honestly by amendment rather than nullification." It was dangerous for the courts to provide cover for nullification by condoning legislation that plainly violated constitutional guarantees.

Justice Stone's *Blaisdell* dissent did not hurt him politically. Like Justice Holt, who authored the majority opinion, he was reelected in 1936 by over 150,000 votes. Then again, it is difficult to assess the influence of partisan politics on the decision because of the selection process for Minnesota Supreme Court justices. Minnesota's original 1857 constitution had required the selection of justices in partisan elections, for terms of seven years. In 1883, the terms were reduced to six years. In 1912, during the peak of the progressive movement's efforts to reduce the power of political parties and promote "direct democracy," the legislature required that judicial candidates appear on the ballot without party designation and inaugurated open primaries for judicial candidates. Both of these reforms still stand today. Prior to the establishment of the judicial primary, often three or more candidates would run for a single seat in the general election, with the largest field occurring in 1898, when nine candidates competed for three seats on the court.

Even after the establishment of nonpartisan judicial elections, most justices were initially appointed by the governor to fill vacancies that occurred because of retirement or death. Appointees served for the remainder of a term but then faced election thereafter. All seven of the justices hearing the *Blaisdell* case were first appointed by the governor, with each serving at least one year in this manner before winning a nonpartisan election.

The Blaisdells' case returned to state district court. In late July 1933, the district court conducted a hearing to determine fair rental value for the Blaisdells' home as stipulated by the law. Judge Mathias Baldwin presided. The proceedings began with George Stiles, the Blaisdells' attorney, offering into evidence Petitioners' Exhibit A: a copy of the original mortgage contract. As before, Karl Covell, the Association's attorney, immediately objected to the introduction of any evidence, claiming that the moratorium law violated the Contract, Due Process, and Equal Protection Clauses of the Constitution. Notwithstanding the decision by the Minnesota Supreme Court, Covell insisted that Chapter 339 was "invalid and null and void" because it failed to establish and define standards or rules by which the courts were to be guided, attempted to delegate legislative powers to the courts, and represented an attempt by the legislature to invade the province of the courts. Judge Baldwin overruled all of the objections.

Both lawyers agreed that, after a regular foreclosure by advertisement, the Home Building and Loan Association bought the property for $3,700.98. They also agreed the property had a fair and reasonable current market value of $6,000. Stiles stated that the petitioners had been and still were the owners of the premises described in the mortgage contract. Covell would not admit to that stipulation. Stiles further stipulated that the taxes on the property had not been paid for 1928 and 1929, but were paid by the Association prior to the foreclosure sale. Those taxes amounted to $508.97. Combining the purchase price paid by the Association at the foreclosure sale, interest, taxes, and insurance, the total cost for the Blaisdells to repossess the house would be $4,056.39. The Blaisdells made three payments in January and February 29, 1932, amounting to $125.40, and no payments had been made since then. Finally, Stiles admitted that the Blaisdells filed for an extension of the redemption period as required by Chapter 339, and that the hearing was to determine the terms of the extension.

Both sides at the hearing presented witnesses in order to determine the "fair and reasonable rental value" that the Blaisdells would pay to the Association to remain on their property. This amount partially turned on what the Blaisdells themselves could secure in rental income from tenants. (The law stipulated that the court determine what the entire property could garner on the open rental market, so the sides were put in the odd situation of debating a hypothetical scenario of what the six-unit apartment building would rent for if it were not broken up, as if many individual families were looking for a fourteen-room house in the depths of the Depression!) The sides conducted an extensive discussion about the condition and rental history of the building, and Rosella claimed that the Blaisdells took home about $41.50 per month in rental income after expenses, a figure very close to the amount of their mortgage payment. Asked by Stiles what the Blaisdells should pay to the Association per month, Rosella cited the current downturn and answered $30. Stiles asked Rosella if she and John had made an effort to refinance the home; such action was not required under the terms of the law, but he wanted to demonstrate that the couple had made a good faith effort to meet their contractual obligations. Rosella replied that the couple had visited the Northwestern Building and Loan Association and inquired about a loan but had not made a formal application.

On cross-examination, Karl Covell pointedly questioned Rosella's proposal of a $30 payment to the Association. He also suggested that if the Blaisdells took better care of their units, they could increase their rental income. Covell then quibbled with Rosella over the cost of repairs and recurring expenses and asked her about vacancies. Rosella admitted that with the exception of one apartment vacant for most of the summer, she was collecting rent from the other apartments, although one tenant was behind in her payments. Next, several witnesses for John and Rosella testified, including the head of a realty company and the owner of several apartment buildings. These witnesses estimated that the house would secure only $28 to $35 per month as a whole on the open rental market. This figure seems very low, given that the average rent that the Blaisdells received from the six rental units was over $30, but it is true that the market was very depressed and that boardinghouses often rented for much less as a whole than the sum of their parts.

Before Covell called his first witnesses for the Association, he again moved to dismiss. Judge Baldwin inexplicably responded, "Regretfully, denied." The attorney proceeded to call to the stand George Carlton, a member of the Real Estate Board of Minneapolis and president of David P. Jones and Company, a real estate, mortgage, and rental business. Carlton testified that he had inspected the Blaisdell home earlier that very day. He estimated the rental value of the property to be

$50 a month, unfurnished. Covell then called Paul Von Kuster, vice president and treasurer of the David C. Bell Company, a real estate firm. Von Kuster testified that he had been in the mortgage business in Minneapolis for forty years and was a member of the appraisal committee of the Minneapolis Real Estate Board. He had inspected the home with Carlton and estimated the rental value to be $55 a month, unfurnished. A third witness, James Moffett, owned a local rental business. He had inspected the home about two months prior to the trial and identified a similar fair market value. Following Moffett's testimony, both lawyers concluded their witness list.

Apparently, John Blaisdell never testified at the second hearing, as there is no record he was called to the witness stand. At the end of the hearing, the counsel for the Association recalled Rosella for cross-examination. Covell introduced a picture of the house. Rosella verified the photo but added that it did not show a new roof and improvements to the grounds. We also learn from this testimony that the house was about eighteen years old in 1933 and in good condition, and that the Blaisdells had added a two-car garage after they purchased the property. With the photo confirmed, Covell introduced a copy of the mortgage foreclosure record, which was admitted into evidence, and that closed the testimony in the case. Before the proceedings were adjourned, Covell made one last motion to dismiss the lawsuit on constitutional grounds. Again, Judge Mathias Baldwin denied the motion.

Baldwin issued his order on July 21, 1933. The court granted the Blaisdells a two-year moratorium on mortgage payments until May 1, 1935. During this period, they would be obligated to pay $40 a month to the Home Building and Loan Association, to be applied to taxes, insurance, interest, and a small amount of the mortgage principal. Although this amount was essentially the same as the Blaisdells' existing mortgage payment, the Association opposed these terms and refused to accept the payments pending another Contract Clause–based appeal to the Minnesota Supreme Court. Even if the Blaisdells had been paying the $50-per-month figure listed on their census form and not the $41.80 noted on the original 1928 contract (which is simply not true, given that court records note payments of $41.80 in early 1932 before the Blaisdells began defaulting), the Home Building and Loan Association seems to have received a favorable settlement. All of this suggests a remarkable irony: the test case that

determined the fate of the Minnesota Mortgage Moratorium Act—
which in turn would remake Contract Clause jurisprudence—involved
a pro-lender settlement that barely reduced monthly payments for the
borrower. It is also important to keep in mind that the law merely
established procedures for extending the redemption period (although
the courts could also strike down any foreclosure sale). The law did
not wipe out foreclosures, and it did not, as some conservative opponents of the *Blaisdell* decision have suggested, provide a grace period
after which debtors could resume normal mortgage payments.

Six days after Judge Baldwin's order, the state high court issued a
per curiam opinion. Latin for "by the court," a per curiam opinion is
one from an appellate court issued in the name of the court rather
than specific judges. Such opinions are usually brief, and this one was
no exception. The court simply stated, "We are of the opinion that
the decision in the first appeal rules this appeal, and on the authority
thereof the judgment is affirmed."

After the Minnesota Supreme Court upheld the moratorium,
experts turned to evaluating both the technical merits of Chapter 339
and the economic assumptions behind it. Ten months after the law's
passage, William Prosser, the University of Minnesota law professor
who had participated in its drafting, offered a few observations on its
operations at the ground level, claiming that "opinions appear to be
more or less agreed." First, Prosser observed that a surprisingly small
number of eligible debtors applied for relief, perhaps only one in
twenty, which he attributed "to the fact that mortgage holders have
adopted a very conciliatory attitude and are disposed to enter into a
reasonable agreement without the necessity of a court order." Indeed,
widespread evidence suggests that while the moratorium law clearly
changed the rules of the game under which lenders and property owners operated, the crisis had already forced lenders toward a more
accommodating posture.

Second, Prosser noted that many debtors simply could not hope to
gain from the act because "they have no hope of ultimate redemption
or because the property produces no income and they are unable to
pay the 'rental value' that the court may require." Prosser's point here
speaks to the basic moderation of the law—it hardly represented a
giveaway to property owners in arrears. Third, the professor observed
that the courts had not become clogged by cases under the new law.

Although there would be more than 4,000 cases pending in the state courts of Minnesota by the time the U.S. Supreme Court ruled in *Blaisdell*, more than half of the applications for relief were resolved by agreement of the parties without the taking of evidence. Fourth, two-thirds of relief applicants secured an extension of their redemption period rather than a change in the method of foreclosure. Fifth, a lack of uniformity in the courts hindered administration of the law. In some cases, the court demanded that the applicant pay rent that exceeded the market rental value of the property, and in some cases only 10 percent of the rental value. "The protection given the creditor probably is greatest in the cities," Prosser noted, but leniency depended upon individual judge and region. "The discretion of the court, like the length of the chancellor's foot, is almost the only controlling factor." Sixth, most of the applicants for relief acted in good faith and only rarely defaulted on negotiated payments.

Regarding the law's economic effects, Professor Prosser identified a reasonable likelihood that, as its critics charged, the moratorium had made mortgage loans harder to come by in Minnesota. Building in Minneapolis (a proxy for lending activity) had dropped in the first four months after the law's passage, although Prosser admitted that the comparison between early 1933 and early 1934 was faulty because the nation had suffered through a banking crisis in 1933. Still, he recounted a "general feeling on the part of lenders that the Act has made mortgage loans much less desirable and that it has increased the necessity for caution. Some insurance companies issued orders that no more loans were to be made in Minnesota, with reference to the moratorium."

On the other hand, Prosser identified ample support for the law within the financial community — and the promise of even more support to come should adjudication of the law improve. He quoted a statement, "typical of opinions expressed by mortgagees," by the president of a mortgage company. "'Where the statute is being properly administered, as it is in Minneapolis and Duluth,'" this particular mortgage executive said, "'we have no fault to find with it. In fact, it is working rather well. The trouble is that some of the country judges cannot be made to see that there are such things as taxes, insurance, and interest, to say nothing of depreciation, and that somebody has to carry them.'" In sum, Prosser painted a picture of a moderate law working moderately well and only moderately interfering with the lending market. "Nothing very revolutionary has occurred in Minnesota, or in the [Minnesota] Supreme Court," he concluded. "The intent of the framers of the contracts clause has been defeated, but only to an extent covered by previous decisions." Revolutionary or not, the fate of the Minnesota Mortgage Moratorium Act would soon rest with the U.S. Supreme Court.

CHAPTER 6

The Hughes Court

Four Horsemen, Three Musketeers, and Two Swingers

At the time of the 1934 *Blaisdell* litigation, the U.S. Supreme Court was led by Charles Evans Hughes, a Republican former governor of New York and unsuccessful candidate for president. Scholars often use the Court during Hughes's tenure as chief justice — 1930 to 1941 — as an entry point into debating the proper role of the Supreme Court in American society, primarily because the Hughes Court shaped the contours of the modern regulatory state by greatly expanding the power of both the federal government and the states to regulate economic activity and respond to economic crises. Although the primary goal of this chapter is to detail the justices, therefore, it is important to bear in mind that *Blaisdell* was a crucial first step on the way to the Constitutional Revolution of 1937.

The Hughes Court was closely divided between conservative and liberal justices, with Chief Justice Hughes and Owen Roberts somewhere in the middle. The conservative bloc consisted of George Sutherland, Willis Van Devanter, James McReynolds, and Pierce Butler. Sutherland and Van Devanter were Republicans, while McReynolds and Butler were Democrats. Three justices constituted the liberal bloc: Louis Brandeis, Harlan Fiske Stone, and Benjamin Cardozo (who replaced Oliver Wendell Holmes in 1932). Until 1937, Chief Justice Hughes and Owen Roberts tended to be moderate "swing voters," and they often held the balance of power. True, the partisan and ideological divisions among the justices were often exaggerated, as they are today. On average, the nine justices reached a unanimous decision in 85 percent of cases each term from 1930 to 1934. Nonetheless, the remaining cases exposed fundamental differences over not just issues of social and economic policy but also the appropriate role of the courts in reviewing state and federal legislation.

If ever a man looked the part of chief justice, it was Charles Evans

Hughes. He was an imposing figure, both physically and mentally; Robert Jackson, who joined the Supreme Court in 1941, once said that he "looks like God and talks like God." With piercing eyes, a thick, white mustache, and a Vandyke beard that had long gone out of fashion, Hughes exuded the moral authority of a stern father figure. His presence in a room could awe and intimidate. "One just did not drool or needlessly talk if Hughes was around," remarked Harvard Law professor Felix Frankfurter, who would join the Court in 1939.

Up until the important 1934 term, Hughes defied characterization as a liberal or conservative. He had served as an associate justice from 1910 to 1916 and generally voted to uphold social and regulatory legislation, including the Pure Food and Drug Act, the Mann Act, and the Employers' Liability Act, which established workers' compensation for injured railroad employees. He often joined Holmes and Brandeis in defending civil rights and liberties. Hughes resigned from the Court in June 1916 to accept the Republican nomination for the presidency, subsequently losing to Woodrow Wilson. After returning to private practice, Hughes was appointed secretary of state in 1921 by President Harding, and he served in that position until 1925, when he resumed private practice. By the 1930s, even as he retained many liberal views, Hughes had become a defender of railroad magnates, insurance companies, and the oil, chemical, and mining industries. His work for powerful corporations led *Time* magazine, upon Hughes's nomination to the position of chief justice, to write that "the pure white flame of Liberalism had burned out in him to a sultry ash of Conservatism."

Upon the death of Chief Justice Howard Taft in 1930, President Hoover nominated Hughes to succeed him. Despite Hughes's legal credentials and political résumé, his confirmation was one of the most contentious in a century. Throughout the 1920s, the Taft Court, armed with liberty of contract doctrine, increasingly had championed corporations and property owners against state efforts to use police power to regulate the economy. Liberals, progressives, and states' rights advocates were deeply concerned with the Court's conservative bent, and their frustrations boiled over after the Hughes nomination.

There was little doubt that Hughes would be confirmed, but progressives used the opportunity of his appointment proceedings to educate the public about the power and influence of the Court over the economic and social life of the people. Senator Clarence Dill (D-Wash.) sought to "call the attention of the people of this country to the fact that if they would free themselves and have justice at the hands of their Government they must reach the Supreme Court of the United States by putting men on that bench who hold economic theories which are fair and just to all, and not in the interest of the privileged few." Progressives did not doubt Hughes's integrity or competence but considered him too pro-business and "reactionary." Senator Dill declared, "Property rights and the great monopolies and the money power in America never had an abler or more effective champion." Many other Senate progressives, such as William Borah of Idaho, George Norris of Nebraska (a Republican who would support the New Deal), and Robert La Follette Jr. of Wisconsin, also opposed his nomination. Senator Norris said that "no man in public life" had so exemplified "the influence of powerful combinations in the political and financial world."

Hughes was confirmed over these objections as the eleventh chief justice of the United States and would eventually prove his detractors wrong. Hughes was well suited to be chief justice. He was organized and detail-oriented, and many scholars suggest that he had a photographic memory. He thought, spoke, and acted with discipline and precision. He valued nonpartisanship and professionalism in public service and sincerely desired to be viewed as a political moderate. As chief, he was often more concerned about the Court's institutional reputation than about the policy consequences of individual decisions. Although a few colleagues and friends found him friendly and affectionate, many people who worked with him considered him cold and unapproachable; Teddy Roosevelt called him the "bearded iceberg," and Hughes himself once commented that the public viewed him as a "human icicle."

The "white flame of liberalism" may have barely flickered during his years as a corporate lawyer, but Hughes retained a progressive perspective on some issues. As he had during his tenure as an associate justice, Chief Justice Hughes demonstrated a "willingness to uphold government regulation of wages, hours, and prices against attacks grounded in substantive due process." Prior to *Blaisdell*, he voted with the three liberals in several cases, including *O'Gorman & Young v. Hartford Insurance Co.* (1931), which sustained a New Jersey regulation of the commissions paid to agents by fire insurance companies. The Court determined that the insurance industry was a business affected with a public interest, and a state's police power allowed it to regulate rates.

Justice Owen Roberts was the wildcard on the Hughes Court. A progressive journal of the day described him as "a conservative with liberal tendencies." His biographer William Ross notes that Roberts shared many corporate clients with Hughes but was not viewed as negatively by liberals. His connections to big business aside, Roberts sometimes represented labor unions for a nominal fee and served as a trustee to the predominantly African American Lincoln College. He was certainly more progressive on racial issues than North Carolinian John J. Parker, whom Hoover had originally nominated for the seat and who actively opposed civil rights.

Three months after the *Blaisdell* decision, Roberts authored the majority opinion in *Nebbia v. New York* (another favorite of progressives, as we will see), and his vote was critical in upholding much New Deal and state regulation. At the same time, Roberts also wrote several restrictive opinions involving government's authority to regulate the market. For example, in *Railroad Retirement Board v. Alton Railroad Co.* (1935), Roberts penned the majority opinion striking down a federally mandated pension system for railroad workers funded by the companies. Justice Roberts's mixed record on issues of federal and state regulation of the market made him completely unpredictable. His personal traits may help explain his contradictory voting record. Scholars describe him as uncertain of his own abilities, easily persuadable, and highly sensitive to personal and public pressure. He did not handle criticism well, often responding by shifting his position.

Hughes's first term as chief justice gave progressives hope that the Court was moving in a liberal direction. At the end of the 1930–31 term, the national periodical *Literary Digest* noted "The Supreme Court's Shift to Liberalism," and *Time* magazine declared, "Liberals Have It." Of course, the term "liberalism" is fraught with ideological and historical peril. American liberalism as we understand it today did not begin to emerge until the early twentieth century; the labels of "conservatism" and "liberalism" were thus in flux in the 1930s, and the placement of some of the Court's justices within these camps was tenuous. In fact, Chief Justice Hughes and Justice Roberts joined the liberal bloc in several cases in 1931, giving the impression of a "shift to liberalism," but they aligned with the conservatives in key cases during the 1932 and 1933 terms. Moreover, we should be cautious about grafting our modern definitions onto past historical actors. Nonetheless, it is fair to conclude that several justices on the New Deal Court articulated a liberalism that looks familiar to us today. Whereas nineteenth-century classical liberalism believed that governments should intervene sparingly in the market and in the lives of citizens, the updated liberalism that developed at the turn of the twentieth century posited an active role for the state in society and economy in order to curb the excesses of industrial capitalism. This new liberalism enjoyed some of its first major victories early in the century via the progressive movement in the United States and the ascendancy of the Liberal Party in England, but the New Deal represented its political triumph and the solidification of the dominant understanding of the word "liberalism" in the United States.

The three liberals in place on the Hughes Supreme Court by 1932 — Benjamin Cardozo, Louis Brandeis, and Harlan Stone — shared an East Coast background and a progressive and pragmatic outlook. Rather than viewing law as certain and consistent in meaning, the liberals regarded law as an instrument to solve social problems. Dubbed the "Three Musketeers," they often met on Friday afternoons at Brandeis's apartment to review files for Saturday's conference discussion of pending cases.

When the venerable Oliver Wendell Holmes announced his retirement in January 1932, after thirty years of service on the Court, a widespread public campaign pressured President Hoover to nominate Cardozo, a distinguished legal scholar and chief judge of the New York Court of Appeals, the state's highest court. Cardozo's opinions on the Court of Appeals altered the common law of torts and contracts and shaped legal thinking throughout the country. Despite broad support for Cardozo, President Hoover was hesitant to nominate him. Two justices on the Court, Hughes and Stone, already hailed from New York. Unlike the situation today, the geographic balance of the Court was a major consideration at this time. The West and the South had legitimate claims to the next open seat, and appointing someone from those areas would have helped the political fortunes of the Republican Party. Moreover, Cardozo was a liberal and Hoover a conservative. According to Joseph Pollard, who wrote an early biography on Cardozo, Hoover resisted the pressure of public and professional opinion and sought alternative candidates. Senator William Borah tried to address Hoover's concern about geographic balance by assuring the president that Cardozo's appointment would win "the applause of the whole country and not merely one part." Hoover then consulted with Justice Stone, his personal friend. Stone counseled that, although other candidates might be able to win Senate confirmation, the appointment of Cardozo would win instant confirmation and tremendous national approval. That advice convinced Hoover, and in February he nominated Cardozo to the Court.

Cardozo's appointment turned out to be a critical one. If Hoover had selected a conservative Republican, the key 1934 decisions of *Blaisdell* and *Nebbia* likely would have gone in the other direction, and much of the New Deal could have been overturned. The junior justice during most of his short, five-year tenure, Cardozo was assigned few major opinions because Chief Justice Hughes controlled assignments when in the majority and often selected himself. (Hughes would assert this prerogative in the *Blaisdell* case.) Cardozo realized that his role on the Supreme Court was more limited than the one he had enjoyed on the New York Court of Appeals. He also was disappointed with the lack of collegiality among the justices. Still, his vote was critical for forming a majority in cases supporting government regulation of the market, and his unpublished opinions and memos often influenced majority opinions.

Cardozo's liberalism was rooted in the intellectual trends of the progressive movement. *The Nature of the Judicial Process*, his classic 1921 book based on four lectures delivered at Yale Law School, articulated a legal theory influential among liberals: sociological jurisprudence. Advocated most famously by Massachusetts and later U.S. Supreme Court Justice Oliver Wendell Holmes, Harvard Law School dean Roscoe Pound, and Cardozo, sociological jurisprudence held that in order for law to remain a vital force in society, the judicial decision-making process should be based on more than legal principles and logical reasoning. Judges should consider the social context of a case or, at the very least, defer to the majoritarian legislature's determination expressed in legislation. Broadly speaking, sociological jurisprudence can be described as pragmatic and utilitarian. Pound once defined sociological jurisprudence as "a movement for pragmatism as a phi-losophy of law," and he argued that law "must be judged by the result it achieves, not by the niceties of its internal structure." Sociological jurisprudence was pragmatic in demonstrating concern for the con-sequences of decision making and in viewing law as flexible in react-ing to social and economic problems, and it was utilitarian in recog-nizing that the public good must sometimes trump individual rights. It was thus often put in the service of liberal reforms.

Cardozo was the first modern judge to candidly explain the com-plexities of the decision-making process. In *The Nature of the Judicial Process*, he emphasized the unpredictable and subjective human ele-ment in judging and described how changing economic and social forces shaped the law's development. He called his approach "the method of sociology" but recognized that judges also must consider history and tradition. Cardozo was not a radical by any means. He emphasized applying the methods of philosophy to judging and the importance of logic, and he stressed that an appellate judge should only rarely depart from established legal doctrine and precedent—that is, apply the method of sociology. Only a strong argument based on history, tradition, or justice should overcome the presumption of logic. Still, in recognizing the need for the law to innovate when con-fronted with social and economic disruptions, and to use social sci-ence evidence in decision making, Cardozo became one of the lead-ing advocates of sociological jurisprudence. As seen especially in his unpublished draft opinion, sociological jurisprudence influenced his approach to the issues in the *Blaisdell* case.

Cardozo had no patience for rigid legal categories and distinctions. He opposed the "direct/indirect effects" test when reviewing con-gressional power to regulate local economic activity under the Con-stitution's Commerce Clause, and he rejected distinctions between manufacturing and commerce. These tests had been used for several decades to limit the power of Congress to regulate interstate and intrastate commerce. Most famously, Congress had designed the 1890 Sherman Anti-Trust Act to break up monopolies in restraint of trade. But in an 8–1 ruling in *U.S. v. E.C. Knight Co.* (1895), the Court held that a company controlling 98 percent of the sugar refining business in the United States could not be regulated by federal authority. The Court characterized sugar refining as manufacturing, not commerce, and concluded that control of almost all refining of sugar had only an indirect effect on interstate commerce. The distinction between an indirect and a direct effect on commerce is subjective, and conservative courts often used it to restrict government regulation. Cardozo also favored statutory and administrative regulation in response to social and economic problems, which made him more receptive to New Deal programs.

Prior to his appointment to the Court by President Wilson in 1916, Louis Brandeis had developed a reputation as a defender of progressive labor and consumer legislation. Known as the "People's Attorney," he spent over two decades fighting the manipulation of stocks and securities, the power of big banks, unfair labor practices, and monopolies. In the U.S. Supreme Court case of *Muller v. Oregon* (1908), Brandeis, then a private attorney representing the state of Oregon, famously defended an Oregon law that limited the number of hours women could work to ten hours per day and sixty hours a week. Curt Muller owned a laundry and worked his laundresses more than ten hours a day. He claimed that the law violated his liberty of contract under the Fourteenth Amendment's Due Process Clause.

In support of the law, Brandeis put together a brief consisting of only a couple of pages of legal precedents and over 100 pages of economic and social science findings on working conditions in sweatshops and factories. We now call legal briefs that lean heavily on social science research "Brandeis briefs." The overwhelming social science data convinced the High Court that the law was a reasonable exercise of the state's police power to protect the physical and maternal health of women. The "Brandeis brief" was sociological jurisprudence in action. It revolutionized the judicial decision-making process, prompting judges to move beyond abstract legal concepts and case precedents to consider real world facts and statistics when reviewing legislation. It also complicated decision making; thereafter, both sides in litigation increasingly presented legal and social science arguments to support their claims and thus thrust judges into the middle of policy disputes.

Brandeis believed that good government was primarily achieved at the state level, where states could act as "laboratories of democracy." Responding to social change required knowledge of varying local conditions. As one who had warned much earlier against the perils of "bigness" in American society, Brandeis was suspicious of expanded

116   { *Chapter 6* }

national government power and distrusted much of the New Deal. Although former chief justice Taft derided him as a socialist, Brandeis was no collectivist. He supported public ownership only of utilities, such as water and electricity. Nonetheless, his ideas about judicial decision making encouraged experimental policy making; he urged judicial restraint and allowing the states flexibility in responding to the Great Depression, which made him inclined to support state legislative initiatives such as moratorium laws and price controls.

Nominated by President Calvin Coolidge to replace Justice Joseph McKenna in 1925, Harlan Fiske Stone was a lifelong Republican and close friend of Herbert Hoover. Stone served as dean of Columbia Law School from 1910 to 1923 and attorney general of the United States from 1924 to 1925. He also had worked at the influential Wall Street firm of Sullivan and Cromwell, and his corporate background generated strong opposition to his appointment from progressives. Chief Justice Taft, a conservative, lobbied Coolidge to appoint Stone because he feared that the president might appoint Benjamin Cardozo or federal judge Learned Hand, two judges he believed would become allies of Brandeis and Holmes, Taft's ideological opponents. Taft would later regret his support for Stone, who indeed often voted with the two liberal giants. Taft sometimes referred to Brandeis, Holmes, and Stone as the "Bolsheviki" because of their support for government regulation. It is ironic that two Republican presidents, Coolidge and Hoover, were responsible for appointing two of the most liberal justices, Stone and Cardozo, on the Hughes Court. As discussed in the following chapter, both justices contributed significantly to the *Blaisdell* decision.

Stone initially opposed sociological jurisprudence. He once said that "abstract or social justice as a test for the correctness of judicial decisions is absolutely without value." By the 1920s, however, he had become convinced "not only of the evolutionary character of the judicial process but also of the importance of social values to it." In a 1923 *Columbia Law Review* article, Stone wrote, "Sociological jurisprudence, rightly understood, ought to give a new inspiration and a new trend to legal development." As an associate justice on the Taft Court, Stone often voted with Brandeis and Holmes, and later, on the Hughes Court, he joined Brandeis and Cardozo to sustain federal and state New Deal programs. Stone shared with Brandeis and Holmes a deep skepticism about judicial activism, and he encouraged the liberals on the Hughes Court to exercise judicial restraint.

Like Holmes and Cardozo, Stone had little patience for the abstract categories that the Court had applied over the years in limiting federal and state intervention in the market. He viewed the various legal doctrines argued by lawyers and applied by the Court as "sterile constitutionalism" oblivious to relevant social and economic forces. In *Disanto v. Pennsylvania* (1927), for example, he criticized the direct/indirect distinction for Commerce Clause questions as "too mechanical, too uncertain in . . . application, and too remote from actualities, to be of value." Stone agreed with Justice Holmes's dissenting observation in *Lochner* that a "constitution is not intended to embody a particular economic theory, whether of paternalism and the organic relation of the citizen to the State or of laissez faire." Stone supported most New Deal programs, although he was more cautious than his fellow liberals on the Court about injecting his personal values in opinions. When Chief Justice Hughes retired in 1941, President Roosevelt nominated Stone to be the twelfth chief justice of the United States.

All four conservatives — Sutherland, Van Devanter, McReynolds, and Butler — were born within a year or two of the Civil War, and their social outlook and judicial philosophy were anchored in the Gilded Age of the late nineteenth century. They shared an unquestioned faith in rugged frontier individualism and free markets. According to William Ross, a contemporary biographer of Chief Justice Hughes, some 1930s critics labeled the conservative bloc "murderer's row" because it killed so much reform legislation. Widely respected federal judge Learned Hand called the four conservatives "the mastiffs" based on their eagerness to bite into and overturn the New Deal's major initiatives. More frequently, the media called them the "Four Horsemen of Reaction," and they were later dubbed the "Four Horsemen of the Apocalypse" because their strident warnings about the evils of government intervention practically prophesied the imminent demise of capitalism and republican government. Ross noted that the "mocking label has forever clung to these men, whose losing battles against the rise of the administrative state have consigned them to low levels in lists that rank justices according to their reputation among scholars." Like the three liberals, the Four Horsemen usually met on Friday evenings before the Court's Saturday conference to work out a consensus position.

Especially in the years preceding *Blaisdell*, however, and at times in those that followed it, the Four Horsemen did not always ride together. Sutherland and Van Devanter sometimes broke ranks with the other conservatives in cases involving economic issues and also took liberal positions on some civil rights and liberties issues. Moreover, the four conservatives were occasionally joined by Justice Roberts and Chief Justice Hughes and, in some cases, even by a few of the liberal justices. In "Secret Lives of the Four Horsemen," historian Barry Cushman shows that the jurisprudence of these four justices was more complicated than their moniker suggests. For example, they did on occasion vote to uphold tax and regulatory legislation. Yet it is undeniable that they consistently voted as an anti-intervention bloc in major cases involving federal or state economic recovery legislation. Indeed, they would vote together in both *Blaisdell* and *Nebbia*.

The four conservatives shared a philosophy that bridged an older American conservatism and the modern conservatism that developed after the watershed years of the Depression. These justices subscribed to a traditional American antistatism and faith in individual entrepreneurship that sought to limit government regulation of market activity. They agreed most strongly on matters involving labor legislation and perceived economic redistribution policies, staunchly opposing maximum-hours, minimum-wage, and price-fixing regulations. Consistent with classical legal thought, the Four Horsemen viewed these policies as class legislation that violated the ideal of the state as a neutral umpire in market relations.

The four conservatives also shared a vision of law as fixed rather than flexible, and they believed that the law should maintain its constancy even in times of severe economic stress. To stray from that interpretation would transform the Constitution into an empty vessel that any generation could fill with the political passions of the day. Finally, the conservatives used a public/private dichotomy to assess government regulation. Some regulation and government programs were permitted as long as they protected a genuine public good, but, for the most part, government should stay out of the private sphere. However, they tended to downplay the fact that the language of the Constitution does not establish a public/private distinction or define the boundaries between the two areas. These attitudes influenced the dissenting opinion of Justice Sutherland in the *Blaisdell* case and form the basis of contemporary conservative and libertarian critiques of the decision.

George Sutherland was the intellectual leader of the conservatives. He wrote many opinions on the Hughes Court, including the *Blaisdell* dissent, which Brandeis stated was "one of the finest opinions he had ever read, although he declined to join it." Sutherland deplored pragmatism in constitutional interpretation, arguing that only by adhering to principle can we maintain a government of laws. He wrote that "every attempt to remedy an undesirable condition by setting aside some great fundamental principle has not only generally failed, but has generated consequences more seriously unfortunate than the original evil itself." Although scholars often view him as a prisoner of laissez-faire economic philosophy, Sutherland's approach to law, economics, and government was more sophisticated than a rigid opposition to all state intervention in the market. He shared with his conservative colleagues an antipathy to government intervention, but he was willing to uphold broader regulatory powers in taxing and spending.

The other conservatives' contributions to constitutional jurisprudence have faded over the years. The papers of Pierce Butler and James McReynolds were largely destroyed after they left the Court, and those of Van Devanter and Sutherland offer few insights into their personal and professional lives. Van Devanter was on the Court for twenty-six years and participated in over 5,000 decisions. Though active in conference discussions and author of 360 opinions, he dissented only four times and wrote just one concurrence. Brandeis believed that he may have suffered from writer's block. Like his fellow conservatives, Van Devanter thought that the Constitution requires clear boundaries between areas of private autonomy and public authority. He supported broad spending powers for Congress and implied powers to conduct investigations but consistently opposed government regulation of prices and wages. Van Devanter "lined up always with the conservatives and voted almost always in favor of big business," observed the *New York Times*.

Like his liberal colleague Justice Brandeis, Justice McReynolds opposed "bigness" in nearly all its forms. While the other conservatives had few problems with monopolies or the bigness of national corporations, McReynolds believed in a maximum size above which no business should be permitted to organize, although this threshold was ill-defined. As President Woodrow Wilson's attorney general, he worked to break up powerful monopolies as mandated by the Sherman Anti-Trust Act, but his arrogance and temper led to a poor working relationship with Congress. Nonetheless, Wilson nominated him for the Supreme Court in 1914. Once he was on the Court, Wilson administration officials were shocked to learn McReynolds had harbored strong pro-business, laissez-faire positions. Although he opposed oversized corporations, he strongly supported private enterprise and viewed corporate mergers as a positive reflection of the material wealth of the United States.

As much as he disliked bigness in the market, McReynolds detested bigness in government. Among the four conservatives, he was probably the staunchest opponent of federal and state efforts to respond to the economic crises of the Depression. "If it were not for the Court," he once told his law clerk, "this country would go too far down the road to socialism ever to return." McReynolds so despised Roosevelt that he vowed not to retire "as long as that crippled son of a bitch is in the White House." Indeed, he was the last of the Four Horsemen to leave the bench, retiring in 1941, and, according to Michael Parrish, author of a comprehensive study of the Hughes Court, McReynolds "dissented to the bitter end against government innovations sanctioned by other members of the Hughes Court."

McReynolds, and to a lesser extent Pierce Butler, are mostly remembered today for their many ethnic prejudices. McReynolds was a rabid anti-Semite; his insulting treatment of Louis Brandeis, the first Jewish justice on the Supreme Court, is widely documented. McReynolds regularly refused to shake hands with Justices Brandeis and Cardozo prior to conference. In 1924, he refused to sit with Brandeis for the official Court photograph; no group picture of the Court exists for that year. McReynolds was, according to Chief Justice Taft, "inconsiderate of his colleagues and others and contemptuous of everybody." Burt Solomon's *FDR v. The Constitution* notes that McReynolds "despised women with red nail polish, men who wore wristwatches, and lady lawyers of both sexes." He also loathed anyone who used tobacco. Oliver Wendell Holmes called him a savage.

A former county prosecutor and prominent railroad attorney from Minnesota, Pierce Butler was nominated by President Warren Harding in 1922. Butler owed his appointment to a lobbying effort by Chief Justice Taft and Justice Van Devanter, both of whom sought to solidify the conservative, pro-business wing of the Court against the liberal Holmes and Brandeis. Correctly fearing that he would vote against their interests, progressives and labor groups opposed his nomination. Like the other conservatives, Butler exalted private property and rugged individualism over the activist state. "Too much paternalism, too much wetnursing by the state," he once remarked, "is destructive of individual initiative and development."

Although he was a Democrat and a Catholic, Butler's conservative views won over conservative Republicans in the Senate confirmation process, and his voting record did not disappoint them. Justice Butler voted to overturn nearly twenty acts of Congress during the New Deal, and he supported only three measures of significance to Roosevelt — an anti–New Deal record second only to that of Justice McReynolds. One of those measures, affirming broad authority for the president to issue an arms embargo in *U.S. v. Curtiss-Wright Export Corporation* (1936), had more to do with the president's power over foreign affairs than with the economy. After the conservatives "lost" the doctrinal debate over the New Deal in 1937, Butler authored an increasing number of dissenting opinions: twenty during the 1938 term and thirty-two during his last year. He passed away while in office in November 1939.

In a speech before the Chamber of Commerce of Elmira, New York, in 1907, Charles Evans Hughes, then governor of New York, remarked, "We are under a Constitution, but the Constitution is what the judges say it is." The nine men discussed in this chapter, who comprised the Supreme Court from March 1932 through August 1937, were the Hughes Court justices who would help determine what the Constitution is by deciding *Blaisdell*. It was a closely divided Court, separated by fundamental differences over both the intrinsic value of regulation and the Court's proper role in reviewing state and congressional actions. Minnesota's mortgage moratorium would reveal these differences exquisitely.

CHAPTER 7

The Supreme Court Decides

A "Rational Compromise between
Individual Rights and Public Welfare"

On October 9, 1933, the Supreme Court granted review of *Home Building and Loan Association v. Blaisdell.* The Minnesota Mortgage Moratorium Act was the first economic recovery legislation, state or federal, to reach the Supreme Court. In sustaining the act, the Supreme Court not only placated Minnesota's farmers but also fired the first shot in the jurisprudential revolution through which it embraced the modern regulatory state.

At about the same time, the Court granted review of *Nebbia v. New York*, the case regarding New York State's law fixing the price of milk. *Blaisdell* and *Nebbia* were closely watched as they made their way through the Court. Although these cases involved state legislation, many observers believed that the decisions in them would have an important bearing on the constitutionality of federal recovery legislation and thus ultimately on the survival of President Roosevelt's New Deal.

Oral arguments in the Minnesota mortgage moratorium case were held on November 8 and 9, 1933. Unfortunately, neither transcripts nor recordings of cases from this era exist, and the media covered the arguments very little. Our understanding of what happened derives from the various briefs filed in the case and memos and draft opinions in the public records of the justices. Because the Home Building and Loan Association lost at the state supreme court level, it was the appellant, or petitioner, and the Blaisdells were the appellees, or respondents. Attorney Alfred Bowen, assisted by Karl Covell, Benjamin Meyers, and George Strong, represented the Association.

In his brief on the merits, Bowen made the same overriding three claims against the Minnesota Mortgage Moratorium Act (Chapter 339) used during the state litigation. The petitioners contended that the law was repugnant to the Contract Clause, a taking of property without due process of law in violation of the Fourteenth Amendment, and a denial of the equal protection of the laws under the Fourteenth Amendment.

Bowen denied that the economic depression justified state impairment of contracts. "Neither the conditions recited in the preamble of the Act," he wrote, "nor the actual prevailing conditions, approximate in degree of depression those conditions prevailing throughout the nation prior to adoption of the contract clause in the federal Constitution." The moratorium act's recitation of economic conditions, he argued, only explained what caused the rash of foreclosures but did not justify government action.

The Minnesota law, the petitioners claimed, produced three deleterious consequences to the economy. First, it was aggravating the Depression because it "tends naturally and inevitably to restrict the extension of credit on real estate security in Minnesota." This market-skewing argument, as we noted in chapter 4, has received a sympathetic hearing from economic historians. The petitioners' related point that the somewhat restricted credit market significantly increased foreclosures on existing mortgages seems more dubious given the complete collapse of the housing market. Second, the act increased unemployment because builders could not borrow the funds needed for improvements or new construction. Third, the moratorium froze assets in banks and other lending institutions that would have become liquid in a normally functioning real estate market. Lead attorney Bowen pointed out that even the majority opinion of the Minnesota Supreme Court had recognized that the act restricted the credit market. In obiter dictum (the portions of a majority opinion not essential to deciding a case), the state high court said that it "may well be argued that legislation which impairs contract obligations defeats its purpose. . . . Lenders will not loan their money in a state where the contract for its repayment may be impaired at the uncontrolled whim of the legislature." In his dissenting opinion, Minnesota Supreme Court justice Royal Stone asked, "Just how or from whom can we borrow if we serve notice, as this law does, that foreclosure of mortgages may be deferred indefinitely at the pleasure of officials owing their office to the favor of the debtors?"

Bowen offered several specifics to back up his assertion that the negative effects predicted by the Minnesota Court had already kicked in. Citing records of the building inspector of the City of Minneapolis, Bowen reported that in the five months since passage of Chapter 339, the volume of construction in the city had fallen by 23 percent. Of course, one cannot prove that the moratorium law caused the building decline. The severe depression significantly reduced demand for new housing just as much as the moratorium law impacted the credit market.

Bowen concluded by denying that Chapter 339 "operates for the benefit or welfare of the state as a whole, or of all of its people as a whole, or even for the particular class of debtors intended to be benefited thereby." This question of whom the law benefited was central. Supporters of the moratorium asserted that in an economic emergency, the public welfare trumps individual property rights. Bowen also believed that public policy should enhance the public good — but argued this particular law was contrary to it. In his view, the public good was advanced best by protecting property rights and respecting contractual obligations.

Bowen combined the Contract Clause and Due Process Clause arguments against the Minnesota law as he believed that the Supreme Court had done in *Bronson v. Kinzie* (1843), *Howard v. Bugbee* (1861), and *Barnitz v. Beverly* (1896). For Bowen, these decisions revealed that Minnesota's more recent moratorium act impaired contract rights — and took lenders' property without due process of law. In addition, the moratorium arbitrarily changed provisions of existing law by allowing foreclosure action in the courts rather than by advertisement and by extending the redemption period from one year to three years. In this vein, the law unconstitutionally reduced the Home Building and Loan Association's property for the benefit of the Blaisdells.

The Court also grappled with the emergency powers doctrine. More specifically, it faced two main questions: what constitutes an economic emergency, and when does one justify state impairment of contracts? At one point in the proceedings, according to *Newsweek*, Justice Brandeis leaned over the bench and interrupted the Association's lawyers. "The situation has led the Federal Government to do what it has never done before," Brandeis stated, and the "universality and magnitude of the situation must be considered. What do you say to that?" The Association's lawyers then replied, "There is no emergency which will suspend the limits of the Federal Constitution." And regardless, the Association's lawyers did not even concede that the economic depression constituted an emergency.

Bowen further asserted that no precedents, not even the *Rent Cases*, had reversed, overruled, or modified the cases cited in support of the appellant. The Minnesota Mortgage Moratorium Act was not a legitimate exercise of the police power, and therefore it was void under the Contract and Due Process Clauses of the Constitution. Finally, Bowen argued that the law denied equal protection, not only to the Association and other creditors but also to other debtors. According to this logic, the law created an artificial distinction between some debtors, who enjoyed the benefits of the act, and others, who were required to fulfill the obligations of their contracts. The appellants denied any "reasonable or valid basis for such classification and discrimination." Here was one of the most important legal arguments in the case, even if it remained unexplored in the ruling. The Home Building and Loan Association was arguing that a macroeconomic crisis could not justifiably trigger the kinds of distinctions among classes of people under the police powers that, say, dangerous health conditions in a mine might.

George Stiles and George Simpson, another Minneapolis attorney, represented the Blaisdells. Harry Peterson, the attorney general of Minnesota, and William S. Ervin, assistant attorney general, contributed to the Blaisdells' brief and presented oral arguments. The appellees' brief viewed the moratorium law as an emergency measure justified under the police power. "Every contract is entered into subject to the implied limitation, that in an emergency its terms may be varied in a reasonable manner under the exercise of the police power of the state," they argued. This implied restriction on contract rights was as much a part of any contract as if it had been expressly written into the terms of the agreement. Moreover, the law did not deprive the Association of its property without due process because it provided procedures for an orderly extension of the time of redemption from the mortgage foreclosure sale. A hearing had been held on the Association's petition, and it had had an opportunity to be heard and defend its rights. In addition, the district court had required the Blaisdells to pay a fee during the extended period of redemption.

The state attorneys conceded that "in normal times and under normal conditions" the moratorium law would be unconstitutional. But the times and conditions were unprecedented. "A great economic emergency" had compelled Minnesota to invoke its police and emergency powers to "protect its people in the possession and ownership of their homes and farms and other real estate from the disastrous effects of the wholesale foreclosure of real estate mortgages which inevitably resulted from the present state wide, nation wide, and world wide economic depression." In the tradition of sociological jurisprudence, the respondents offered numerous statistics on the depressed state of Minnesota's economy. More than half of Minnesotans lived on farms, and when the moratorium law was enacted, "the prices of farm products had fallen to a point where most persons engaged in farming could not realize enough from their products to support their families, and pay taxes and interest on the mortgages on their homes." By the spring of 1933, the number of mortgage foreclosures in the state had reached an all-time high, and many serious breaches of the peace took place in connection with the foreclosure sales, especially in rural districts. The *Chicago Daily Tribune* reported that during oral argument, Attorney General Peterson claimed that the Minnesota law was "made necessary by a menacing state of unrest among farmers who had organized to stop foreclosure sales," and that "farmers were being evicted by the thousands."

The brief by George Simpson, one of the Blaisdells' lawyers, relied primarily on all four of the *Rent Cases: Block v. Hirsch* (1921), *Marcus Brown Holding Company v. Feldman* (1921), *Levy Leasing Co. v. Siegel* (1922), and *810 West End Avenue, Inc. v. Stern* (1922). According to the Blaisdells, the emergency recognized by the Supreme Court when it justified the New York rent-control laws was far less severe than the current depression. When the rent laws were passed, housing was scarce and rents were high; now, thousands of farmers had lost or were in danger of losing their homes, and urban homeowners were no better off. Savings had been wiped out, unemployment was high, and "there is the ever present menacing danger of widespread rioting and lawlessness by people otherwise peaceful and law-abiding about to be rendered homeless and shelterless." State legislatures, the Blaisdells concluded, have the power to determine when social and economic conditions rise to the level of an emergency, triggering the authority to take remedial action for the public good.

The Blaisdells rejected the claim that the law violated the Equal Protection Clause of the Fourteenth Amendment by discriminating not only against real estate lenders (e.g., the Home Building and Loan Association) but also debtors whose indebtedness was not secured by home mortgages. In this vein, for instance, the moratorium act did not provide relief to debtors who borrowed to purchase commercial property or an automobile. The Blaisdells' brief, however, cited several precedents upholding state policies that grouped citizens into various categories. It maintained that if a law serves a reasonable public policy purpose and applies impartially to all within the same class, the court must sustain it.

The Blaisdells next contended that the only question before the Court concerned the redemption period extension. More specifically, they urged the Court to respect the intent of the legislature to make the Minnesota Mortgage Moratorium Act severable, meaning that an individual provision could be reviewed and overturned if deemed unconstitutional without affecting other parts of the law. The Blaisdells likely hoped that other aspects of the law would stand if the Court struck down the redemption extension, which indeed would be the only provision adjudicated.

Finally, the Blaisdells' brief held that the Minnesota Mortgage Moratorium Act was just, fair, and reasonable because it benefited both the mortgagor and the mortgagee and merely vested in the courts equitable powers to cope with an emergency. Equity is a concept based on fairness. Rather than demanding the strict application of statutes or common law doctrine, equitable powers permit judges to "do justice" in a case. The Minnesota act, for example, gave judges the power to determine, after a hearing, fair rental value for a property so that the interests of both the creditor and the debtor were protected. As an emergency measure, Chapter 339 was "an extremely conservative law." It protected the mortgagee as well as the mortgagor. "It does not wipe out the mortgagee's security or impair that security," the brief noted. "It merely gives the court the power, in cases where it is equitable, to postpone for a limited time, the mortgagee's right to realize on his security by requiring reasonable payments to be made." The relief provided was limited to the period of distress, gave fair consideration to both parties, and allowed the courts to decide what is fair and reasonable between the mortgagor and mortgagee. The brief did not consider that the creditor would never get back the payments forgone during the period of distress.

An amicus curiae (friend of the court) brief, sympathetic to the Blaisdells, was filed by Vernon Vrooman, a professor of constitutional law at Drake University Law School in Des Moines. His was the only amicus brief filed. Unlike today, when contentious cases before the Court can generate dozens of amicus briefs, this low number was not atypical for the time. Vrooman's brief was long and rambling, citing over 280 federal and state precedents and legal treatises. Vrooman wrote in "the spirit and attitude" of the New York Court of Appeals, which, in *People v. Nebbia*, held that legislative authority to abridge property rights and the Contract Clause can be "justified only by exceptional circumstances, and even then, by reasonable regulation only." The law professor concluded that the conditions underlying passage of the Minnesota Mortgage Moratorium Act met the requirements for "exceptional circumstances" and that the law represented a reasonable regulation under the police powers. A grave economic emergency undoubtedly existed, especially as President Roosevelt had proclaimed the existence of one on March 6, 1933.

Vrooman emphasized that the Court should defer to state legislatures, the "first judge of what is for the greatest good of the greatest number, and so for the true ultimate good of all." On matters of general welfare, a legislature enjoys wide discretion, and may even extend emergency legislation "sufficiently beyond the emergency" to prevent the return of the crisis. Vrooman acknowledged the difficulties in defining the scope of these broad police powers but proposed a "balance-of-welfare theory" that weighed the letter of the Constitution against the public good according to the times and circumstances. The Contract Clause did not automatically override the police powers.

Vrooman's brief also claimed, without any evidence, that the founders wrote the Contract Clause solely to prevent repudiation of debts by the states rather than to protect contractual rights against state action. The brief thus rejected a strict interpretation of the Contract Clause in favor of the Constitution's exhortation to "promote the general Welfare." It was incorrect to assume that "any legislative act which impairs the obligation of contracts or trenches upon due process or savors of class legislation is a violation of the organic law." This argument cut to a core constitutional issue at stake in the *Blaisdell* case: whether the courts should interpret the Constitution literally, so as to prohibit any legislative act in direct conflict with the language of the Constitution, or liberally, so as to permit legislation contrary to the text if consistent with the purpose and spirit of the document.

Vrooman's brief, finally, dismissed the due process argument against the moratorium law. Advancing its most extreme argument, it even suggested that all property is held "subject to the possibility that under the police power it may be taken" regardless of the protections of due process. But even if it enjoyed the right to do so, the legislature did not deprive the "appellant of anything without such process," because the Association had a fair hearing according to the requirements of the statute. And the moratorium law was not "class legislation" in violation of the Equal Protection Clause. State legislatures maintain wide discretion to promote the general welfare by making reasonable distinctions among citizens, and "the greater the emergency, the wider the discretion."

The lawyers for the Home Building and Loan Association filed a supplemental brief. Lead attorney Bowen again noted that both the Minnesota Supreme Court and the lawyers representing Blaisdell had acknowledged that Chapter 339 violated provisions of the federal Constitution, even as they claimed that the law was a valid exercise of emergency police power. But, Bowen insisted, the Supreme Court never established that emergencies enhanced the police powers, and the *Rent Cases* had not "reversed, overruled, or modified" the protections of the Contract Clause and Fourteenth Amendment.

The Association's supplemental brief also reminded the Court that even the war-related powers of the federal government are subject to limitations. It cited *Ex Parte Milligan* (1866), which overturned President Lincoln's suspension of habeas corpus protections during the Civil War. True, since the famous case of *Munn v. Illinois* (1877), in which the Court had permitted the regulation of grain elevators critical to the storage and distribution of wheat, and more recently in *Wolff Packing Company v. Court of Industrial Relations* (1923), which identified multiple industries suitable for state regulation, the Supreme Court had upheld the common law principle that the states could regulate industries "clothed" with a public interest. The question of what constitutes a business affected with a public interest, however, does not end with a legislature — it is subject to judicial review. And, according to the Association, "The relationship of a mortgagor and mortgagee in a contract and the enforcement of the agreed remedies therein are clearly private matters and are not affected with a public interest." In this vein, the act did not regulate the business of lending money or, in fact, any type of business. The only business regulated by the act was the enforcement of mortgage security in existing mortgages. Whereas the Blaisdells' argument, based on the *Rent Cases*, was that enforcement of agreed-upon remedies is a "business affected with a public interest," Bowen denied that remedies fell into that category. This argument, however, conveniently glided over the fact that if the act were set aside, mortgage foreclosures could displace tens of thousands of farmers and urban dwellers from their homes, with severe consequences for the public interest.

Finally, the Association denied that the *Rent Cases* supported the mortgage moratorium. Those cases "unquestionably went to the extreme in sustaining as valid the exercise of the police power" and, as Justice Holmes admitted in *Pennsylvania Coal Company v. Mahon* (1922), "went to the verge of the law." The New York rent-control laws were more limited in duration and scope than Minnesota's law and applied only to rented residential property. The rent-control laws "restrained and prevented inequitable and oppressive conduct by landlords" and thus represented a valid exercise of the police power. Chapter 339, however, did not. The contractual agreement between mortgagor and mortgagee was contemplated by the parties, voluntary, and fair, and involved no extortion or abuse of process that injured public health, safety, and morals.

On Monday, January 8, 1934, the Supreme Court announced its decision in *Home Building and Loan Association v. Blaisdell*. In a personal letter that he wrote two weeks later, Justice Van Devanter reported that the case had been debated hotly by the justices at conference and that he had taken the lead in arguing against sustaining the moratorium law, speaking for an hour. Following a robust exchange of viewpoints, the justices voted 5–4 to uphold the law, with Chief Justice Hughes and Owen Roberts joining the three liberals on the Court (Brandeis, Cardozo, and Stone). As he often did when in the majority of an important case, Hughes assigned the majority opinion to himself.

The Court held that the Minnesota Mortgage Moratorium Act did not violate the Contract Clause, stressing that because of its temporary, reasonable, and limited nature, and the unusual character of the emergency, the law was within the reserved police powers of the states to protect the security and welfare of the people. Hughes reported that the Court was concerned only with the section of the law authorizing district courts to extend the period of redemption. The overall legality of the extension – and the court judgment that the Blaisdells pay a $40 rental fee during their extension – were the only issues under review. Hughes also took judicial notice that the moratorium law did not impair the integrity of mortgage indebtedness. The obligation for interest remained, as did the right of the mortgagee to obtain a deficiency judgment if the mortgagor failed to redeem within the prescribed period. In deciding that the law did not violate the Contract Clause, Hughes wrote that the Court had considered the relation of emergency to constitutional power, the historical setting of the Contract Clause, and, of course, precedents and established principles of constitutional interpretation.

In one of the most quoted and subsequently debated sections of the opinion, the chief justice explained the nature of emergency power. "While emergency does not create power," Hughes declared, "emergency may furnish the occasion for the exercise of power." Economic emergencies trigger broad discretion to promote the general welfare, as occurs during wartime. "The war power of the Federal Government," he said, "is not created by the emergency of war, but it is a power given to meet the emergency" and to "wage war successfully." Hughes noted, however, that even the war power does not remove constitutional limitations protecting civil liberties. A similar limitation holds true for economic emergencies.

Hughes then made a dubious distinction, given the unambiguous language of the Contract Clause. Where the Constitution is "specific," he proposed, there can be no departure from its provisions. For example, an emergency would not permit a state to "coin money" or "make anything but gold and silver coin tender in payment of debts." But clauses general enough to admit some interpretation provide room for the emergency exercise of powers. And, according to Hughes, "the reservation of the reasonable exercise of the protective power of the State is read into all contracts."

Although he noted that the historical record of the Constitutional Convention offers few clues about the founders' intent behind the

Contract Clause, the chief justice conceded that "the reasons which led to the adoption of that clause, and of the other prohibitions of Section 10 of Article 1, are not left in doubt." The widespread economic distress in the post-Revolutionary period prompted states to intervene with laws to assist debtors at the expense of creditors and contrary to contractual obligations. Legislative interference to protect debtors was so pervasive and extreme that it undermined the confidence necessary for trade and threatened the destruction of credit. As evidence of the framers' intent with respect to the Contract Clause, he cited Madison's *Federalist No. 44* and Chief Justice John Marshall's dissenting opinion in *Ogden v. Saunders* (1827).

Yet, Hughes asserted, full recognition of the origins and purpose of the Contract Clause is not needed to fix its precise scope. The clause did not create an absolute prohibition "and is not to be read with literal exactness like a mathematical formula." The chief justice cited a series of precedents in which the Court recognized exceptions to a strict interpretation of the clause. Writing for the majority in *Ogden*, for example, Justice William Johnson rejected strict adherence to the intent of the framers by arguing that "to assign to contracts, universally, a literal purport, and to exact for them a rigid literal fulfillment, could not have been the intent of the constitution." In *Stone v. Mississippi* (1880), moreover, the Court concluded that the legislature cannot "bargain away the public health or the public morals." An amendment to Mississippi's constitution that eliminated a lottery authorized by a previous legislature, therefore, did not violate the Contract Clause. Similarly, the Court acknowledged that states have reserved powers to control the sale of intoxicating liquors, to protect the public safety, to protect the public health against nuisances, and to exercise the power of eminent domain regardless of contractual obligations.

The lawyers for the Home Building and Loan Association argued that the contracts in the above cases were affected only incidentally, while the moratorium law was a direct and substantial impairment. But to Hughes, "Whatever doubt there may have been that the protective power of the State, its police power, may be exercised — without violating the true intent of the provision of the Federal Constitution — in directly preventing the immediate and literal enforcement of contractual obligations . . . where vital public interests would otherwise suffer, was removed by our decisions relating to the enforcement of provisions of leases during a period of scarcity of housing." Hughes then devoted several pages of the opinion to discussing the *Rent Cases*.

Explaining that the Court had long recognized limits to the police power, Hughes observed "a growing appreciation of public needs and of the necessity of finding ground for a rational compromise between individual rights and public welfare." Hughes noted that most of Minnesota's rural mortgages were held by insurance companies, banks, and investment companies, institutions not interested in taking possession of foreclosed farms and growing crops. They simply wanted a return on their investment. By enacting the moratorium, the Minnesota legislature sought to prevent the ruin of both the mortgagor and mortgagee.

As it rejected an emphasis on the founders' intent, the Court logically accentuated the need to interpret the Constitution broadly so that it can be adapted to the needs of the times. Put another way, the majority rejected the notion that the Constitution should be interpreted strictly according to the literal meaning of the text and supposed intent of the framers. The majority also stressed the changes in the relationship between citizens and the state that had occurred since the Constitution was written. These changes justified a new compromise between individual rights and the public welfare.

Hughes finished the opinion by summarizing its five conclusions. First, an emergency existed in Minnesota that furnished a proper occasion for the exercise of the reserved powers of the state to protect the vital interests of the community. Second, the legislation promoted the public interest and did not privilege any particular group. Third, the relief afforded by the act was commensurate with the emergency. Fourth, the redemption extension and the conditions accompanying it were reasonable. Under the act, the integrity of mortgage indebtedness was not impaired, the validity of the sale and the right of a lender to lay claim to the property if the borrower failed to redeem within the extended period were maintained, and the conditions of redemption stood as they did under the prior law. True, the homeowner was not forced from the home during the extension, but he or she had to pay a rental amount determined by the courts. Finally, the legislation was temporary and limited to the exigency that called it forth. Although the period of redemption from the Blaisdells' fore-closure sale had been extended to May 1, 1935, that period could be reduced by the order of the court under the statute, in case of a change in circumstance. The statute could not validly outlast the emergency or be so extended as to virtually destroy the contracts.

The Court's findings hinged on its conclusion that the "Minnesota statute as here applied" did not violate the Contract Clause. "Whether the legislation is wise or unwise as a matter of policy," Hughes said, "is a question with which we are not concerned." Hughes similarly and hastily dismissed the Due Process Clause argument against the act but did not provide much rationale. The majority opinion ended by asserting that the Minnesota Mortgage Moratorium Act did not arbitrarily classify citizens into groups and therefore did not deny the Association the equal protection of the laws.

Justice Cardozo and Justice Stone influenced many of the key points in Chief Justice Hughes's opinion. When Hughes circulated his draft opinion among his colleagues, Justice Brandeis wrote on his copy, "Yes. Strongly put and interesting. I approve of the changes proposed." But not everyone in the majority was happy. Justices Stone and Cardozo were deeply disappointed with the first draft of the majority opinion, and both considered writing a concurring opinion. Hughes's initial draft opinion was based on a distinction between unacceptable laws, which impaired the substantive rights of a creditor, and acceptable ones (including the Minnesota act), which merely altered the remedy. U.S. courts had made this distinction throughout the nineteenth century. Wishing to place the decision squarely within liberal Fourteenth Amendment jurisprudence, Stone and Cardozo rejected Hughes's resort to the right/remedy distinction, which asserted that the government cannot alter or impair contractual obligations but merely can adjust the remedies for enforcement. They wanted a broader basis for governmental action. Cardozo began writing a separate concurring opinion while Stone prepared a long memorandum.

Justice Cardozo's unpublished concurrence rejected the static view of the Constitution based on original intent of the framers and emphasized the necessity of interpreting constitutional provisions in light of changing social and economic circumstances. This approach to the law followed the argument Cardozo made in his classic treatise,

The Nature of the Judicial Process (1921). The opening paragraph of his draft opinion, which made its way into the formal opinion, quoted Chief Justice John Marshall's famous dictum from *McCulloch v. Maryland* (1819): "We must never forget that it is a constitution we are expounding," a document "intended to endure for ages to come and, consequently, to be adapted to the various crises of human affairs." Cardozo's unpublished concurrence also cited Justice Holmes's clear statement in the 1920 case *Missouri v. Holland*: "The case before us must be considered in light of our whole experience and not merely what was said a hundred years ago." Holmes added, "We must realize that they [the founders] have called into life a being the development of which could not have been foreseen completely by the most gifted of its begetters." Echoing Holmes, Cardozo insisted that the founders realized that they were creating a document that needed to be malleable to endure.

Unlike Hughes's majority opinion, Justice Cardozo's proposed concurring opinion made no attempt to reconcile the Minnesota statute with the literal text of the Contract Clause. Neither did Cardozo rest his argument on a distinction between right and remedy. Rather, he saw the general provisions of the Fourteenth Amendment as leading "toward a rational compromise between private rights and public welfare." The nation had changed dramatically since its founding. Cardozo proclaimed:

> Upon the basis of that amendment a vast body of law unknown to the fathers has been developed and expounded by the judges of the nation. The economic and social changes wrought by the industrial revolution and by the growth of the population have made it necessary for government at this day to do a thousand things that were beyond the experience or the thought of a century ago. With the growing recognition of this need, courts have awakened to the truth that the contract clause is perverted from its proper meaning when it throttles the capacity of the states to exert their governmental power to deal with matters which are basically the concern of government. . . . A gospel of *laissez faire* — of individual initiative — of thrift and industry and sacrifice — may be inadequate in the great society that we live in to point the way to salvation, at least for economic life. The state when it acts today by statutes like

the one before us is not furthering the selfish good of individuals or classes as ends of ultimate validity. It is furthering its own good by maintaining the economic structure on which the good of all depends. Such at least is its endeavor, however much it miss the mark.

Cardozo biographer Andrew Kaufman proposed that this statement was the closest the justice ever came to expressing support for the welfare state. Cardozo admitted that the Minnesota law might be inconsistent with what the framers intended or believed in 1787, but he maintained that "their beliefs to be significant must be adjusted to the world they knew. It is not . . . inconsistent with what they would say today, nor with what they would believe, if they were called upon to interpret in light of our whole experience." A contractual relationship, Cardozo concluded, "was not to paralyze the state in its endeavor at times of direful crises to keep its life-blood flowing." According to historian Michael Parrish, no member of the Court "wrote a more radical statement of constitutional interpretation rejecting the notion that jurists should strictly apply the original intent of the framers." Cardozo usually avoided such sweeping statements, but he may have been influenced by the consequences of the Depression. Although Cardozo's comments were not published, it is clear that he targeted his arguments at Sutherland's dissenting opinion, discussed below.

On December 12, 1933, Justice Stone sent Hughes a memo suggesting improvements in the majority opinion. Stone wrote that he had "taken more than the usual time to study your opinion because of the great importance to the public and to the court of the questions involved." He defended the moratorium law more strongly than either Hughes or Cardozo, and his memo and personal notes emphasized the social context and economic imperatives for increased local regulation of private contracts. Anticipating the waning of the present emergency as well as future challenges to the New Deal, Stone did not want to establish a hard-and-fast rule based on the emergency powers that would limit the Court's ability to review the constitutionality of other state laws. He wrote:

I am not inclined to join in so much of the [opinion] . . . as states that the relief afforded could only be of a temporary character. . . .

We may yet have to deal with cases where the moratorium is for longer periods and where the law itself is made applicable for longer periods than those involved in this case. . . . Therefore, it seems to me that we should leave ourselves absolutely unhampered by pronouncements which might be taken to affect situations not presented to us in this case.

Stone's biographer Alpheus Mason notes that Chief Justice Hughes disregarded Stone's suggestion that the Court develop a flexible rationale in the *Blaisdell* ruling.

Stone wrote in his memo that he was uncomfortable, like Cardozo, with the right/remedy distinction regarding contracts. He observed:

I think the part of the opinion which discusses what the Court has sometimes treated as a distinction between obligation and remedy is somewhat confusing, and, to some extent, obscures the point with which we have to deal in the present case. The distinction . . . comes to nothing more than a question of degree, and the net result of the cases seems to be unreasonable. Our present case has no complications of this character, since the statute does cut down both obligation and remedy to a material extent, and the sole question is whether private parties, by their contract, may tie the hands of the state so that it is powerless to deal with a problem vital to the Government itself. I think the opinion would gain in power and directness if the discussion of the right-remedy phase were very much condensed or relegated to a footnote.

Hughes subsequently condensed his discussion of the right/remedy distinction in the final draft opinion.

Stone's memorandum, finally, emphasized the dire economic problems facing the country. He wrote:

Today, when the whole economic structure of society is threatened with widespread foreclosures, the state has afforded a measure of relief which tends to prevent the impending ruin of mortgagees, as well as mortgagors, and to preserve the stake of the former as well as the latter in land mortgages, viewed as a form of investment security. . . . It is, I think, desirable to emphasize the special character of the mortgage situation as [it] affects both mortgagors and mortgagees, to show that, looked at collectively, the legislation protects the interests of both and harms neither.

Stone continued, "Once conceded, as it must be, that the contract clause is not an absolute and unyielding restriction upon the state, such legislation is demonstrated to be so reasonable in character as to be plainly within state competency."

Hughes willingly embraced many of the changes recommended by Cardozo and Stone. A January 4, 1934, memo from Hughes informed Stone of his plans to incorporate several paragraphs from Justice Cardozo's proposed concurrence into the majority opinion. Justice Stone replied to Hughes's memo immediately, writing that the proposed changes met "very effectively the chief point in Justice Sutherland's dissent," and he felt the revisions strengthened the prevailing opinion. The final opinion was announced on January 8, and its memorable phrase "a rational compromise between individual rights and public welfare" was adopted word for word from Cardozo's draft. Two sections of the majority opinion also use the phrase "a growing recognition of public need" in the discussion of the public interest and private contracts. Indeed, Justice Cardozo did not issue his separate concurrence because the opinion of the Court written by the Chief Justice contained many of his points. Although he did not receive any recognition for the *Blaisdell* decision when it was announced, Cardozo's influence on the majority opinion was significant, and his ideas would eventually dominate judicial interpretations of the Contract Clause. In the decades following *Blaisdell*, federal courts became more deferential to state regulation that impacted contract rights.

Nonetheless, Hughes's final opinion retained some of the arguments from his draft to which Cardozo and Stone had objected. Privately, Justice Stone was not completely satisfied with the published opinion. In a February 1934 letter to his friend Sterling Carr, Stone remarked, "Just between ourselves I feel it was too long and discursive . . . if I had been doing the writing, I should have presented the matter in somewhat different form." According to Stone's biographer, the justice worried that the Court had not advanced the justifications for state regulation beyond those offered in the *Rent Cases*. Stone further complained that the chief justice's views could have been expressed more forcefully. Stone's law clerk, Howard Westwood, and his secretary, Gertrude Jenkins, were upset that he had decided not to write a separate concurrence. A note from Jenkins recalled, "Stone was inclined, at first, to write a concurring opinion, stronger than the majority opinion written by Hughes, C. J. He changed his mind and wrote the memorandum, taking it down personally to the Chief." Jenkins also mentioned that Westwood was "quite disturbed that H. F. S. did not write his own concurring opinion" because Hughes had received so much publicity and accolades, and Jenkins thought that Stone was now "cured and will write his dissents and concurrences in the future, for all his hesitation to do so."

The dissenters went down swinging. Justice George Sutherland wrote the dissent, joined by the other three members of the Court's conservative bloc: Pierce Butler, James McReynolds, and Willis Van Devanter. Compared to the maneuvering that took place behind the scenes with respect to the majority opinion, there is no evidence that much negotiation or collaboration took place among the dissenters. The only material in Sutherland's public papers relevant to the *Blaisdell* case is a collection of letters praising the justice for his original-meaning argument in defense of property rights.

Sutherland's disdainful *Blaisdell* dissent disparaged the majority as "bewildered travelers lost in a wood" and predicted doom for contract rights and constitutional democracy. He argued for an originalist interpretation of the Constitution that would promote consistency in meaning regardless of economic exigency. He did not contest the nature of the emergency confronting Minnesota's lawmakers or challenge the ability of a state legislature to respond to local economic conditions because he considered those issues inconsequential. Instead, he asserted that the framers' intent was clear. The Contract Clause "was framed and adopted with the specific and studied purpose of preventing legislation designed to relieve debtors *especially* in time of financial distress." How then, he asked, can the clause be interpreted to mean exactly the opposite of what the framers intended? It makes no sense to say, Sutherland argued, that the "conditions which produced the rule may now be invoked to destroy it." Justice Sutherland's opinion cited works by several famous historians, including Charles Warren, Charles Beard, and George Bancroft, who described how state efforts to help debtors during the Confederation period led to the restrictions placed upon states in Article 1, Section 10, including the prohibition against impairing the obligation of contracts. In other words, the framers wrote the Contract Clause for the very reason that they feared emergencies unwisely tempt legislatures to loosen contract rights. Sutherland insisted that the "meaning of constitutional provisions is changeless; it is only their application which is extensible."

Rejecting the majority's conclusion that an emergency justified some leeway in interpretation, Sutherland declared that a constitutional provision cannot "mean one thing at one time and an entirely different thing at another time." He also downplayed the seriousness of the Depression, the worst economic crisis in the nation's history; he claimed that the "present exigency" was "nothing new" and that "periods of depression, of industrial failure, of financial distress, of unpaid and unpayable indebtedness" had always "alternated with years of plenty." Recovery from these economic crises, Sutherland editorialized, comes from "self-denial and painful effort."

Sutherland rejected the contention that the Minnesota Mortgage Moratorium Act merely modified the remedy for a contractual obligation. The law, he argued, "effects a material and injurious change in the obligation." The extension of the redemption period for two years, regardless of compensation or rent paid in its place, destroys the "legally enforceable right of the creditor" to become the owner of the property upon default of the redemption. Sutherland observed that the Court had previously recognized that "whatever tends to postpone or retard the enforcement of a contract, to that extent weakens the obligation."

Conceding that governments have the right to interfere in the marketplace in some cases to protect public safety and health, Sutherland's dissent distinguished laws that make something illegal for the entire community, such as the sale of liquor, from laws that interfere with a legal activity that in fact remains legal (in this case, a home loan). The Association's contract with the Blaisdells was "lawful when made and it has never been anything else." Thus, the Minnesota law was not a reasonable exercise of the state's police power. Sutherland noted with alarm that the "effect of the Minnesota legislation, though serious enough in itself, is of trivial significance compared with the far more serious and dangerous inroads upon the limitations of the Constitution which are almost certain to ensue as a consequence naturally following any step beyond the boundaries by that fixed instrument." He predicted that the majority decision would lead to "gradual but ever-advancing encroachments upon the sanctity of public and private contracts." Finally, Sutherland exhorted the court to consider that if the "provisions of the Constitution be not upheld when they pinch as well as when they comfort, they may as well be abandoned."

Sutherland's dissenting opinion exemplified classical legal thought. It treated the Constitution as static—what many of today's conservatives, such as Justice Antonin Scalia, call "dead"—rather than as a living document. According to this view, the Court must not alter the text of the Constitution and the intent of the framers (or the authors of subsequent amendments) because of social or economic changes, no matter how severe. The natural right to property guaranteed by the Contract Clause must be protected against majoritarian pressures.

Almost one month after the decision in *Home Building and Loan Association v. Blaisdell* was announced, the Association's lawyers petitioned for a rehearing. They claimed that the counsel for Minnesota, Attorney General Peterson, made misleading statements they did not have time to dispute, including statements quoted in the majority opinion. Specifically, they referred to an alleged statement by Peterson that "mortgage foreclosures had been prevented by mob violence." Alfred Bowen, one of the Association's lawyers, had attempted, unsuccessfully, to downplay the threat of violence in Minnesota in order to weaken the Blaisdells' argument that dire circumstances necessitated the moratorium law. The Court denied the petition for a rehearing on February 5, officially bringing to an end the Minnesota mortgage moratorium case.

CHAPTER 8

Reaction to the *Blaisdell* Decision

The 4,000 homeowners seeking relief under the moratorium law were no doubt happy with the *Blaisdell* decision. And throughout the nation, reaction to the opinion was passionate and overwhelmingly supportive. One week after the decision, the *Washington Post* reviewed the editorials of fifteen major newspapers throughout the country. These editorials "uniformly" approved the decision, although many cautioned that the opinion did not necessarily augur the Court's complete acceptance of the New Deal.

Commentators across the political spectrum quickly recognized the decision's significance, describing it as "far reaching," "epochal," "momentous," and "landmark." Several editorials compared its reach to that of *Scott v. Sandford* (1857) — a case that contributed to the onset of the American Civil War! In that case, Dred Scott, a slave from Missouri, claimed that his prior residence in the free areas of Illinois and Wisconsin Territory made him a free man. The Taney Court ruled, however, that no one but a citizen of the United States could be a citizen of a state, and that only Congress could confer national citizenship. By winning his case, *Newsweek* argued, John Blaisdell avoided becoming the Dred Scott of the New Deal.

Officials responsible for drafting and defending the Minnesota Mortgage Moratorium Act were elated. Minnesota attorney general Harry Peterson hailed the decision as "a victory for the people of Minnesota that will enable many farmers and city dwellers to hold onto [*sic*] their homes." He claimed that "the temporary respite afforded homeowners by such emergency legislation will give them a chance to refinance their obligations through the [federal] farm credit and home loan corporations, and consequently will save thousands of homes from foreclosure." Peterson called the decision one of the five most important in U.S. history and predicted that it would enable the federal government to continue implementing recovery legislation, especially the National Recovery Act, without fear of the Court. He also praised Chief Justice Hughes's legal reasoning. "The majority opinion," Peterson said, "was not only a sound statement of the legal phases involved, but was statesmanlike in that it interpreted the constitution as a living document that must be adapted to current conditions." Assistant Attorney General William Ervin, who defended the law with Peterson, said, "We felt that this law is beneficial both to the mortgagees and mortgagors of this state, and that the law is a step in the right direction." George Stiles, the Minneapolis attorney who helped draft the moratorium legislation and who represented the Blaisdells in the Minnesota courts, was "extremely pleased with the decision, which upholds the right of an individual to safeguard his property," reported the *Minneapolis Star*.

Governor Floyd Olson, who came to Washington for some of the proceedings, indulged in a bit of constitutional interpretation. "The decision," he boldly stated, "represents more than a triumph of the police power clause of the constitution over the due process of law and obligation of contract clauses. . . . It really represents a triumph of human rights over property rights." Clearly overstating the scope of state powers recognized by the Court, Governor Olson added, "It also indicates that we can change the system under which we live in any manner we desire and keep within the constitution." Despite Governor Olson's enthusiasm for the outcome, a close reading of Hughes's opinion does not reveal support for such unfettered police powers.

Two days after the opinion was announced, a U.S. congressman from Minnesota, Ernest Lundeen (Farmer-Labor), offered special recognition on the floor of the House to his fellow Farmer-Laborite Harry Peterson for drafting the moratorium law and arguing the case before the Supreme Court. Lundeen also praised Governor Olson's role in shepherding the legislation and described the Minnesota Mortgage Moratorium Act as "an outstanding achievement of the Farmer-Labor Party." If the moratorium had not been upheld, Representative Lundeen claimed, an estimated 50,000 farms and homes could have been lost in 1933 alone. Lundeen used the decision in *Blaisdell* to help build support for the federal Frazier-Lemke bill (see chapter 4), which provided for moratoriums on mortgage payments and refinancing of farm and home loans. Congress passed Frazier-Lemke six months later, only to see it struck down by a unanimous Supreme Court in May 1935.

Many thoughtful commentators recognized the battle between the living-Constitution approach of the majority opinion and the strict-interpretation-of-the-framers approach of Sutherland's dissent, and they approved of what they characterized as the Court's pragmatic, flexible interpretation. In an editorial entitled "The Adaptable Constitution," the *St. Paul Pioneer Press* explained that the Court in effect had declared that "the Constitution is not to be regarded as a dead hand of the past on the shoulder of legislative authorities, but as a living body of fundamental law which shall adapt itself to the necessities of the times and not inhibit the Legislatures from socially useful acts. . . . Far from weakening the Constitution, such a rule of interpretation strengthens it." The editors warned, "Had the decision been the other way, then indeed the fundamentals of the American political structure would have been in danger. What is hard and brittle breaks; what is tough and yielding stands."

The *New York Times* correspondingly supported what it saw as a pragmatic interpretation of the Constitution. It argued, "A growing nation meeting ever new problems and emergencies simply cannot be confined to a legalistic strait-jacket. If the Constitution is a prison, our Nation must escape it or die." The *New York Evening Post* similarly observed, "We are free of a great danger. Legalism will not tie our hands as we move forward to a better America. The Constitution is protecting the country, not tying it hand and foot." The *Philadelphia Record* opined that the *Blaisdell* decision freed America "from the slavish subservience to a literal interpretation of the Constitution, which has for years served to stifle liberalism, block progress, and protect vested interests." Even the conservative *Wall Street Journal* expressed qualified support. Its editorial asserted that *Blaisdell* had "not altered or changed the spirit of the constitution, nor is that instrument passing away from us." The decision confirmed that "within the constitution are the powers to deal with every emergency." In upholding the legislation, the Court "did no violence to the contract clause of the constitution. . . . What the present decision means, above everything else, is that the Constitution never was the rigid instrument that so many of us have supposed it to be."

Liberal newspapers stressed that a victory for the Home Building and Loan Association would have produced drastic consequences. A *Washington Post* editorial concluded that an "adverse opinion on this Minnesota case would have had repercussions far beyond the confines of that State and far deeper in character than the particular law in issue. The legality of large parts of the recovery program . . . would have been immediately called into question." "In other words," continued the editors, "the general reaction to the historic decision is likely to be that it was foreordained by circumstances." The *Post* recognized the strengths of both sides of the argument and praised each for their earnestness, integrity, and scholarship. "When a rigid Constitution comes into direct opposition with an inflexible economic situation," the newspaper suggested, "it is not difficult to predict which of the two will yield. The merit of the legal mind lies in its ability to find precedents to show that it is constitutional for rigidity to become temporarily malleable." *Collier's* magazine commented that the decision was "fortunate for both the country and the Supreme Court" because a contrary ruling would have made the Court "an object of bitter political controversy."

Although newspapers imagined what would have happened had the Court decided the other way, a sense of inevitability surrounded the decision, something that today's critics of *Blaisdell* often miss. The *Nation* suggested that Chief Justice Hughes and the majority "bowed to the inevitable rather than expounded the certain." Justice Sutherland's dissent was "an impressive statement of cold logic," but it had to be discarded in order to protect the basic interests of society. Still, the *Nation's* editors lamented that a policy vital to 120 million people depended on a 5–4 vote among nine men.

As might be expected, liberal-leaning newspapers not only celebrated the Minnesota mortgage-moratorium decision but also suggested that it vindicated the New Deal. The *Farmer-Labor Leader* in St. Paul praised Attorney General Peterson for delivering a "solar plexus blow" to the "methods of exploitation treasured by the capitalist system." The *New York Evening Post* was certain the decision dealt a "paralyzing blow" to Republican opponents of the New Deal, whom the paper described as "the small coterie of ultrapartisan tories." The paper found it ironic that on the same day Chief Justice Hughes read his decision from the bench, on Capitol Hill, the "Republican professional 'viewers-with-alarm' were denouncing such [mortgage-relief] legislation in the Senate." Trumpeting the decision, the *St. Louis Dispatch* declared that the Court "has broken chains which have bound the American people for sixty years." The *Minneapolis Tribune* described the decision as "a broad and liberal view of constitutional powers which may presage general upholding of national recovery legislation." The *New York Evening Post* proffered that the Supreme Court had "joined the ranks of the New Deal." Homer Cummings, Roosevelt's attorney general, exclaimed that it was "a red-letter day." He called the president on the evening of the decision and found him "exceedingly gratified and happy." Cummings was certain that the Court now had a liberal majority, at least as far as emergency legislation was concerned.

On Capitol Hill, Speaker of the House Henry Rainey (D-Ill.), Roosevelt's ally, assumed that the decision indicated the Supreme Court would "sustain every [National Recovery Administration] code thus far enacted or hereafter enacted to get the country out of the depression." (Rainey would not live long enough to witness the implementation of many New Deal policies. Shortly after returning home from a tour promoting the New Deal, he contracted pneumonia and died in St. Louis in August 1934.) Senator Hiram Johnson (R-Calif.), a pro-Roosevelt Republican, was quoted in the *Chicago Daily Tribune* as saying that the "far-reaching opinion will have a tremendous effect in strengthening the recovery program." Senator George Norris remarked, "It [the decision] will convince everybody, including the Supreme Court itself, that we are trying to save this country." Senator Robert Wagner (D-N.Y.), chairman of the National Labor Board and coauthor of the National Industrial Recovery Act, declared that it was "highly gratifying to see the Supreme Court's complete appreciation of the great economic and social problems that confronted Minnesota." He believed that the Court henceforth would demonstrate the same appreciation for the national problems that confronted Congress and the president.

Average Americans chimed in on constitutional questions, too. W. A. Jakel of Mathis, Texas, wrote Governor Olson to "note with a full measure of pleasure your successful handing before the U.S. Supreme Court the Minnesota Moratorium law." Jakel vilified existing state foreclosure law, "by which Foreclosures are consummated 'without trial by jury,'" as the "rankest kind of class legislation, for the benefit of Real Estate Racketeers and Shyster 10% Attorney Fee Lawyers." Jakel added, "The 7th Amendment [which guarantees a trial by jury in civil cases] stands out all alone, nothing else mixed with it, while the Contract clause in the Constitution is mentioned among a number of things, hence the 7th Amendment is entitled far more consideration, than the Contract Clause, its holiness only being based upon the 10% Attorney fee clauses in Contracts."

Many commentators believed that the *Blaisdell* decision finally revealed Chief Justice Hughes's liberal preferences unambiguously. Although Hughes had voted with the three liberals in several key cases dating back to the 1930–31 term, it had remained unclear where he would fall when the first economic recovery cases reached the Court. Now, the *Minneapolis Tribune* concluded that Hughes's vote and the arguments he used in the ruling "definitely placed [him] among the liberal group" on the Court. The *Dallas News* described *Blaisdell* as "one of the most remarkable displays of liberal thought in the entire history of the usually conservative tribunal."

It is impossible to understand reaction to *Blaisdell* without remembering that it was the first blow in a one-two punch the Supreme Court dealt in favor of state economic regulation. Two months after *Blaisdell*, *Nebbia v. New York* upheld the New York Milk Control Act of 1933 by the same 5–4 margin and voting alignment. During the Depression, price cutting by distributors damaged dairy farmers, and the resulting farmers' strikes and unrest threatened the industry. Under the Milk Control Act, New York's Milk Control Board set the retail price of a quart of milk at 9 cents. Leo Nebbia, a grocery store owner in Rochester, was convicted of violating the board's order when he bundled two quarts of milk and a 5-cent loaf of bread for 18 cents, essentially lowering his milk price to 6½ cents. Nebbia claimed that the law violated the Due Process Clause because state-mandated milk prices interfered with his right to conduct business and were per se unreasonable and unconstitutional. Just as Minnesota insisted that it had the authority to pass a moratorium law, New York State maintained that the milk industry was a business affected with a public interest and that it could regulate milk prices under its police power. The High Court agreed.

By allowing a state to set prices, the *Nebbia* decision significantly confirmed *Blaisdell*'s acceptance of broad police powers. This time,

Justice Owen Roberts wrote the majority opinion and McReynolds authored the dissent. Roberts acknowledged that property use and contracts are usually private matters. "The general rule is that both should be free of governmental influence," Roberts stated. "But neither property rights nor contract rights are absolute," he continued, "for government cannot exist if the citizen may at will use his property to the detriment of his fellows, or exercise his freedom of contract to work them harm." As in *Blaisdell*, the Court determined that "equally fundamental with the private right is that of the public to regulate it in the common interest." These correlative rights are always in collision, Roberts noted, but, since the nation's founding, the Court had affirmed that the power to promote the general welfare is inherent in government.

Like *Blaisdell*, *Nebbia* in and of itself did not cement the constitutional revolution. After all, the states had long regulated the milk industry in the public interest. Nonetheless, the ruling seemed to suggest that the Court had embraced anti–laissez-faire ideas. Roberts noted that a legislative investigation of the milk industry conducted by New York in 1932 concluded that "unrestricted competition aggravated existing evils, and the normal laws of supply and demand were insufficient to correct maladjustments detrimental to the community." The legislature had believed that preventing destructive price cutting would improve economic conditions. "We do not understand the appellant to deny that in these circumstances the legislature might reasonably consider further regulation and control for the protection of the milk industry and the consuming public," Roberts suggested. "In light of the facts of the case the order is not unreasonable or arbitrary."

Moreover, *Nebbia* broadened the police powers doctrine by effectively throwing out the requirement that a regulated industry be affected with the public interest. Leo Nebbia's lawyers conceded a regulatory exception for the narrow category of businesses affected with a public interest but denied that the milk industry fell within that category. Justice Roberts was not convinced. First, he cited the Court's upholding of price regulation of grain elevators in *Munn v. Illinois*. Then he moved beyond *Munn*'s traditional understanding of public-interest industries (usually public utilities and those making products that affected public health). "There is no closed class or category of businesses affected with a public interest," Roberts wrote. In other words, any industry can be controlled for the public good. Therefore, Roberts continued, the role of the courts "in the application of the Fifth and Fourteenth Amendments is to determine in each case whether the circumstances vindicate the challenged regulation as a reasonable exertion of governmental authority." A state is free to adopt whatever economic policy it chooses to promote public welfare if it is not arbitrary or discriminatory and meets the requirements of due process.

In stark contrast, Justice McReynolds saw in the majority *Nebbia* opinion nothing less than the destruction of liberty. "This is not regulation, but management, control, dictation — it amounts to the deprivation of the fundamental right which one has to conduct his own affairs honestly and along customary lines," McReynolds warned in his dissent. He also took direct aim at the emergency powers doctrine: "The theory that legislative action which ordinarily would be ineffective because of conflict with the Constitution may become potent if intended to meet peculiar conditions and properly limited was lucidly discussed, and its weakness disclosed, by the dissenting opinion in *Home Building & Loan Association v. Blaisdell.*" He further argued that to claim that a legislature has broad authority to determine when it can control property rights and dictate prices is equivalent to declaring that the rights under the Constitution "exist only for so long as the public interest does not require their extinction." McReynolds contended that New York's price regulation interfered not just with the right of the "little grocer" to conduct his business but also with the right of millions of consumers "to buy a necessity of life on the open market." Invoking the specter of socialism, the justice exclaimed, "A superabundance; but no child can purchase from a willing storekeeper below the figure appointed by three men at headquarters!" The result of such excessive economic regulation, he concluded, is the destruction of the rule of law under the Constitution.

Prior to *Blaisdell* and *Nebbia*, some prescient commentators had predicted that Roosevelt would try to "pack" the Court with justices more favorable to New Deal policies. Reacting to the votes of Hughes and Roberts in these cases, however, most commentators now speculated (incorrectly) that Roosevelt would not pursue such action. The *Nation* suggested that *Blaisdell* and *Nebbia* made "certain that President Roosevelt can carry through his policies without having to pack the Supreme Court with new justices in order to do it."

The *Blaisdell* and *Nebbia* voting alignments did not last, however. As we detail in the next chapter, on "Black Monday," May 27, 1935, the Court unanimously struck down three New Deal policies. The Roosevelt administration became increasingly frustrated with the Court's decisions, and, on February 5, 1937, more than three years after *Blaisdell*, President Roosevelt unveiled his plan to reorganize the federal judiciary, dubbed by critics the "court-packing plan."

In the meantime, in the wake of *Blaisdell* and *Nebbia*, many legal experts expressed support for emergency legislation and the flexible interpretation of the Constitution that they believed the High Court had embraced. Princeton political scientist Edward Corwin attacked Sutherland's dissenting opinion as "too literal an interpretation of the Constitution," and he accused Sutherland of being "inconsistent with his own opinion in *Funk v. United States*." *Funk* (1933) centered on the question of witness competency in criminal trials, but it is important for us because in it Sutherland applied an evolutionary, flexible view of common law doctrine. Sutherland wrote that the "common law is not immutable, but flexible, and by its own principles adapted itself to varying conditions." He even suggested that a public policy right for one generation may not be right for the next.

Corwin provided a more elaborate defense of the *Blaisdell* decision in the *University of Pennsylvania Law Review*. Here he admitted that Chief Justice Hughes "appeared to be a trifle shy of his own argument," which produced a majority opinion not as neatly argued as Sutherland's dissent. Corwin also acknowledged that *Blaisdell* confronted two legitimate points of view about government power that could yield widely divergent paths of constitutional law. In the main, however, he lamented that Justice Sutherland was an "unconvinced, unconvincible, rugged individualist" who believed unrealistically that individual distress during the Great Depression should be relieved only by "industry and frugality, not by relaxation of law." In any event, that the Blaisdells were renting eleven rooms in a fourteen-room house suggested that they were doing everything they could to make ends meet.

Other experts applauded the judicial concern for struggling homeowners. In the *Kansas City Law Review*, John Fitzsimmons, commissioner of the Supreme Court of Missouri, praised Hughes's "humanism" in considering the desperate circumstances of the mortgagee. He compared the economic crisis of the Depression to the Panic of 1837, which actually persisted for several years. Following the panic, Illinois, Indiana, and other states passed mortgage relief for hard-pressed debtors. The legislation led to the Taney Court decisions of *Bronson v. Kinzie* and *Howard v. Bugbee*, in which the Court struck down both relief measures via a strict interpretation of the Contract Clause. But unlike these decisions, Fitzsimmons noted, the *Blaisdell* majority opinion took judicial notice of the dismal economic conditions. Chief Justice Hughes's attitude differed from the "classic coldness" of most of his predecessors. Fitzsimmons described the opinion as "visionary and a brilliant expression of the flexibility of the Constitution." It was a "noble example of the humanism of a great court." In contrast, Justice Sutherland's dissenting opinion was "stern, unbending, able and comprehensive." The majority opinion in *Blaisdell*, Fitzsimmons concluded, promised that the Constitution would enjoy "a fresh and green old age" and therefore that the republic would continue to flourish.

In the *North American Review*, constitutional scholar Alpheus Mason declared the *Blaisdell* and *Nebbia* decisions solidly pro–New Deal but decidedly less than revolutionary. He put forward that supporters of the New Deal would find comfort in the majority opinions, especially Hughes's reference to the Court's "growing appreciation of public needs and of the necessity of finding ground for a rational compromise between individual rights and public welfare." Yet opponents of federal recovery legislation could find some solace in the emphasis the Chief Justice placed upon the emergency character of the Minnesota law, even if this emphasis was noticeably absent from the *Nebbia* decision.

Mason further identified the deeper significance of the decisions— they were central to the survival of the New Deal. For the dissenters, the "disturbing aspect of these decisions is their threat to the existence of the Constitution itself, and to our unique and venerable principle of judicial review." To Mason, however, a majority of Supreme Court justices "now recognize[d] so openly that the Constitution is not a self-declaring document, and that in constitutional interpretation judges may mold, change, or even destroy the Constitution itself." It was neither the foundations of the Constitution nor the intent of the framers that *Blaisdell* and *Nebbia* overthrew, Mason concluded, but only "the then dissenting view of what constitutes sound economic and social policy." Indeed, the triumphant theory in these two cases enjoyed no clear permanence. America did not possess a static government of laws, Mason concluded, but "a system wherein all law must conform to certain standards of constitutional morality" determined by nine individuals on the Supreme Court.

Roscoe Pound, one of the founders of sociological jurisprudence, echoed Mason's views on constitutional change in the *New York Times*. Pound described the early twentieth century as an "Era of Transition" between two ideals of justice under law. The nineteenth-century ideal of justice, rooted in individual liberty and a competitive, acquisitive society, was yielding to a new and inchoate ideal of justice that assumed an interconnected economy in which the national government sometimes had to regulate local economic conditions for the benefit of all. The transition between the two forms of justice explained the current vacillation between doctrines such as "liberty of contract" and "businesses affected with a public interest" and the tendency of the Court to issue closely divided decisions, even as much progress had been made toward the new conception of justice. In his view, therefore, the *Blaisdell* and *Nebbia* decisions did not represent a radical departure from precedents but instead fell "in line with an established view of what is reasonable, demanded by the very conception of reasonableness."

According to Pound, shifts in legal thinking mirrored society's evolving sense of justice. An abstract nineteenth-century concept of reasonableness — analytical jurisprudence — gave way to a more concrete concept of reasonableness — sociological jurisprudence. Pound rooted this evolution in the changing relationship between the states and the federal government; because local economic activities increasingly had national implications, the federal government had to assume more regulatory control. Responding to critics of *Blaisdell* and *Nebbia*, Pound proposed that it was not the Constitution that had been overturned but a "superconstitution erected in its name on the basis of ideals which have ceased to give an adequate picture of our social and economic order."

Despite the broad support in the press and among scholars, *Blais-*

dell had its share of detractors. Conservative Democrats and anti–New Deal Republicans were deeply concerned about its consequences. The *Los Angeles Times* editorialized, "Since the power to interfere with the obligation of contracts is specifically denied to the States . . . it is difficult for laymen to understand how even 'rational' interference can be assumed to be among the reserved powers [of the Tenth Amendment]." In a letter to his sister, Justice Van Devanter worried that the decision could generate "incalculable harm and instability." Kansas lawyer F. Dumont Smith, former chair of the American Bar Association Committee on American Citizenship, wrote to Justice Sutherland several weeks after the decision. Smith claimed that the decision "throws a cloud, a doubt upon every contract executed in the future, and even upon existing contracts. The effect upon the business world and especially upon the debtor class will be deplorable. Few will care to loan money if the legislature may declare an emergency and deny their remedy for one, two or three years." A Connecticut lawyer wrote to Sutherland expressing alarm at the scope of emergency police powers recognized by the decision. If a state, by a preamble to a statute, can declare an emergency to exist and abrogate one provision of the Constitution, he wrote, "I do not see why all provisions and guarantees of our Constitution may not be nullified at the whim of a majority in any state legislature."

The *Chicago Daily Tribune* quoted the following warning from Senator Henry Hatfield (R-W.V.), a prominent critic of the New Deal: "There is grave danger that (the decision) will establish a precedent and give rise to innumerable unconstitutional laws under the pretext of an emergency, which would wreck the Constitution." Senator Hatfield lamented the violation of property rights. "This decision serves notice upon the individual who heretofore had trusted in the constitution for protection and believed in the sanctity of contract that the constitution is no longer a guarantee nor security against the abrogation of a proper and legal contract." An editorial from Helena, Montana, warned, "The decision is hailed by farmers and their political friends as a great victory when as a matter of fact it will eventually be a costly decision to the class moratoriums are supposed to benefit."

Despite these misgivings, conservative Republicans were unwilling to concede that the decision forecast anything about the constitutionality of federal recovery legislation. It was one thing to argue that a state could use its emergency powers to promote the general welfare, quite another to assert that Congress had such powers to impose remedies on the entire nation. James Beck, a Republican congressman from Pennsylvania and former solicitor general of the United States, warned that the "alphabetical excrescences [abnormal outgrowths] of our already swollen bureaucracy should not take too much encouragement from the Supreme Court decision in the recent Minnesota case." In his opinion, the decision did not validate any of the emergency legislation Congress had passed or was considering because the Court did not consider the powers of Congress under the Constitution, only state police powers.

Bankers' Magazine concluded that all the attention paid to the majority opinion unfortunately obscured the importance and wisdom of the economic philosophy contained in Sutherland's dissent. The "severity of depressions could be avoided" if Americans learned to be more frugal. This editorial admitted that during severe economic times it was human nature to seek to shift the burden of debt to the shoulders of creditors, especially when debtors felt victimized by circumstances they did not create. But a better course of action was to anticipate the potential consequences of assuming debt. *Bankers' Magazine* also proposed reforms to avoid future mortgage crises. At the time, many real estate mortgages were of the type in which, after a term of years, the entire cost of the house was due and payable (although the federal farm land banks were pushing the industry toward amortized loans). Moreover, annual or semiannual payments of taxes and interest called for large sums of money, causing distress to debtors. Anticipating many of the changes that would take place in the mortgage industry, the editors recommended making all real estate mortgages amortize, with monthly or quarterly payments that included interest, taxes, and a moderate reduction of the principal. Debtors, creditors, and local governments, it was argued, would all benefit from the reforms. Mortgage debtors would find it easier to make smaller payments, creditors would enjoy more predictable income, and states and municipalities would be relieved of collecting so many delinquent taxes.

Although the *Blaisdell* decision whipped up a storm of publicity, noticeably absent from the historical record is any reaction from John and Rosella Blaisdell themselves. As for many other average citizens fortunate enough to take a legal dispute all the way to the Supreme Court, their legacy is that of bit players in a constitutional drama. Although they won their case, the Blaisdells did not enjoy a fairy tale ending. John and Rosella divorced on February 13, 1935, and, one day later, John married Minneapolitan Mabel Albares in Grant County, South Dakota. Following the divorce, ownership of the house was transferred to Rosella on February 25, 1935. After the moratorium law was renewed for two years in early 1935, Rosella sought and received an extension on her redemption period from May 1, 1935, to March 1, 1937. As the couple had done since 1933, she alone would pay the $40 fee during that period. It is uncertain how long Rosella continued to live in the house after the divorce. The location of the house, 1518 Linden Avenue, is now a parking lot for a small business.

CHAPTER 9

The Death of
the Contract Clause?

Home Building and Loan Association v. Blaisdell did not instantaneously gut the Contract Clause. The first few relevant decisions after *Blaisdell* demonstrated that the case was neither as revolutionary as its admirers thought nor as devastating to property rights as its critics argued. By 1937, however, the revolution that *Blaisdell* helped plant was in full bloom — and for much of the remainder of the twentieth century, the Contract Clause would remain moribund.

Initially, supporters and opponents of the New Deal both could find comfort in the majority opinion. According to legal scholar Samuel Olken, *Blaisdell* "merely represented an application of the Court's long-standing mediation between vested contract rights and the state's power to regulate for the public interest." In this vein, the Court simply upheld an unremarkable exercise of state police power during an economic emergency. A few commentators, particularly those critical of the decision, even suggested that the 5–4 split in both *Blaisdell* and *Nebbia* portended trouble for New Deal legislation. After all, the Minnesota moratorium law was temporary and limited, but much New Deal legislation was designed to be permanent. At the least, it was unclear how the Hughes Court and state courts would apply the *Blaisdell* precedent to regulatory laws that did not closely mirror Minnesota's statute.

It seemed at first as if the Supreme Court would stunt *Blaisdell's* reach. A few months after *Blaisdell*, the *W. B. Worthen Co. v. Thomas* decision unanimously struck down an Arkansas law that exempted the life insurance of a defaulting debtor from garnishment. Ralph Thomas and his wife were partners in a harness business in Little Rock, Arkansas, and rented their business space from the W. B. Worthen Company. When the Thomases fell behind in their payments, the company secured a $1,200 judgment against them. After Mr. Thomas died on March 5, 1933, the company obtained a writ of garnishment against the $5,000 policy that the harness dealer left his wife. Several days later, the Arkansas legislature enacted a law exempting life insurance from seizure.

Writing for the Court, Chief Justice Hughes argued, "Such an exemption applied in the case of debts owing before the exemption was created by the legislature constitutes an unwarrantable interference with the obligation of contracts in violation of the constitutional provisions." Like Minnesota, Arkansas claimed that an economic emergency necessitated the relief measure. The chief justice, however, distinguished the Arkansas insurance law from the Minnesota moratorium by reasoning that the former lacked the "temporary and conditional quality" that permitted the Court to find the latter a reasonable emergency exercise of the police power. In *Blaisdell*, Hughes noted, the Court had found the relief to be reasonable, from the standpoint of both mortgagor and mortgagee, because it was limited to the exigency to which the legislation was addressed. "By placing insurance moneys beyond the reach of existing creditors," Hughes explained, the Arkansas law contained "no limitations as to time, amount, circumstances, or need."

Justice Sutherland, writing a concurrence for the same four who had dissented in *Blaisdell*, agreed "unreservedly" in the decision striking down the Arkansas statute, but he disagreed that the differences between the Minnesota and Arkansas statutes were material. Both laws, Sutherland suggested, were governed by the same principles. He wrote:

We were unable then, as we are now, to concur in the view that an emergency can ever justify, or what is really the same thing, can ever furnish an occasion for justifying, a nullification of the constitutional restriction upon state power in respect of the impairment of contractual obligations. . . . We reject as unsound and dangerous doctrine . . . the notion that violations of those provisions may be measured by the length of time they are to continue or the extent of the infraction. . . . The power of this court is not to amend but only to expound the constitution as an agency of the sovereign people who made it and who alone have the authority to alter or unmake it.

The following year, the Court had another opportunity to determine the reach of the *Blaisdell* precedent—and once again limited it. In *W. B. Worthen Co. v. Kavanaugh* (1935), Justice Cardozo wrote for a unanimous Court in striking down three Arkansas statutes that helped borrowers by reducing penalties for late payment of mandatory fees related to improvements on property and also substantially extended the period during which a delinquent owner could occupy a property from a minimum of sixty-five days to six and one-half years. Justice Cardozo noted that the "catalogue of changes imposed on the mortgage" by the Arkansas laws demonstrated "studied indifference" to the interests of creditors. The modifications to the mortgage agreement were so onerous that *Blaisdell* could not be used to support the new laws. None of the limitations in the Minnesota act, nor anything approaching them, was present in the Arkansas statutes. Cardozo acknowledged that the courts long had recognized a distinction between the substance of a contract and changes to its remedy, but "not even changes of the remedy may be pressed so far as to cut down the security of a mortgage without moderation of reason or in a spirit of oppression. Even when the public welfare is invoked as an excuse, these bounds must be respected." This decision limited *Blaisdell*'s reach, but the central tenets of *Blaisdell* were largely untested because the law under review gave such generous terms to debtors. Even the liberals agreed that Arkansas overreached.

Although it did not involve a moratorium issue, the High Court also used the Contract Clause to strike down a law that abrogated shareholders' rights in *Treigle v. ACME Homestead Association* (1936). Here the Court overturned a Louisiana law that changed a building and loan association's obligation to maintain a fund to pay shareholders. Prior to the enactment of the law, building and loan associations were required to set aside 50 percent of the receipts to pay members who withdrew from the association. The new law abolished this requirement and left it to the discretion of the directors whether receipts would be used to make loans, pay old or new debts, pay dividends to continuing members, or serve as cash reserves for future dividends. As a consequence, some stockholders who withdrew had not been paid. Writing for a unanimous Court, Justice Roberts concluded that the law impaired the obligation of a stockholder's contract and his or her vested rights. The law did not purport to deal with an existing emergency, the restrictions were neither temporary nor conditional, and the use of the police power was unconnected to the public interest, as distinguished from purely private rights.

Clearly, then, the *Blaisdell* precedent was not an open invitation for the states to enact broad debtor relief without respecting the rights of creditors. The Court demanded that relief laws be reasonable in light of an economic emergency, and the scope of the legislation and the nature of the emergency were critical in determining the validity of these laws.

Meanwhile, the political stakes surrounding Contract Clause jurisprudence grew dramatically. In 1935 and 1936, the Supreme Court invalidated several federal programs designed to reform the American economy; these decisions did not directly affect *Blaisdell* but portended trouble for it. On Monday, May 27, 1935, which liberals called "Black Monday," the Court unanimously attacked the New Deal on three fronts. In *A. L. A. Schechter Poultry Corp. v. United States*, the Court overturned the National Industrial Recovery Act (which established the production and price codes in hundreds of industries that farmer-activists unsuccessfully sought to emulate in agriculture), primarily because it unconstitutionally delegated authority to the executive branch. In *Humphrey's Executor v. United States*, the Court declared that President Roosevelt did not have the authority to remove a commissioner from the Federal Trade Commission (and replace him with a New Deal supporter).

Finally, in *Louisville Joint Stock Land Bank v. Radford*, the Court overturned the 1934 Frazier-Lemke Act. As we introduced earlier, Frazier-Lemke amended the Bankruptcy Act to compel holders of existing mortgages to relinquish farm property to mortgagors without full payment of mortgage debt. The law applied retroactively and permitted extensions lasting ten years. Radford, the mortgagee, relied heavily on *Blaisdell* and the emergency powers doctrine. Arguing before the Court, Radford's lawyer said, "Emergency calls forth dormant powers. An emergency is here. There is a distinct menace that ownership of farmlands will pass into the hands of a privileged few."

Justice Brandeis's majority opinion distinguished the laws at issue in *Louisville Joint Stock Land Bank v. Radford* and *Blaisdell*. Brandeis deemed the Frazier-Lemke Act unacceptable because it granted an overly generous ten-year extension and excessively expanded the rights of debtors by depriving creditors of their security (the property) for a mortgage loan. The Minnesota Mortgage Moratorium Act was acceptable, however, because it offered a stingy extension and under it mortgagors continued to make payments. The Court did not apply the Contract Clause in this case because the clause does not apply to Congress; instead, the Court held that Frazier-Lemke represented an unconstitutional taking of property without just compensation in violation of the Fifth Amendment. Brandeis concluded, "If the public interest requires, and permits the taking of property of individual mortgagees in order to relieve the necessities of individual mortgagors," the government must resort to proceedings by eminent domain, "so that, through taxation, the burden of the relief afforded in the public interest may be borne by the public." Congress subsequently passed the new Farm Mortgage Moratorium Act of August 1935, which altered the terms of the moratorium and limited it to a three-year period. This revised law was unanimously sustained by the Supreme Court on March 29, 1937.

As the U.S. Supreme Court narrowed the scope of *Blaisdell*, the states reassessed their mortgage-relief legislation in light of the decision. Although some states moved in a more conservative direction, overall the trend was toward sustaining and expanding mortgage relief. *Blaisdell* encouraged several state legislatures to amend their debtor-relief laws to conform to the features of the Minnesota statute, and many state supreme courts used the decision to validate mortgage-relief legislation. South Carolina, Mississippi, and Louisiana enacted moratoriums soon after *Blaisdell*. One study of *Blaisdell*'s influence a year after the decision identified eleven cases in which state supreme courts had reviewed the constitutionality of emergency legislation. Of those eleven, eight statutes had been confirmed as constitutional on the basis of *Blaisdell*.

Statutes especially similar to the Minnesota law were reviewed in Michigan, Iowa, and Texas. In a per curiam opinion, the Michigan Supreme Court upheld that state's law and suggested that *Blaisdell* had settled the issue with respect to mortgage-relief legislation. The Iowa court sustained relief in *Des Moines Joint Stock Land Bank v. Nordholm* after citing a significant portion of the *Blaisdell* majority opinion. In

1939, however, the Iowa Supreme Court found an extension of that state's moratorium law unconstitutional under the federal and state contract clause, observing, "If a so-called emergency exists beyond a temporary period then it is no longer an emergency but a status." Nebraska's Supreme Court also invalidated an extension of that state's mortgage-moratorium law.

Some of the state laws upheld differed significantly from the Minnesota moratorium law—and many were even more generous to debtors. One common form of mortgage relief allowed the courts to refuse confirmation of a foreclosure sale because of the inadequacy of the price. North Carolina passed such legislation, but unlike the Minnesota law it contained no declaration of an emergency and appeared to be permanent. North Carolina's Supreme Court upheld the law in *Hopkins v. Swain* (1934). The court made no attempt to discuss the temporal character of the law; it simply concluded that it was constitutional in light of *Blaisdell*. Various provisions of statutes dealing with liquidation of closed banks and defaulted mortgage guarantee companies were also upheld in Mississippi, New Jersey, and New York with reference to *Blaisdell*.

Three state supreme courts, however, followed Justice Sutherland's dissent in *Blaisdell* in rejecting mortgage-relief legislation. In *Blagg v. Harrigan* (1934), the Texas Supreme Court held a statute similar to the Minnesota law unconstitutional because it authorized the courts to stay foreclosure proceedings. Although the contract clause of the Texas constitution was modeled after the federal provision, the court accepted interpretations of the federal clause only prior to 1875–1876, when the Texas provision was enacted. Under judicial federalism, the Texas Supreme Court can construe the state's contract clause to afford more protection to contracts than the federal Constitution, but it is unusual for a state supreme court to accept interpretations of the U.S. Constitution only prior to a certain year. The Texas Supreme Court found no emergency exception in the Texas constitution's contract clause. The opinion even failed to cite the Minnesota mortgage moratorium case. In *U.S. Mortgage Company v. Matthews* (1934), the Maryland Court of Appeals (the state supreme court) also declared unconstitutional two laws that deprived the holder of less than 25 percent of the entire mortgage debt the use of two remedies, an immediate foreclosure by a trustee and a power of sale on default. The law upheld in

Blaisdell had provided payment of a rental value applied to the carrying of the property and payment of the mortgage indebtedness. But Maryland law provided no substitute remedy, the court reasoned, so the statute could not be upheld. In Wisconsin, a law denied a bondholder the power to sue on the bond until the trustee foreclosed on the mortgage. The Wisconsin Supreme Court maintained in *Hanauer v. Republic Building Co.* that the law did not satisfy the criteria of reasonableness established in *Blaisdell* because it was not limited in time and did not compensate the bondholder for the denial of his remedy.

Although state courts applied the *Blaisdell* precedent variously, on balance the opinion strengthened the constitutional validity of state mortgage-relief laws, encouraged additional states to enact moratorium legislation, and even was used to justify emergency legislation in other areas of law such as the liquidation of closed banks and defaulted mortgage-guarantee companies. Yet the limitations embedded in Chief Justice Hughes's opinion, emphasized by several state supreme courts, threatened *Blaisdell*'s long-term impact.

If liberal supporters of economic regulation were dismayed during the 1934–35 Supreme Court term, they were horrified during the 1935–36 one. In the spring of 1936, Justice Owen Roberts, sometimes joined by Chief Justice Hughes, joined the four conservatives in overturning several pieces of federal and state legislation. In *United States v. Butler* (1936), Roberts wrote for a majority of six in striking down the 1933 Agricultural Adjustment Act, more specifically its provision that imposed a tax on food processors in order to fund benefit payments to farmers who participated in the government's voluntary crop-reduction program. While holding that the federal government has broad taxing and spending powers to promote the general welfare, Roberts relied on the commerce-versus-production distinction to characterize agriculture as a local productive activity that Congress could not regulate under the Commerce Clause. In the same term, the Court dealt a further blow to economic regulation in *Morehead v. New York ex rel. Tipaldo* (1936); here Justice Roberts joined the four conservatives in striking down New York's law mandating minimum wages for women and children on the grounds that it violated the liberty of contract protected by the Due Process Clause.

The liberals on the Court seemed to be not only outnumbered but also running out of time. By 1936, the Great Depression had lasted seven years. Laws enacted to respond to an economic emergency carried with them the expectation that the relief would end once the crisis had passed. In addition, the economy showed signs of life at mid-decade. Several states' moratorium laws, including those in Idaho, Kansas, Maryland, New Hampshire, and Vermont, reached their expiration date in 1937 and were not renewed (although Minnesota's was). Even after the economy dipped significantly again during the "Roosevelt Recession" of 1937–1938, additional proposed economic regulations simply could not be justified as emergency measures. Liberals needed a new rationale.

That rationale emerged in 1937, in the form of a new stress on judicial deference to legislatures on matters of economic regulation. Although liberals hardly could have guessed it at the time, *Morehead* turned out to be the last gasp for liberty of contract doctrine. The decision was rebuked by media throughout the country, criticized in the Republican Party's 1936 platform, and overturned within just one year. How this remarkable transformation took place is one of the most important stories in American constitutional history.

Soon after Roosevelt won a landslide reelection in 1936 and unveiled his plan to "reorganize" the federal judiciary, Justice Roberts performed his so-called switch in time. In *West Coast Hotel v. Parrish* (1937), he joined Hughes, Cardozo, Stone, and Brandeis in upholding Washington State's minimum wage law for women. *West Coast Hotel v. Parrish* dealt a major blow to substantive due process. In rejecting the freedom-of-contract challenge to this Washington State law, Chief Justice Hughes stressed that the Constitution neither refers to a liberty of contract nor recognizes "an absolute uncontrollable liberty." The Court thus overturned the precedent of *Adkins v. Children's Hospital* (1923), which had invalidated an almost identical minimum wage law in the District of Columbia.

On March 29, the same day as the *West Coast Hotel* decision — "White Monday" to liberals — the High Court upheld several acts of Congress that expanded federal power, including the revised Frazier-Lemke Act. Writing for the Court in *Wright v. Vinton Branch of Mountain Trust Bank of Roanoke* (1937), Justice Brandeis sustained the revised federal farm-bankruptcy law because it limited moratoriums to three years (recall that the original Frazier-Lemke Act offered ten-year extensions) and gave secured creditors the opportunity to force a public sale. Additionally, in *Virginian Railway v. Railway Employees* (1937), the Court upheld labor regulations for the railroad industry.

Two weeks later, the Court handed the Roosevelt administration a victory in five consolidated cases involving the 1935 National Labor Relations Act, a seminal law that recognized the rights of organized labor to collectively bargain and to strike. In *NLRB v. Jones and Laughlin Steel Corp.*, Chief Justice Hughes declared, "Although activities may be intrastate in character when separately considered, if they have such a close and substantial relation to interstate commerce that their control is essential and appropriate to protect that commerce from burdens and obstructions, Congress cannot be denied the power to exercise that control." A month later, in *Helvering v. Davis* (1937), the Court sustained the 1935 Social Security Act, the grandfather of the modern American welfare state. In upholding Washington's minimum wage, the National Labor Relations Act, the Social Security Act, and other seminal New Deal programs in a span of just a few months, the Court applied a new deferential stance to government regulation of economic activity. States now had significant authority to regulate intrastate commerce using their police powers, and Congress had broad powers under the Commerce Clause to regulate the economy and enact social welfare programs. Hughes and Roberts voted with the liberals in both *NLRB v. Jones and Laughlin Steel* and *Helvering v. Davis*.

Why did Justice Roberts switch his votes in 1937 to affirm state and federal regulation of the market? The question has generated volumes of scholarly research and contentious debate. A traditional interpretation, articulated by many observers in the 1930s and historians thereafter, narrowly dates the Constitutional Revolution in favor of the New Deal to the 1937 victories for state and federal regulation in *West Coast Hotel v. Parrish* and *National Labor Relations Board v. Jones and Laughlin Steel*. This interpretation assumes that Roosevelt's plan to "pack" the High Court with justices more receptive to the constitutionality of New Deal initiatives was the catalyst for Roberts's reversal. Traditionalists stress other external factors as well, such as public protests for relief and the Democrats' landslide victory in the 1936 elections.

A second camp identifies a more gradual change in constitutional doctrine dating back to the early years of the Hughes Court — and indeed decades earlier. This camp sees the Constitutional Revolution as the culmination of a decades-long intellectual struggle against a system of legal orthodoxy that characterized law as neutral and nonpolitical. Barry Cushman and G. Edward White are among the leading revisionists who assert that the change in constitutional jurisprudence was gradual and not marked by a sudden shift in 1937.

Revisionists note that Roberts had voted in conference in December 1936 to sustain wage regulation in *West Coast Hotel*, two months before the Court-packing plan was made public. To be sure, it is not implausible that Roberts was influenced by the Democrats' overwhelming victory in 1936. Justice Sutherland suggested as much in his *West Coast Hotel* dissent, accusing the majority of bending to popular will. Roosevelt administration officials also suspected that electoral politics played a role. Burt Solomon, however, proposes that Roberts may have changed his mind even before the election. On October 10, 1936, weeks before the fall elections, the Court granted review of the *West Coast Hotel* case. Roberts joined the three liberals and Chief Justice Hughes in voting to consider the case. According to Solomon, Roberts's action prompted one of the Four Horsemen to ask, "What is the matter with Roberts?" No one had an answer, including Roberts. He probably changed his mind on his own, for reasons known only to himself, although various explanations have been offered: Chief Justice Hughes successfully lobbied him to change his mind, he had ambitions to receive the Republican nomination for president, and he was stung by criticisms of his earlier decisions.

Owen Roberts waited eighteen years to offer an explanation of his "somersault," as future justice Felix Frankfurter termed it. Roberts attributed his switch to a legal technicality in the *Morehead* minimum wage case, but few scholars find this explanation convincing. The truth is that we may never know for certain. Justice Roberts burned all of his personal and judicial papers because, as a friend explained, "he did not want them subject to interpretation which he would not approve or correct."

Beyond the mystery of Roberts's switch, the *Blaisdell* decision remains central to the debate over the origins and significance of the Constitutional Revolution of 1937. To the traditionalists, *Blaisdell* and

Nebbia may have been harbingers of the revolution, but few jurispru-dential signs indicated that the Court would engage in its dramatic reversal in 1937 after stepping back in 1935 and 1936. In this vein, the revolution was an abrupt response to external political pressure. To the revisionists, however, *Blaisdell* and *Nebbia* were crucial stepping-stones on a much older and ongoing path of gradual constitutional change (and indeed Roberts himself had been shifting his thinking for some time). G. Edward White, for example, proposes that the Court had been relaxing scrutiny over legislative actions since early in the twentieth century.

The present study agrees with the evolutionary model of the rev-olution of 1937 — and suggests that *Blaisdell* deserves as much attention as *Nebbia*. *Blaisdell* was the first Supreme Court decision to uphold a law designed to combat the economic crisis — "recovery legislation" in the language of the day. Although the police powers had always been broad enough to encompass the "public welfare," *Blaisdell* took the dramatic step of moving beyond the traditional police powers emphasis on health and safety to supporting a widespread impairment of contracts based on macroeconomic conditions. Certainly the Court's path from 1934 to 1937 was rocky and marked by ruts and false trailheads. The Court oscillated back and forth from 1934 to 1936, many decisions were 5–4, and nothing was inevitable. Yet, the pro-regulation ideas at the heart of the 1937 Constitutional Revolution were hinted at in early Hughes Court decisions and clearly displayed in *Blaisdell* and *Nebbia*. In addition, these pro-regulation ideas have deep roots in the common law and early American jurisprudence. Finally, they sprang in part from a newer body of liberal legal ideas that had been rising to the surface since before the New Deal.

More specifically, the Court's liberal turn in the 1930s reflected the maturation of legal realism, a doctrine that emerged in the late 1920s and early 1930s at Yale and Columbia law schools. The leading advo-cates of legal realism included Karl Llewellyn, Robert Lee Hale, Arthur Corbin, and Jerome Frank. An important extension of turn-of-the-century sociological jurisprudence, legal realism claimed that the decision-making process is not merely a formal, analytical exer-cise separate from social or economic forces; it is subjective, political, and often unpredictable. According to the realists, the language of the Constitution and statutes is often ambiguous and requires interpretation. Precedents can help narrow the range of choices judges face when they resolve cases, but they can never provide complete certainty because a precedent can be found to support most arguments. Reasoned choice, not the application of law in an analytical vacuum, drives decision making. Choice involves subjective decisions as to the meaning of the text, the intent of the Constitution's framers, and the value and relevancy of past precedents. According to the legal realist school, judges decide cases based on their subjective personal preferences — which are shaped by external influences — and use legal criteria to defend the decision. Judicial decision making, in short, is reduced to politics.

Legal realism promoted judicial deference and shared many intellectual affinities with the Court's ascendant pro–New Deal position. Each expressed skepticism over abstract legal principles and acknowledged the complex nature of a modern, industrial economy. Realists and New Dealers supported using technical experts and administrative regulation to address social and economic problems. In fact, a large number of legal realists served in the Roosevelt administration, including Thurman Arnold, William O. Douglas, Felix Frankfurter, and Jerome Frank. The Court, admitting that it lacked the capacity to understand the economic complexity of modern society, had removed itself as an obstacle to legislative experimentation. The principles of judicial deference to legislatures and skepticism of rigid legal doctrines such as liberty of contract had been articulated by Justice Oliver Wendell Holmes decades earlier in substantive due process cases such as *Lochner v. New York* (1905) and *Adkins v. Children's Hospital* (1923) — but only in dissenting opinions.

As the Court moved toward a deferential stance toward laws regulating economic activity in the 1930s, at first haltingly but then, after 1937, decisively, it was able to sever the Due Process Clauses of the Fourteenth and Fifth Amendments from the accumulated weight of liberty of contract doctrine. Under the new, deferential approach, laws regulating the market needed to possess only a reasonable connection to whatever problem the state was trying to address. This fundamental change defines the 1937 Constitutional Revolution. Constitutional scholar Daniel Hulsebosch argues that judicial deference to legislative intent on economic policy was the "new reason" or rationale that emerged from the New Deal. In some ways, judicial deference was more radical than invocation of emergency powers doctrine, a device that at least had a decent body of precedent behind it.

In 1937, the conservative justices on the Supreme Court began to retire, beginning with Willis Van Devanter. By 1941, the Four Horsemen were gone, replaced by such ardent New Deal supporters as Hugo Black, Stanley Reed, and Felix Frankfurter. James W. Ely Jr. notes that the "advent of New Deal constitutionalism completed the effective destruction of Contract Clause jurisprudence," as the new justices "stressed heavy deference to legislative judgments about economic policy." Ely seeks to rejuvenate the Contract Clause, but few scholars of any ilk disagree with his conclusions here. At least for the next forty years, the Contract Clause appeared to be in a constitutional graveyard. Liberals rejoiced at the increasingly narrow interpretation of the Contract Clause – the New Deal was now on firm constitutional ground.

Dramatically broadening the potential for state interventions, the High Court soon ruled that an emergency was no longer a necessary prerequisite for regulating contracts along police power lines. In *Veix v. Sixth Ward Building and Loan Association* (1940), it rejected a Contract Clause challenge in sustaining permanent legislation that restricted the right of customers to withdraw funds from building and loan associations. Justice Stanley Reed wrote, "Such legislation may be classified as emergency in one sense but it need not be temporary." Permanent legislation was also upheld in *Gelfert v. National City Bank* (1941), in which new Justice William O. Douglas declared that the absence of a legislative declaration of emergency did not bring the mortgagee's rights within the scope of the Contract Clause. In *East New York Savings Bank v. Hahn* (1945), Justice Felix Frankfurter wrote that the "incidence of mortgage-moratorium legislation on an isolated contract must be considered in the light of the right of the State to safeguard the interests of its people." In upholding the tenth extension of a mortgage-moratorium law, Frankfurter stressed that the Court must respect the "wide discretion on the part of the legislature in determining what is and what is not necessary," even if a private contract may be affected.

In the decades following the New Deal, the Supreme Court was dominated by justices who took liberal positions on economic regulation. Between 1941 and 1977, the Supreme Court heard few cases involving the Contract Clause and found no violations of the provision. In *El Paso v. Simmons* (1965), the Contract Clause was used unsuccessfully to challenge a Texas law governing public land sales. Under the original law, a purchaser who missed an interest payment immediately forfeited the land back to the state. However, a purchaser could reinstate his or her claim on written request and payment of interest if the owner made the payment before the land could be resold. In 1941, Texas amended the law, limiting reinstatement rights to five years from the forfeiture date. Greenbury Simmons purchased and then forfeited some land in 1947. A little over five years later, he offered to pay the interest to reacquire the property, but the state refused to comply, citing the 1941 amendment. Simmons's land was sold to the City of El Paso in 1955. By an 8–1 vote, the Court upheld the amendment. Quoting Chief Justice Hughes in *Blaisdell*, Justice Byron White wrote that the prohibition against impairment of the obligation of contract "is not an absolute one and is not to be read with literal exactness like a mathematical formula."

In a lone dissenting opinion, Justice Hugo Black, known for his literal interpretation of the Constitution, criticized the majority's "balancing away" the property protections of both the Contract Clause and Fifth Amendment's Takings Clause. Justice Black agreed with the interpretation of the Court of Appeals, which held that Texas's original contractual promise to permit reinstatement created an obligation that the state was bound by contract to honor. Neither the history of the Contract Clause nor Court precedents, he argued, supported the majority opinion. Justice Black read the *Blaisdell* decision narrowly, as he believed that Chief Justice Hughes intended, by pointing out that the case upheld only a temporary restraint that provided for some compensation. To bolster his narrow interpretation of *Blaisdell*, Justice Black observed that the Court used the precedent to strike down several state laws subsequent to the decision. He felt that the majority in the *El Paso* case was "balancing away" property rights under a reasonableness test in much the same way that it had diminished First Amendment rights.

Although it is true that the Contract Clause lost most of its relevance during the middle decades of the twentieth century, it had not been completely eliminated from the Constitution. In the late 1970s, the Court breathed some life back into it. President Nixon's appointment of Chief Justice Warren Burger in 1969 and subsequent conservative appointments brought more business-oriented justices to the Court and increased the prospects for revitalizing the Contract Clause. In *United States Trust Co. v. New Jersey* (1977), a narrow majority held that the Contract Clause prohibited the retroactive repeal of a 1962 covenant agreed to by New York and New Jersey. In 1921, these two states entered into a compact to create the Port Authority of New York, a financially independent body responsible for developing and coordinating transportation and commerce in the New York metropolitan area. In 1962, in response to increased public interest in mass transit, the Port Authority took control of the Hudson and Manhattan Railroad, but the states agreed that none of the Port Authority's revenues pledged as security for existing bonds would be used for any additional railroad expenditures. In the early 1970s, the United States faced an energy crisis. Under pressure to develop mass transit, both states freed funds to expand their mass transit systems by repealing the original pledge. The United States Trust Company, a holder of bonds harmed by the repeal, claimed that the repeal was a contractual impairment in violation of the Contract Clause.

The Supreme Court found the repeal of the 1962 covenant both unreasonable and unnecessary, and thereby a violation of the Contract Clause. *United States Trust Co. v. New Jersey* was the first decision in almost forty years in which the Court used the Contract Clause to overturn a state law. Justice Harry Blackmun argued that the impairment was "neither necessary to achieve the States' plan to encourage private automobile users to shift to public transportation nor reasonable in light of changed circumstances." Total repeal of the 1962 covenant was not essential, he asserted, because New York and New Jersey's plan could have been implemented with a less drastic modification of the covenant. In addition, the states could have adopted alternative means of achieving their shared goal of discouraging automobile use and improving mass transit without modifying the covenant at all. Reaffirming the police powers doctrine, Blackmun argued that the repeal was not a response to an unforeseen crisis or emergency situation; the 1962 covenant was adopted with knowledge of the need for mass transportation, energy conservation, and environmental protection in the New York metropolitan area.

In his dissenting opinion, Justice William Brennan concluded that the majority decision was contrary to the established principle that the state police power to enact laws "in furtherance of the health, safety, and similar collective interests of the policy" qualifies the Contract Cause. The decision, he claimed, "remolds the Contract Clause into a potent instrument for overseeing important policy determinations of the state legislature" and "distorts modern constitutional jurisprudence governing regulation of private economic interests." Brennan felt that the Court's review of policy decisions made by the legislature was "unwise as it is unnecessary," and he professed to be mystified by the decision. He warned that the decision signaled "a return to substantive constitutional review of States' policies" reminiscent of the substantive due process jurisprudence of the *Lochner* era.

In *Allied Structural Steel Co. v. Spannaus* (1978), the Court again struck down a state law under the Contract Clause. Under Minnesota's Private Pension Benefits Law, a company that terminated a pension plan or closed down its offices in Minnesota would be subject to a charge to the extent that retirement funds did not assure full pensions to all workers employed by the company for ten years or more. Writing for a slim five-justice majority, Justice Potter Stewart acknowledged that the Contract Clause had receded into "comparative desuetude" with the ratification of the Fourteenth Amendment and development of liberty of contract jurisprudence, but he pointed out that the Contract Clause is still "part of the Constitution . . . it is not dead letter." The Court also reminded the legal community that the *Blaisdell* decision implied that the Court would not have upheld Minnesota's moratorium had it not possessed several moderating characteristics. The Court concluded that the Minnesota pension law severely disrupted contractual expectations, and it saw no evidence the law was designed to meet an important social problem. Rather, the law nullified the express terms of a company's labor contract with its employees and imposed a completely unexpected liability upon the company in potentially disabling amounts. Of course, in at least one major way, this law was crucially different from the one upheld in *Blaisdell*. The pension law was not enacted to deal with a situation remotely as desperate as the emergency of the Great Depression.

Justice Brennan delivered a strong dissent, asserting that until *Allied Structural Steel*, the Court had interpreted the Contract Clause to prohibit only state acts that effectively diminished or nullified the obligation due a party under the terms of a contract. He claimed that the Minnesota pension act did not abrogate or dilute any obligation but instead imposed additional, new obligations. The word "impair," Justice Brennan asserted, cannot be interpreted to include new laws that add obligations. He suggested that the authors of the Constitution never contemplated that the clause would limit the legislative power of states to enact laws creating duties that might burden some individuals in order to benefit others. Brennan claimed that the Contract Clause did not apply to the Minnesota act and that the act could be challenged only under the Due Process Clause. But the due process claim had no merit. Brennan argued in sum that the majority opinion in *Spannaus* was "a distortion" of Contract Clause jurisprudence.

Although these 1970s decisions breathed some life back into the Contract Clause, they did not restore it as the primary protection for property rights. In the words of Justice Stewart, the Contract Clause may not be "dead letter," but neither is there much life left in the provision. Many observers suggest that the clause will never hold the same status that it once had under the Marshall Court. Indeed, despite the ascendancy of a more conservative, pro-corporate political economy in the past forty years, the Supreme Court continues to use a deferential approach with regard to regulation that affects contracts.

In *Energy Reserves Group v. Kansas Power and Light* (1983), the Court unanimously upheld a Kansas law that dictated an energy-pricing system in conflict with existing contracts. The Court held that the Contract Clause prohibits only state actions "that substantially impair the contractual arrangement." Even such a substantial impairment can be justified if a significant and legitimate public purpose supports the regulation, such as remedying a broad economic or social problem. Once such a purpose has been identified, concluded Justice Harry Blackmun, "the adjustment of the contracting parties' rights and responsibilities must be based upon reasonable conditions, and must be of a character appropriate to the public purpose justifying the legislation's adoption."

Subsequent decisions have applied a highly deferential approach to the reasonableness standard. *Keystone Bituminous Coal Association v. DeBenedictis* (1987) raised both Contract Clause and Fifth Amendment Takings Clause issues. A closely divided Court upheld a Pennsylvania law that required coal mine operators to leave 50 percent of the coal in the ground beneath certain structures to provide surface support. This mandate conflicted with contracts between mining companies and the landowners that allowed companies to extract a much higher proportion of coal. The Court supported the right of the state, pursuant to its police powers, to impose such a regulation to protect a legitimate public interest, with Justice John Paul Stevens claiming that the Contract Clause "is not to be read literally."

Today, state and federal courts sometimes apply Contract Clause provisions in striking down government regulations. But even the recent conservative Supreme Courts under Chief Justice William Rehnquist (1986–2005) and Chief Justice John Roberts (2005–present) have done little to resuscitate the clause, even as the Rehnquist Court strengthened the Takings Clause as a protection for property rights. The Supreme Court has not decided a major Contract Clause case in the past thirty years. Indeed, the Contract Clause has been on life support since *Home Building and Loan Association v. Blaisdell.*

The moribund status of the Contract Clause has prompted contemporary conservatives and libertarians to single out the *Blaisdell* decision for criticism and to call for a revitalization of the provision as a bulwark of property rights. For example, Robert Levy of the conservative-libertarian Cato Institute and William Mellor of the Institute of Justice (according to its webpage, the "nation's only libertarian public interest law firm") include *Blaisdell* in their book on the *Dirty Dozen* Supreme Court decisions that, they argue, have most eroded Americans' constitutional freedoms.

The current hostility toward *Blaisdell*, like Justice Sutherland's blistering dissent, draws upon traditional strands of American conservatism and antistatism. For example, three overriding beliefs guide Levy and Mellor's defense of liberty of contract and hostility to *Blaisdell*. The first is the "principle of private autonomy," because, they write, "When governments abrogate private contracts, it intrudes upon private liberty." Second, *Blaisdell* harmed the "rule-of-law ideal." Government must enact laws faithfully, and apply them equally to all people and in all circumstances, and not make any retroactive changes to them. Third, the Contract Clause is closely connected to the principle of the separation of powers embodied in the Constitution; it was designed partially as "a check against concentrated political power." In this vein, *The Dirty Dozen* contends, "the Contracts Clause prevents the legislature from assuming the institutional role of the Courts — reserving to the judiciary the job of resolving individual contractual disputes."

Anti-*Blaisdell* sentiment also springs from recent shifts in economic thinking. For more than four decades, conservative economists and theorists have successfully counterattacked the economic liberalism that reigned among academics and policy makers in the United States from the 1930s through the 1960s. Contemporary American conservatism holds that markets almost always work, and work best when left alone. Accordingly, even conservatives who consider *Blaisdell* constitutional believe that state interventions such as the Minnesota Mortgage Moratorium Act deleteriously distort markets. From this antistate perspective, such laws may help some lucky people in the short term — in our case, the Minnesota farmers who retained their farms thanks to state largesse or the owners of a Minneapolis boardinghouse — but in the long term they engender a host of unintended and destructive economic consequences — in our case, a stunted lending market and a new unhealthy reliance upon the state.

Theorists who emphasize personal liberty claim that laws interfering with contracts unconstitutionally and unethically favor one group of citizens over another, what nineteenth-century judges called "class legislation." The Federalist Society is an influential legal think tank that briefly captured national headlines during the George W. Bush administration for unofficially wresting control of vetting federal judges away from the centrist American Bar Association. At a Federalist Society forum, Nadine Strossen, then president of the American Civil Liberties Union, reserved special vitriol for what she saw as Chief Justice Hughes's creation of a two-tiered society that privileged the property rights of some property owners (homeowners) over those of others (lenders). Strossen referred specifically to Hughes's comment in *Blaisdell* that lenders "are predominantly corporations, such as insurance companies, banks, and investment and mortgage companies. [They] are not seeking homes or the opportunity to engage in farming. Their chief concern is the reasonable protection of their investment security." Similarly rejecting Hughes's distinction between corporations and farmers, Robert Levy wrote,

"There you have it, a new hierarchy of rights based on class and found nowhere in the Constitution: Corporate shareholders and employees are second-class citizens whose rights can be sacrificed to protect homeowners and farmers."

Conservatives and libertarians insist that special treatment for certain groups helped *Blaisdell* stretch and twist the police powers doctrine beyond recognition. "Few would object if a state, acting under a police power exception to the Contracts Clause, annuls a contract to pollute or to bribe that might injure nonconsenting third parties," *The Dirty Dozen* notes. "But the more complex problem, described by University of Chicago law professor Richard A. Epstein, is that 'the New Deal constitutional transformation . . . greatly expanded the scope of the police power beyond these broadly libertarian objectives, so that it was no longer possible to distinguish between general welfare and special interests.'" Distressed Minnesotans who had defaulted on their mortgages constituted the special interest who received special favor at the "expense of creditors who had provided the capital and who were surely not to blame for the economic conditions that led to default."

Conservatives also emphasize that the Constitution contains no emergency powers provision, even if the executive branch has constructed one throughout the nation's history, especially during wars. To conservatives, then, the Court's identification of emergency conditions in the post–World War I *Rent Cases*, vital precedents for *Blaisdell*, was an especially unfortunate aberration. In the *Charleston Law Review*, James Ely Jr. wrote that the *Rent Cases* subordinated contract rights to the will of legislatures during emergencies in a "cursory opinion, which really never came to grips with the question of contractual impairment." In contrast, Ely avers, the dissenting opinion in the *Rent Cases* correctly deemed the Contract Clause "paramount." It also should be recalled that the Supreme Court dropped the criterion of emergency for interfering in contracts soon after *Blaisdell*; some conservatives claim that the talk of emergency was always a cynical front to mask statist objectives and was easily abandoned by the Court when no longer needed.

Ironically, however, even as libertarians single out *Blaisdell* for complaint, they sometimes dip into its language to buttress their arguments. In the Federalist Society forum mentioned above, Nadine

Strossen used the *Blaisdell* decision to support her contention that beyond the high threshold of existential threat to the nation, individual rights must prevail even in times of emergency. She quoted the following portion of Hughes's opinion: "Emergency does not create power. Emergency does not increase granted power or remove or diminish the restrictions imposed upon power granted or reserved. The Constitution was adopted in a period of grave emergency. Its grants of power to the Federal Government and its limitations of the power of the States were determined in the light of emergency and they are not altered by emergency." The ACLU's president neglected to mention that even as Hughes acknowledged that emergency did not make power, he further wrote that "emergency may furnish the occasion for the exercise of power. Although an emergency may not call into life a power which has never lived, nevertheless emergency may afford a reason for the exertion of a living power already enjoyed."

Few linguists give Hughes's tortured syntax high marks. Yet his ambiguous insistence that emergency does not create but rather "calls into life" power somehow captures ably, perhaps even eloquently, America's never-ending struggle to balance individual liberty and the common good in the framework of the Constitution. The lines between protecting the needs of the few and the needs of the many, between contract rights and the general welfare, and between the intent of the founders and the exigencies of modern America are as ambiguous today as they were in 1787 and 1934.

Postscript on the Great Recession's Mortgage Crisis

In the fall of 2008, home prices in the United States plummeted from their historic peak after a perfect storm of factors converged to spur the worst credit and mortgage crisis since the 1930s. A speculative bubble collapsed for hundreds of billions of dollars of mortgage-backed investments, many of them newly invented financial products completely undecipherable to almost all Americans, including bank regulators. The stock market plummeted. Lehman Brothers and several other leading investment banks and insurance companies went belly-up, promoting a massive government bailout. The normal economy sputtered, and unemployment quickly soared. Many Americans would have found themselves burdened with too much home even if the economic landing had been soft; for decades, both political parties had promoted deregulation of financial markets and sometimes unwise policies designed to increase homeownership with little regard for how a downturn would alter the landscape. The investment community and mortgage industry, convinced that the housing boom would last forever, made millions of irresponsible "subprime" loans.

When the housing bubble burst, millions of Americans suffered through foreclosure. Millions more found themselves "under water" in the sense that their mortgage obligation exceeded the value of their home—and saw their interest rates rise dramatically from low introductory levels. In 2008, nearly 1 percent of American homes went into foreclosure; in a few states, the rate exceeded 10 percent. In 2009, there were about 2.7 million foreclosures, which increased to 2.9 million in 2010, a number that likely would have been much worse were it not for a $787 billion federal stimulus package enacted in 2009 and, to a more modest degree, for the government programs enacted to provide homeowner relief detailed below. While the Great Recession was not as dire as the 1930s Depression, foreclosure rates in 2011 stood at their worst levels since the 1930s, and only in this year did prices bottom out.

The policy responses to the Great Recession and subprime crisis were a far cry from the mortgage-relief initiatives of the 1930s. This inactivity was a blessing to conservatives who emphasized the need to protect contract rights and let markets recover on their own and a curse to liberals who emphasized that millions of Americans were thrown out of their jobs and homes due to the runaway speculation of millionaires. In 2008, several states, including Massachusetts, New York, and Minnesota, considered mortgage-moratorium legislation reminiscent of the 1930s. Many states rewrote their rules covering the fine print of underwriting and selling of loans. Some tweaked the edges of the mortgage contract, for example by extending the period of pre-foreclosure notice, allowing tenants to stay in foreclosed rental properties for longer periods of time, and requiring mandatory mediation between lenders and borrowers in default. But no state passed a moratorium that came close to matching the laws discussed in this book.

Minnesota's ambivalent response to the Great Recession demonstrates perfectly how the nation's political-economic climate has changed since the 1930s. Foreclosures in Minnesota jumped from 6,500 in 2005 to almost 28,000 in 2008. As in the 1930s, the crisis permeated both urban and rural areas. In late 2008, nearly 9,000 foreclosed properties dotted the Twin Cities metro area, and a record number of homes were auctioned in the seven metro counties. In middle- and working-class north Minneapolis, about one-fifth of mortgaged homes were in foreclosure by the end of 2008. One study of subprime lending in the Twin Cities found that African American borrowers, irrespective of income and neighborhood characteristics, were four times more likely to receive a subprime loan than whites and that Hispanics were twice as likely to receive such loans. The next two years brought stability but not improvement.

When foreclosures began rising in 2007, even before the financial crisis began in earnest, Minnesota ACORN, part of a now-defunct liberal community-advocacy organization that came under intense scrutiny for its dubious signature-gathering practices, endorsed a three-month voluntary freeze on home foreclosures. After the Hennepin County Commission rejected the idea, the group turned to the

Minneapolis City Council. In an October 2007 editorial, the *Star Tribune* (the leading paper in the Twin Cities) urged the city council to refrain from supporting a freeze on mortgage foreclosures. The editors contended that a "one-size-fits-all moratorium solution was not the answer" to the foreclosure crisis because each buyer's circumstances varied. The *Star Tribune* noted that some distressed homeowners were victims of predatory lending schemes while others were speculators who took risks to "flip" properties and turn a quick profit in the overheated housing market. City officials estimated that "about half" of the foreclosures had been among investors/speculators, and in those situations, the editorial argued, "it's not up to the government to save them, even temporarily, from a shaky business deal."

Instead of a foreclosure ban, the *Star Tribune* editors recommended that local governments provide counseling to assist struggling homeowners. They proposed that city, county, and state entities "take lessons from the Minnesota farm crisis of the 1980s," during which thousands of farmers were in danger of losing their land and the legislature responded with the state's second historic mortgage-relief law. Among other provisions, this moratorium had required mediation between the landowners and creditors. R. T. Rybak, the Democratic-Farmer-Labor mayor of Minneapolis (the Farmer-Labor and Democratic parties merged after World War II), also opposed a local moratorium on foreclosures. "A ban on foreclosures," he said, "would unfortunately only be a temporary Band-Aid for a longer-term problem. It is not the best of solutions. Cities need to help with foreclosure prevention and focus on filling those vacant properties with responsible homeowners." Toward those objectives, the city established an $11 million fund with support from the Minnesota Family Housing Fund, a state entity.

As the housing crisis persisted, however, calls for stronger action increased. In November 2008, Minneapolis attorney Marshall Tanick invoked the *Blaisdell* decision in the *Star Tribune*, calling for the legislature to "take a page from constitutional law and historical lore" and enact a new mortgage-foreclosure moratorium. Lawmakers, he said, should "heed the edict" of Chief Justice Hughes in *Blaisdell*: "While emergency does not create power, emergency may furnish the occasion for the exercise of power."

Liberal and even some centrist state legislators responded. In the 2008 session, the Minnesota legislature passed the Minnesota Subprime Borrower Relief Act by significant majorities in both chambers. The law would have placed a temporary one-year hold on mortgage foreclosures while requiring homeowners to make loan payments equal to the minimum monthly payment at origination or 65 percent of the payment at the time of default, whichever was lower. A borrower who did not pay would lose the right to deferment, and the lender could go ahead and foreclose. "We have a crisis in mortgage foreclosures, and this seemed like the boldest way that we could respond to the problem," said State Senator Ellen Anderson, who sponsored the bill. Anderson explained that the legislation would have let some borrowers with subprime loans or negative-amortization mortgages defer paying a portion of the amount owed, without being considered delinquent. (A negative-amortization mortgage is one in which the loan balance can grow even if the borrower keeps up with the payments.) Minnesota attorney and consumer advocate Sam Glover also supported the measure, arguing that "the law would give borrowers valuable time to sell their home or refinance their loan. This is not a bailout, just a little encouragement for homeowners."

But the Subprime Borrower Relief Act faced strong opposition from the credit industry. Tom Deutsch, deputy executive director of the American Securitization Forum, a financial industry advocacy group, claimed that the measure "would significantly erode the confidence lenders and borrowers have about the stability of contracts in Minnesota." Bowing to the opposition, Republican governor Tim Pawlenty vetoed the measure on May 29, 2008, arguing that it would damage credit markets. Citing the Contract, Due Process, and Equal Protection Clauses of the U.S. Constitution, he also said that the bill raised "significant legal and philosophical concerns." Kieran Quinn, chairman of the Mortgage Bankers Association, applauded the veto. "While the MBA continues to work with state and local policymakers to explore all reasonable avenues for alleviating the foreclosure problem nationwide," Quinn announced, "we applaud Governor Pawlenty for his leadership in promoting solutions to aid troubled borrowers and correctly deciding to veto this bill." The legislature did not attempt to override.

On February 9, 2009, the Minnesota People's Bailout Act was introduced in the state Senate and House. Authored by Senator David J. Tomassoni (DFL-Chisholm) and Representative David Bly (DFL-

Northfield), this legislation sought to protect the interests of low-income Minnesotans from the worst effects of the deepening economic crisis. Among its many provisions, the bill called for a two-year moratorium on housing foreclosures. It would have required banks and mortgage companies that foreclose on rental property to honor existing tenants' leases. Several other bills providing different kinds of mortgage relief were also considered during the 2009 legislative session. Yet all of them died in committee. Lawmakers introduced additional bills during the 2010 legislative session that variously sought to provide mediation or counseling, require fair notice of foreclosure, and streamline the process of connecting a homeowner facing foreclosure with a foreclosure-prevention agency. Another pair of bills would have established a two-year moratorium on mortgage foreclosures on residential property, both rental and owner-occupied, and enhanced the rights of tenants who rent properties subject to foreclosure. All of these bills languished in committee until the session ended.

The fall 2010 elections changed the political landscape across the nation and in Minnesota. DFLer Mark Dayton won a close gubernatorial race against Republican Tom Emmer, but Republicans regained control of the state house as part of the national Republican (and Tea Party) tidal wave. The DFL Party lost twenty-five seats in the Minnesota House, leaving Republicans with a ten-seat majority. Minnesota now seems unlikely to duplicate its Depression-era homeowners' relief.

The federal government dipped into mortgage-relief policy, as well, but its programs have been largely ineffectual or only modestly successful, depending upon whom one asks. In any event, they petered out. Both the Bush and Obama administrations emphasized stimulating the macroeconomy and providing incentives to lenders rather than directly aiding individual homeowners.

In the summer of 2008, President Bush signed the Housing and Economic Recovery Act, which boosted Federal Housing Administration (FHA) loan guarantees for creditors that refinanced delinquent loans. This law also created the Hope for Homeowners program, under which the FHA backed up delinquent loans if debtors refinanced. This refinancing program was voluntary for lending companies — and thus, not surprisingly, little used.

On February 24, 2009, U.S. Representative Marcy Kaptur (D-Ohio) introduced a resolution expressing the sense of the House of Representatives that the individual states should enact temporary mortgage moratoriums on residential mortgage foreclosures. The resolution estimated that 2.4 million homes would be foreclosed in the United States before the end of 2009, and it cited the Minnesota mortgage moratorium case as justification for states to address the crisis under their police powers. Congress did not pass the resolution, and Representative Kaptur reintroduced the legislation in subsequent sessions.

In February 2009, the newly elected Obama administration unveiled the Making Home Affordable plan, and more specifically the Home Affordable Modification Program (HAMP), as the president's signature anti-foreclosure initiative. When introducing it, the administration claimed that HAMP would "enable three to four million homeowners to modify the terms of their mortgages to avoid foreclosure." The $75 billion plan, funded with $50 billion from the Trouble Assets Relief Program fund (TARP was the bank bailout program) and $25 billion from (now) government-owned mortgage lenders Fannie Mae and Freddie Mac, was designed to "induce lenders, servicers, and investors to modify distressed mortgages through a series of cash incentives." One year into the implementation of the plan, however, signs emerged that it was not working as billed, and by the second year, a chorus of critics had denounced the plan as a failure.

In its first year, HAMP invited 1.5 million Americans to participate in "trial" modifications of their mortgages. Homeowners were approved for trial modifications if they met core requirements: their house payments were more than 31 percent of their monthly pretax income; they lived in their home; they owed less than $729,000; and they were at risk of default. A HAMP trial is supposed to become permanent after three months. By June 2011, HAMP had resulted in about 540,000 permanent modifications. Writing in the *American Prospect*, Marcus Stanley, the policy director of Americans for Financial Reform, noted encouragingly that many of those modifications substantially lowered monthly payments (by an average of $527). But he lamented that the number of permanent modifications was a far cry from the 3 to 4 million promised by the Obama administration. More troublesome, Stanley warned, was the 50 percent drop in monthly modifications between June 2010 and May 2011, indicating that the program was fizzling out.

Almost from its inception, families struggled with arcane and incomprehensible HAMP regulations. Homeowners seeking a modification had to first contact the mortgage servicer—the private company that collects mortgage checks. The servicer, often a subsidiary of a large bank, handled the entire HAMP process and, for example, was responsible for verifying borrower income. Under its initial structure, HAMP gave mortgage servicers and investors $1,000 incentive payments for permanent modifications, and additional payments each year a borrower stayed current. But, Stanley noted, "servicers rejected more than a fifth of the applications for paperwork reasons—often due to lost paperwork by the servicer itself." A survey conducted by ProPublica, a nonprofit watchdog organization, found that homeowners seeking modification had to send documents "an average of six times before they were received." The length of the application process was another problem. One report found that "of 364,077 trial plans, 166,000 dragged on for longer than six months." Needless to say, the excessively bureaucratic process left many homeowners frustrated and angry. Teresa Follmer, an interior designer from Mesa, Arizona, tried for over a year to modify her mortgage with Countrywide (now Bank of America) before she learned in May 2009 that she met HAMP's requirements—only to be told by Countrywide that it did not service HAMP modifications. Homeowners throughout the country told countless such horror stories.

In March 2010 testimony before the House Oversight and Government Reform Committee, Troubled Assets Relief Program inspector general Neil Barofsky said that HAMP had been "plagued with inconsistent goals and requirements for prospective participants." Barofsky announced that the Treasury Department had changed its goal to "granting 3 to 4 million temporary mortgage adjustments by 2012, rather than trying to achieve that number of permanent modifications." Treasury officials at the hearing defended the program. The Treasury undersecretary for financial stability, Herbert Allison, claimed that the program was on track to reach its goal of 3 to 4 million trial modifications by 2012, with participants saving an average of $500 per month. "A groundbreaking program of this scale," he added, "will have problems." He said HAMP officials were working to make the application process quicker with a standard set of documents. The HAMP program had resulted in a not insignificant total of 675,000 permanent modifications for homeowners as of July 2011, while over 850,000 modifications were canceled. The Republican-controlled House of Representatives voted to end HAMP in 2011, and although the Senate did not follow suit, the program is scheduled to end on December 31, 2013.

In July 2011, with unemployment holding steady at 9 percent, the Obama administration announced that the Federal Housing Administration would help unemployed homeowners behind on their payments or at risk of default by requiring servicers to extend to twelve months the forbearance period during which their monthly payments could be reduced or suspended. But as the federal deficit continued to surge (and to frame national discussion of the economy), and as many Americans across the political spectrum came to agree that federal and state efforts to combat the housing crisis had failed, the Obama administration lost its appetite for large-scale mortgage relief. "Congress and the White House have run out of ideas to save those homes," said Mark Zandi, chief economist for Moody's Analytics. "There's no political appetite to do anything," he lamented. "So we're on our own."

In 2012, Republicans continued to automatically oppose any proposal by President Obama. For example, the White House proposed a new plan to allow underwater homeowners to refinance private loans at lower rates with Fannie Mae or Freddie Mac, but it barely made a ripple on Capitol Hill. Speaker of the House John Boehner (R-Ohio) claimed, "None of these [federal mortgage-relief] programs have worked and I don't know why anyone would think that this next idea's going to work and all they've done is delay the clearing of the market." The president, still suggesting that the housing crisis was the "single biggest drag" on the economy, then turned to relatively minor devices such as cutting fees on government-backed loans.

Notwithstanding the political stalemate, a major breakthrough for borrowers occurred in February 2012. After dramatic evidence emerged in 2010 that five large banks had engaged in abusive loan servicing and foreclosure practices, including inflating fees and robo-signing thousands of foreclosure documents without properly reviewing paperwork, a coalition of state attorneys general and federal agencies launched an investigation that resulted sixteen months later in the largest joint state-federal settlement in the nation's history. Bank of America Corp, Wells Fargo and Co., JPMorgan Chase & Co., Citigroup Inc., and Allied Financial Inc., which together service almost 60 percent of the nation's mortgages, agreed to pay $25 billion to settle the claims. Washington, D.C., and every state but Oklahoma signed the agreement. A multipronged effort to hold banks accountable for past mortgage practices and to bring some order to a troubled housing market, the agreement required loan servicers to commit a minimum of $17 billion directly to borrowers for homeowner relief, including principal reduction. As much as $32 billion may ultimately go to aid homeowners. Additionally, the five banks must commit $3 billion to an underwater mortgage refinancing program and pay $5 billion to the states and federal government. Finally, the settlement established new protections for mortgage loan servicing and standards for foreclosure proceedings.

Democratic and Republican state attorneys alike hailed the agreement. "This is a big first step toward addressing the wrongs," said North Carolina attorney general Roy Cooper. "After many months of investigation and negotiation, I've concluded that this settlement accomplishes two major goals: it provides timely help for struggling homeowners, and it establishes new rules for mortgage servicing that will protect homeowners in the future," remarked Illinois attorney general Lisa Madigan.

Not everyone was happy with the settlement, however. "You're hardly skimming the surface," claimed one prominent housing expert. State and federal officials estimated that the agreement could help over a million homeowners, with about 750,000 borrowers who lost their homes between 2008 and 2011 receiving a cash payment of $2,000. Critics, however, contended that the agreement did little to help the 11 million homeowners who were underwater and the 6 million who were in foreclosure or behind on their payments. "While a significant step toward fixing the foreclosure crisis, this settlement was never intended or able to provide a comprehensive remedy," said Michael Calhoun, president of the Center for Responsible Lending. "Much more work is required." Whether the agreement will produce substantial reforms in the lending market remains to be seen, and the United States will likely have millions of distressed homeowners for years to come.

How can we account for the difference between the recent tepid and ineffectual state response to the housing crisis and the robust and,

186

on balance, successful response during the 1930s? Many of today's victims created their own problems by speculating in real estate, and they seem very different from the farmers of the Dust Bowl (although speculation surely took place in the 1930s, as well). Poorly designed and administered Bush and Obama administration policies contributed to the lack of interest in aggressive policy making, too.

Yet recent speculation and policy failures both may be less cause than symptom of a long-standing ideological shift. In the past generation, conservatives have set the terms of the nation's major policy discussions, especially those regarding the economy, and today, Americans are much less enamored of state intervention — and trust the market more — than their counterparts who endured the Great Depression. A concomitant reevaluation of whether New Deal policies worked has taken place. On the specific matter of mortgage moratoriums (which happens to be a good proxy for what took place in dozens of policy areas), conservative economists and historians have shown that such state interventions in credit markets impose real costs and create both winners and losers. And, more subjectively, conservatives have convinced many Americans that the gains in keeping people in their homes and even of propping up the macroeconomy are not worth the costs of skewing credit markets and abrogating property rights.

Then again, perhaps the recent lukewarm support for moratoriums reflects, to some degree, the success of the liberal coalition forged in the New Deal. Americans who lose their jobs and houses today enjoy benefits, such as unemployment insurance, that derive from the 1930s creation of America's modest welfare state. And, of course, farmers now occupy a very different position in the United States than they did eighty years ago. Less than 2 percent of the population, they enjoy the protection of federal subsidies that also date from the 1930s.

Another irony in our story, as the continued vitriol hurled at *Blaisdell* illustrates, is that the case continues to provide constitutional legitimacy for interventionist state actions. Although the courts are as pro-business as they have been at any time since the Gilded Age, the Contract Clause remains dormant, especially as many other legal devices, such as the Fifth Amendment's Takings Clause, are readily available to market-oriented judges. Of course, the Court is not faced with many Contract Clause cases because, in the past generation, legislatures have enacted few interventionist measures that might invoke *Home Building and Loan Association v. Blaisdell*'s constitutional protections. And the prevailing political economy leaves little appetite for new regulations on property or distinctions among property holders. For now, conservatives can afford a quiescent Contract Clause, and liberals can take solace in the fact that the Minnesota mortgage moratorium case still stands. From the vantage point of the current political stalemate, it may be left to the next generation of Americans to determine whether the Contract Clause will be firmed up as the bulwark of a new laissez-faire regime or made a dead letter entirely.

RELEVANT CASES

Adams v. Spillyards, 187 Ark. 641, 61 S.W. 686 (1933)

Adkins v. Children's Hospital, 261 U.S. 525 (1923)

A. L. A. Schechter Poultry Corp. v. United States, 295 U.S. 495 (1935)

Allgeyer v. Louisiana, 165 U.S. 578 (1897)

Allied Structural Steel Co. v. Spannaus, 438 U.S. 234 (1978)

Barnitz v. Beverly, 163 U.S. 118 (1896)

Blagg v. Harrigan, 74 S.W. 2d 324 (1934)

Blaisdell v. Home Building and Loan Association, 249 N.W. 334 (Minn. 1933)

Block v. Hirsh, 256 U.S. 135 (1921)

Bronson v. Kinzie, 1 How. 311 (1843)

Champion v. Casey, Cir. Ct., Rhode Island (1792)

Charles River Bridge v. Warren Bridge, 11 Pet. 420 (1837)

Chicago Alton R.R. v. Tranbarger, 238 U.S. 67 (1915)

Dartmouth College v. Woodward, 4 Wheat. 518 (1819)

Des Moines Joint Stock Land Bank v. Nordholm, 253 N.W. 701 (Iowa 1934)

Disanto v. Pennsylvania, 273 U.S. 34 (1927)

E. C. Knight Co. v. United States, 156 U.S. 1 (1895)

East New York Savings Bank v. Hahn, 326 U.S. 230 (1945)

Edgar A. Leasing Co. v. Siegel, 258 U.S. 242 (1922)

Edwards v. Kearzy, 96 U.S. 595 (1878)

810 West End Avenue, Inc. v. Stern, 186 N.Y.S. 56 (1922)

El Paso, City of v. Simmons, 379 U.S. 497 (1965)

Energy Reserves Group v. Kansas Power and Light, 459 U.S. 400 (1983)

Ex Parte Milligan, 4 Wall. 2 (1866)

First Trust Co. of Lincoln v. Smith, 277 N.W. 762 (Neb. 1938)

Fletcher v. Peck, 6 Cranch 87 (1810)

Funk v. United States, 290 U.S. 371 (1933)

Gantley's Lessee v. Ewing, 44 U.S. 707 (1845)

Gelfert v. National City Bank, 313 U.S. 221 (1941)

Gibbons v. Ogden, 9 Wheat. 1 (1824)

Goenen v. Schroder, 8 Minn. 387 (1863)

Hanauer v. Republic Building Co., 255 N.W. 136 (Wis. 1934)

Helvering v. Davis, 301 U.S. 609 (1937)

Heyward v. Judd, 4 Minn. 483 (1860)

Home Building and Loan Association v. Blaisdell, 290 U.S. 398 (1934)

Hopkins v. Swain, 206 N.C. 439, 174 S.E. 409 (1934)

Howard v. Bugbee, 65 U.S. 461 (1860)

Hudson County Water Co. v. McCarter, 209 U.S. 349 (1908)

Humphrey's Executor v. United States, 295 U.S. 602 (1935)

Keystone Bituminous Coal Association v. DeBenedictis, 480 U.S. 470 (1987)

Levy Leasing Co. v. Siegel, 258 U.S. 242 (1922)

License Cases, 5 How. 504 (1847)

Life Insurance Co. v. Sanders, 62 S.W. 2d 348 (1933)

Lochner v. New York, 198 U.S. 45 (1905)

Louisville Joint Stock Land Bank v. Radford, 295 U.S. 555 (1935)

Manigault v. Springs, 199 U.S. 473 (1905)

Marcus Brown Holding Company, Inc. v. Feldman, 256 U.S. 170 (1921)

McCracken v. Hayward, 43 U.S. 608 (1844)

McCulloch v. Maryland, 4 Wheat. 316 (1819)

McMillan v. McNeill, 17 U.S. 209 (1819)

Missouri v. Holland, 252 U.S. 416 (1920)

Morehead v. New York ex rel. Tipaldo, 298 U.S. 587 (1936)

Mulford v. Smith, 307 U.S. 38 (1939)

Muller v. Oregon, 208 U.S. 412 (1908)

Munn v. Illinois, 94 U.S. 113 (1877)

National Labor Relations Board (NLRB) v. Jones and Laughlin Steel, 301 U.S. 1 (1937)

Nebbia v. New York, 291 U.S. 502 (1934)

New Jersey v. Wilson, 7 Cranch 164 (1812)

O'Brien v. Krenz, 36 Minn. 136, 30 N.W. 458 (1886)

O'Gorman & Young v. Hartford Insurance, 282 U.S. 251 (1931)

Ogden v. Saunders, 12 Wheat. 213 (1827)

Orr v. Bennett, 135 Minn. 443 N.W. (1917)

Owings v. Speed, 18 U.S. 420 (1820)

Pennsylvania Coal Co. v. Mahon, 260 U.S. 393 (1922)

People v. Nebbia, 262 N.Y. 259, 186 N.E. 694 (1933)

Planter's Bank v. Sharp, 47 U.S. 6 How. 301 (1847)

Railroad Retirement Board v. Alton Railroad Company, 295 U.S. 230 (1935)

Scott v. Sandford, 19 How. 393 (1857)

Slaughterhouse Cases, 83 U.S. 36 (1873)

Sproles v. Binford, 286 U.S. 374 (1932)

State ex rel. Cleveringa v. Klein, N.D. 249 N.W. 118 (1933)

State ex rel. Lichtscheidl v. Moeller, 249 N.W. 330 (Minn. 1933)

Stone v. Mississippi, 101 U.S. 814 (1880)

Sturges v. Crowninshield, 4 Wheat. 122 (1819)

Traveler's Insurance Co. v. Marshall, 76 S.W.2d 1007 (1934)

Treigle v. ACME Homestead Association, 297 U.S. 189 (1936)

Trevett v. Weeden, Rhode Island (1786)

Union Dry Goods v. Georgia Public Service Corp., 248 U.S. 372 (1919)

United States v. Butler, 297 U.S. 1 (1936)

United States v. Curtis-Wright Export Corp., 299 U.S. 304 (1936)

U.S. v. E.C. Knight Co., 156 U.S. 1 (1895)

U.S. Mortgage Co. v. Matthews, 173 Atl. 903 (Md. 1934)

United States Trust Co. v. New Jersey, 431 U.S. 1 (1977)

Van Horne's Lessee v. Dorrance, 2 U.S. (Dallas) 304 (1795)

Veix v. Sixth Ward Building and Loan Association, 310 U.S. 32 (1940)

Virginian Railway v. Railway Employees, 300 U.S. 515 (1937)

W. B. Worthen Co. v. Kavanaugh, 295 U.S. 56 (1935)

W. B. Worthen Co. v. Thomas, 292 U.S. 426 (1934)

West Coast Hotel v. Parrish, 300 U.S. 379 (1937)

Wilson v. New, 243 U.S. 332 (1917)

Wolf Packing Co. v. Court of Industrial Relations, 262 U.S. 522 (1923)

Wright v. Vinton Branch Bank, 300 U.S. 440 (1937)

CHRONOLOGY

August 1, 1928	John H. and Rosella Blaisdell purchase a two-story residential building in Minneapolis, Minnesota. The mortgage is held with the Home Building and Loan Association.
October 24–28, 1929	The stock market crashes.
May 2, 1932	The mortgage on John and Rosella Blaisdell's home is foreclosed and sold to the Home Building and Loan Association for $3,700.98. Under existing Minnesota law, the Blaisdells have one year to redeem their property by paying the full amount owed, but they are unable to raise the funds.
May 3, 1932	Several thousand farmers meet in Des Moines, Iowa, form the National Farmers' Holiday Association, and select Milo Reno as president.
July 29, 1932	The Minnesota Farmers' Holiday Association forms in St. Cloud, Minnesota.
Late August 1932	Major commodity-withholding strikes — "holidays" — break out across the Midwest.
September 9, 1932	Nine midwestern states are represented at a governors' conference in Sioux City, Iowa, on farm policy and the farmers' strikes.
Late September 1932	Minnesota's most significant commodity strike begins.
January 28, 1933	The Farmers' Holiday Association engages in several foreclosure-stoppage actions across Minnesota.
February 17, 1933	The Minnesota Legislature debates several mortgage-relief bills.
	Iowa governor Clyde Herrings signs the nation's first significant mortgage moratorium into law.
February 24, 1933	Concerned about potential violence, Governor Floyd B. Olson issues an executive order imposing a

moratorium on mortgage foreclosures in Minnesota until May 1.

March 2, 1933   The Minnesota Legislature passes a temporary measure legalizing the postponement of foreclosures by Governor Olson and relieving sheriffs of the requirement to publish foreclosure announcements.

March 22, 1933   Three thousand farmers converge on the legislature in St. Paul demanding farm relief and making threats and predictions of bloodshed.

April 15, 1933   Addressing a crowd of farmers in the state capitol building, Governor Olson renews his threat to declare martial law in Minnesota and confiscate wealth to prevent "human misery" in the absence of farm relief.

April 18, 1933   By a unanimous vote in both chambers, the Minnesota Legislature passes the Minnesota Mortgage Moratorium Act on the last day of the legislative session.

May 12, 1933   The National Farmers' Holiday Association agrees to postpone a planned nationwide farm strike following pressure from Governor Olson and a statement by President Roosevelt urging holders of mortgages to be lenient.

May 17, 1933   District Judge Arthur W. Selover holds the Minnesota Mortgage Moratorium Act unconstitutional.

July 7, 1933   The Minnesota Supreme Court upholds the moratorium act by a 6–1 vote. At the same time, the court holds that Governor Olson exceeded his executive powers by issuing a ninety-day mortgage moratorium, although the legislature had validated his act by a curative law.

July 21, 1933   Minnesota judge Mathias Baldwin issues an order granting the Blaisdells a two-year extension on their redemption period, with the requirement that they

	pay a monthly fee of $40. The Home Building and Loan Association appeals to the U.S. Supreme Court.
October 9, 1933	The Supreme Court grants review of the Minnesota Mortgage Moratorium Act.
November 8, 9, 1933	The Court hears oral arguments in *Home Building and Loan Association v. Blaisdell*.
December 12, 1933	Justice Harlan Fiske Stone sends Chief Justice Hughes a memo suggesting improvements in the draft of the majority opinion.
January 4, 1934	Chief Justice Hughes sends Justice Stone a memo informing him of his plans to incorporate several paragraphs from Justice Cardozo into the majority opinion.
January 8, 1934	In a 5–4 decision, the U.S. Supreme Court upholds the Minnesota Mortgage Moratorium Act in *Home Building and Loan Association v. Blaisdell*.
January 9, 1934	Governor Olson calls the decision in *Blaisdell* a "triumph of human rights over property rights."
March 5, 1934	In a 5–4 decision, the Supreme Court in *Nebbia v. New York* upholds state price controls on milk.
May 28, 1934	In *W. B. Worthen Co. v. Thomas*, the Supreme Court unanimously strikes down an Arkansas law that exempted the life insurance of a defaulting debtor from garnishment.
June 28, 1934	Congress passes the Frazier-Lemke Farm Bankruptcy Act, giving courts the discretion to provide mortgage relief under some circumstances.
November 23, 1934	The Texas Supreme Court rules that a state law providing a moratorium on mortgage foreclosures violates the state constitution.
December 26, 1934	Minnesota attorney general Harry Peterson recommends a two-year extension of the Minnesota moratorium law.
February 13, 1935	John and Rosella Blaisdell divorce.

February 25, 1935	Ownership of 1518 Linden Avenue is transferred to Rosella Blaisdell.
	Rosella Blaisdell receives an extension on the period of redemption from May 1, 1935, to March 1, 1937.
March 15, 1935	The Minnesota Legislature extends the moratorium law for two years. The law will be extended repeatedly, finally expiring in July 1942.
May 27, 1935	In three 9–0 decisions, the Supreme Court invalidates the National Recovery Act and the Frazier-Lemke Act and restricts the president's power to remove members of independent regulatory commissions.
May 5, 1936	Milo Reno, leader of the Farmers' Holiday Association, dies.
August 22, 1936	Governor Floyd B. Olson dies in office at age forty-four.
March 29, 1937	In *West Coast Hotel v. Parrish*, the Supreme Court upholds a Washington State minimum wage law by a 5–4 margin and solidifies the Constitutional Revolution in favor of the New Deal.
November 8, 1975	John Hoyt Blaisdell dies from heart disease in Minneapolis.
June 15, 1984	Rosella Blaisdell dies in Hennepin County, Minnesota.

BIBLIOGRAPHICAL ESSAY

Note from the Series Editors: The following bibliographic essay contains the major primary and secondary sources the authors consulted for this volume. We have asked all authors in the series to omit formal citations in order to make our volumes more readable, inexpensive, and appealing for students and general readers. In adopting this format, Landmark Law Cases and American Society follows the precedent of a number of highly regarded and widely consulted series.

Moratorium laws date back to the classical period, and the American states used them even before the creation of the United States. For their early history, see Charles Bunn, "The Impairment of Contracts: Mortgage and Insurance Moratoria," *University of Chicago Law Review* 1 (1933): 249–65; "Constitutional Law: Mortgage Foreclosure Moratorium Statutes," *Michigan Law Review* 32 (1933): 71–80; Edward S. Corwin, "Moratorium over Minnesota," *University of Pennsylvania Law Review* 82 (1934): 311–16; A. H. Feller, "Moratory Legislation: A Comparative Study," *Harvard Law Review* 46 (1933): 1061–85; and "Mortgage Relief during the Depression," *Harvard Law Review* 47 (1933): 299–307. For a survey of the moratorium laws enacted during the Great Depression, see Robert H. Skilton, "Mortgage Moratoria since 1933," *University of Pennsylvania Law Review* 92 (1943): 53–90.

The Contract Clause emerged from the unique political economy of the Critical Period of the 1780s, when the Articles of Confederation governed the new nation. For the problems facing individual states during this period, consult Merrill Jenson, *The New Nation: A History of the United States during the Confederation 1781–1789* (New York: Random House, 1966; reprint, New York: Alfred A. Knopf, 1981); Peter J. Albert, *Sovereign States in an Age of Uncertainty* (Charlottesville: University of Virginia Press, 1981); and Florence Parker Simister, *The Fire's Center: Rhode Island in the Revolutionary Era, 1763–1790* (Providence: Rhode Island Bicentennial Foundation, 1978). Bruce H. Mann examines debtors and bankruptcy laws in *Republic of Debtors: Bankruptcy in the Age of American Independence* (Cambridge, Mass.: Harvard University Press, 2002). Also see Patrick T. Conley, "Rhode Island's Paper Money Issue and *Trevett v. Weeden*," *Rhode Island History* 30 (1971): 95–108. On Shays' Rebellion, see Robert A. Gross, ed., *In Debt to Shays: The Bicentennial of an Agrarian Revolution* (Charlottesville: University of Virginia Press, 1993), and Leonard Richards, *Shays' Rebellion: The American Revolution's Final Battle* (Philadelphia: University of Pennsylvania Press, 2002).

The best source for the 1787 Constitutional Convention remains Max Farrand, ed., *The Records of the Federal Convention of 1787*, 4 vols. (1911–1937; rev. ed., New Haven: Yale University Press, 1966). A number of articles in this collection describe the founders' debate over the Contract Clause. One of the most famous history books ever written, Charles Beard's *An Economic Interpretation of the Constitution* (New York: Macmillan, 1913; reprint, Mineola, N.Y.: Dover, 2004), argues that personal financial interests motivated the framers. Beard's thesis is critiqued by Forrest McDonald, *We the People: The Economic Origins of the Constitution* (New York: Transaction Publishers, 1991), and Robert A. McGuire, *To Form a More Perfect Union: A New Economic Interpretation of the Constitution* (New York: Oxford University Press, 2003). See also Ellen Nore, "Charles A. Beard's Economic Interpretation of the Origins of the Constitution," in *This Constitution: A Bicentennial Chronicle*, vol. 17 (Washington, D.C.: Project 87, 1987), 39–44. Pauline Maier, *Ratification: The People Debate the Constitution, 1787–1788* (New York: Simon and Schuster, 2010), provides an excellent overview of the state ratifying conventions, although its discussion of the Contract Clause is limited.

Although the present volume is the first book-length study on *Blaisdell*, a wealth of sources trace the evolution of the Contract Clause. For debtor-relief laws in the decades immediately following ratification of the Constitution, see Steven R. Boyd, "The Contract Clause and the Evolution of American Federalism, 1789–1815," *William and Mary Quarterly* 44 (1987): 529–48. Warren B. Hunting's *The Obligation of Contracts Clause of the United States Constitution* (Baltimore: Johns Hopkins University Press, 1919) was the first attempt to offer a comprehensive history of the clause, but it is incomplete because the author died in World War I midway through writing it. For Chief Justice John Marshall's Contract Clause jurisprudence, we found especially useful Charles F. Hobson, *The Great Chief Justice: John Marshall and the Rule of Law* (Lawrence: University Press of Kansas, 1996), and Herbert Johnson, *The Chief Justiceship of John Marshall, 1801–1835* (Columbia: University of South Carolina Press, 1997). See also James W. Ely Jr., "The Marshall Court and Property Rights: A Reappraisal," *John Marshall Law Review* 33 (2000): 1023–61, and Morgan D. Dowd, "Justice Story, the Supreme Court, and the Obligation of Contract," *Case Western Reserve Law Review* 19 (1968): 493–527. Nineteenth-century views on the Contract Clause include Joseph Story's *Commentaries on the Constitution of the United States* (Minneapolis: Legacy Filiquarian, 2010), and Thomas M. Cooley, *A Treatise on the Constitutional Limitations Which Rest upon the Legislative Power of the States of the American Union* (Boston: Little, Brown, 1883). Cooley also discusses the Contract Clause in *The General Principles of Constitutional Law*, 3rd ed. (Boston: Little, Brown, 1898).

Scholars have engaged in a lively debate regarding the public/private distinction under the Contract Clause. Benjamin Fletcher Wright, *The Contract Clause and the Constitution* (Cambridge, Mass.: Harvard University Press, 1938; reprint, Westport, Conn.: Greenwood Press, 1982), remains indispensable. Wright argues that the framers originally intended the clause to deny states authority over monetary policy and that judicial interpretation has expanded the original meaning. Wallace Mendelson critiques Benjamin Wright's views on the public/private dichotomy in "B. F. Wright on the Contract Clause: A Progressive Misreading of the Marshall-Taney Era," *Western Political Quarterly* 38 (1985): 262–75. Robert C. Palmer, "Obligation of Contracts: Intent and Distortion," *Case Western Reserve Law Review* 37 (1987): 631–73, maintains that Chief Justice John Marshall's protection of land grants against impairment in *Fletcher v. Peck* actually contributed to the demise of the Contract Clause. Palmer argues that protection of public contracts led to recognition of reserved state powers, which then had to be "balanced" against private contractual rights — *Blaisdell* subsequently represented the triumph of state police power over private rights. Thomas W. Merrill, "Public Contracts, Private Rights, and the Transformation of the Constitutional Order," *Case Western Reserve Law Review* 37 (1987): 597–627, suggests that the public/private distinction led to a double standard of review in Contract Clause cases, with the Supreme Court exercising more deference to legislative power in public-contract cases. An excellent discussion of the framers' intent and the public/private interpretation of the Contract Clause is Robert L. Clinton, "The Obligation Clause of the United States Constitution: Public and/or Private Contracts," *University of Arkansas Little Rock Law Journal* 11 (1988–89): 343–67.

A number of works have reviewed the major Contract Clause cases prior to *Blaisdell*. See John G. Hervey, "The Impairment of the Obligation of Contracts," *Annals of the American Academy of Political and Social Science* 195 (1938): 87–120. A collection of law journal articles on the Contract Clause is found in James W. Ely Jr., ed., *The Contract Clause in American History* (London: Routledge, 1997). Also see James W. Ely Jr., *The Guardian of Every Other Right: A Constitutional History of Property Rights*, 2nd ed. (New York: Oxford University Press, 1998); Robert L. Hale, "The Supreme Court and the Contracts Clause," *Harvard Law Review* 57 (1944): 621–74; and J. Michael Veron, "The Contracts Clause and the Court: A View of Precedent and Practice in Constitutional Adjudication," *Tulane Law Review* 54 (1979): 117–62.

More general works on property rights and American economic development include Kermit L. Hall, ed., *Law, Economy, and the Power of Contract: Major Historical Interpretations* (New York: Garland, 1987); Ellen Paul and Howard Dickman, *Liberty, Property, and Government: Constitutional Interpretation before the New Deal* (Albany: State University of New York Press, 1989); Harry N. Scheiber, ed., *The State and Freedom of Contract* (Stanford, Calif.: Stanford University Press, 1999); James Willard Hurst, *Law and the Conditions of Freedom in the Nineteenth-Century United States* (Madison: University of Wisconsin Press, 1964); and Stanley I. Kutler, *Privilege and Creative Destruction: The Charles River Bridge Case* (Baltimore: Johns Hopkins University Press,

1971). William J. Novak challenges conventional wisdom in *The People's Welfare: Law and Regulation in Nineteenth-Century America* (Chapel Hill: University of North Carolina Press, 1996), arguing that from the post-Revolutionary period until after the Civil War, American society was not a laissez-faire paradise in which individual liberty reigned supreme but rather was highly regulated by both public and private law.

For the liberty of contract and substantive due process debates at the turn of the twentieth century, see Howard Gillman, *The Constitution Besieged: The Rise and Demise of* Lochner *Era Police Powers Jurisprudence* (Durham, N.C.: Duke University Press, 1993) and three works by Paul Kens: Lochner v. New York: *Economic Regulation on Trial* (Lawrence: University Press of Kansas, 1998); "The Source of a Myth: Police Powers of the States and Laissez Faire Constitutionalism, 1900–1937," *American Journal of Legal History* 35 (1991): 70–98; and "*Lochner v. New York*: Tradition or Change in Constitutional Law?" *NYU Journal of Law and Liberty* 1 (2005): 404–31. For a closer look at the *Rent Cases*, essential precedents behind *Blaisdell*, see Joseph A. Spencer, "New York City Tenant Organizations and the Post–World War I Housing Crisis," in ed. Ronald Lawson, *The Tenant Movement in New York City, 1904–1984* (New Brunswick: Rutgers University Press, 1986), and George W. Wickersham, "The Police Power and the New York Emergency Rent Laws," *University of Pennsylvania Law Review* 69 (1921): 301–16. Early discussions include Harold G. Aron, "The New York Landlord and Tenant Laws of 1920," *Cornell Law Quarterly* 6 (1920): 1–35.

For a readable general history of Minnesota, consult William E. Lass, *Minnesota: A History*, 2nd ed. (New York: Norton, 1988). For the nitty-gritty of Minnesota politics during the first half of the twentieth century, try Richard M. Vallely, *Radicalism in the States: The Minnesota Farmer-Labor Party and the American Political Economy* (Chicago: University of Chicago Press, 1989); John Earl Hayes, *Dubious Alliance: The Making of Minnesota's DFL Party* (Minneapolis: University of Minnesota Press, 1984); and George H. Mayer, *The Political Career of Floyd B. Olson* (St. Paul: Minnesota Historical Society, 1987). Much of our discussion in chapter 5 is based on court documents and published opinions found in the Minnesota Law Library, St. Paul, Minnesota. The state litigation materials are located in *Cases and Briefs Minnesota Supreme Court*, vol. 189, 409–22.

State-level rural-credit policy in the 1920s may be explored in Gilbert Cooke, "The North Dakota Rural Credit System," *Journal of Land and Public Utility Economics* 14 (1938): 273–83, and Gilbert C. Fite, "South Dakota's Rural Credit System: A Venture in State Socialism, 1917–1946," *Agricultural History* 21 (1947): 239–49. For the Farmers' Holiday Association and other farm protest movements, see David Nass, ed., *Holiday: Minnesotans Remember the Farmers' Holiday Association* (Marshall, Minn.: Plains Press, 1984); John L.

Shover, *Cornbelt Rebellion: The Farmers' Holiday Association* (Urbana: University of Illinois Press, 1965); and Lowell K. Dyson, *Red Harvest: The Communist Party and American Farmers* (Lincoln: University of Nebraska Press, 1982).

For the political economy of the New Deal, see Alan Brinkley, *The End of Reform: New Deal Liberalism in Recession and War* (New York: Vintage, 1996), and Anthony J. Badger, *The New Deal: The Depression Years, 1933–1940* (Chicago: Ivan R. Dee, 2002). For New Deal farm policy, see Theodore Saloutos, *The American Farmer and the New Deal* (Ames: Iowa State University Press, 1982). For broader overviews of American agricultural history, see R. Douglas Hurt, *Problems of Plenty: The American Farmer in the Twentieth Century* (Chicago: Ivan Dee, 2002), and Grant McConnell, *The Decline of Agrarian Democracy* (Berkeley: University of California Press, 1953).

Oliver Wendell Holmes Jr.'s critique of classical legal thought is reprinted in *The Common Law* (Mineola, N.Y.: Dover Publications, 1991). See also Richard A. Posner, ed., *The Essential Holmes: Selections from Letters, Speeches, Judicial Opinions, and Other Writings of O.W. Holmes Jr.* (Chicago, Ill.: University of Chicago Press, 1997). For the most complete biography of Holmes, consult G. Edward White, *Justice Oliver Wendell Holmes: Law and the Inner Self* (New York: Oxford University Press, 1993). Roscoe Pound published his ideas on sociological jurisprudence in a series of three articles entitled "The Scope and Purpose of Sociological Jurisprudence": *Harvard Law Review* 24 (June 1911): 591–619; *Harvard Law Review* 25 (December 1911): 140–68; and "The Scope and Purpose of Sociological Jurisprudence," *Harvard Law Review* 25 (April 1912): 489–516. See also Roscoe Pound, "The Call for a Realist Jurisprudence," *Harvard Law Review* 44 (1931): 697–711.

The *Blaisdell* decision is reviewed in Samuel Hendel, *Charles Evans Hughes and the Supreme Court* (New York: Russell & Russell, 1968). An excellent reference work on the major decisions of the Hughes Court is Michael Parrish, *The Hughes Court: Justices, Rulings, and Legacy* (Santa Barbara, Calif.: ABC-CLIO, 2002). See also William G. Ross, *The Chief Justiceship of Charles Evans Hughes* (Columbia: University of South Carolina Press, 2007). Richard A. Maidment defends the majority opinion in *Blaisdell* in *The Judicial Response to the New Deal* (Manchester, UK: University of Manchester Press, 1991). See also Gary Jacobsohn, *Pragmatism, Statesmanship, and the Supreme Court* (Ithaca, N.Y.: Cornell University Press, 1977). The briefs submitted to the Court in *Blaisdell* are found in *Landmark Briefs and Arguments of the Supreme Court of the United States: Constitutional Law* (Bethesda, Md.: University Publications of America, 1975).

We consulted numerous newspapers and periodicals to gauge public reaction to the *Blaisdell* decision. Dozens of them were entered into the *Congressional Record* by U.S. Representative Ernest Lundeen of Minnesota. The entire texts of the Minnesota Mortgage Moratorium Act and the U.S. Supreme

Court decision were also submitted into the record. See *Congressional Record*, House, January 10, 1934 (Washington, D.C.: U.S. Government Printing Office), 364–89. Most contemporary law review articles merely summarized the Court's decision in *Blaisdell* without providing critical commentary. An exception is Joseph V. Heffernan, "The Minnesota Mortgage Moratorium Case," *Indiana Law Journal* 9 (1934): 337–56, which commends the "brilliance of the decision of the Chief Justice." For other early commentary, see Alpheus T. Mason, "Has the Supreme Court Abdicated?" *North American Review* 238 (1934): 353–360, and John T. Fitzimmons, "Constitutionality of Emergency Legislation," *Kansas City Law Review* 2 (1934): 72–75.

For contemporary interpretations of *Blaisdell*, see William L. Prosser, "The Minnesota Mortgage Moratorium," *Southern California Law Review* 7 (1934): 353–71; "Constitutionality of Mortgage Relief Legislation: *Home Building and Loan Assn. v. Blaisdell*," *Harvard Law Review* 47 (1934): 660–68; and J. Douglass Poteat, "State Legislative Relief for the Mortgage Debtor during the Depression," *Law and Contemporary Problems* 5 (1938): 517–44. More recently, Samuel R. Olken, "Charles Evans Hughes and the *Blaisdell* Decision: A Historical Study of Contract Clause Jurisprudence," *Oregon Law Review* 72 (1993): 513–602, views the decision as the culmination of evolving Contract Clause jurisprudence. Also see Charles A. Bieneman, "Legal Interpretation and a Constitutional Case: *Home Building and Loan Association v. Blaisdell*," *Michigan Law Review* 90 (1992): 2534–64. Economic analyses of 1930s moratoriums include Randal R. Rucker and Lee J. Alston, "Farm Failures and Government Intervention: A Case Study of the 1930s," *American Economic Review* 77 (1987): 724–30; Randal A. Rucker, "The Effects of State Farm Relief Legislation on Private Lenders and Borrowers: The Experiences of the 1930s," *American Journal of Agricultural Economics* 72 (1990): 24–34; and Lee J. Alston, "Farm Foreclosure Moratorium Legislation: A Lesson from the Past," *American Economic Review* 74 (1984): 445–57.

Excellent works on the Hughes Court justices abound. The premier modern biography on Benjamin Cardozo is Andrew L. Kaufman, *Cardozo* (Cambridge, Mass.: Harvard University Press, 2000). See also Kaufman's foreword to a recent reprint of Benjamin N. Cardozo, *The Nature of the Judicial Process* (New Orleans: Quid Pro Quo Books, 2010), in which he highlights the significance of Cardozo's unpublished draft opinion. For the most complete treatment of the personal life and professional contributions of Justice Louis Brandeis, see Melvin I. Urofsky, *Louis D. Brandeis: A Life* (New York: Pantheon Books, 2009). Urofsky examined the connection between Brandeis and the progressive movement in *Louis D. Brandeis and the Progressive Tradition* (Boston: Little, Brown, 1981). Brandeis's progressive jurisprudence and the significance of his decision in *Erie Railroad Co. v. Tompkins* are analyzed in Edward A. Purcell Jr., *Brandeis and the Progressive Constitution* (New Haven,

Conn.: Yale University Press, 2000). Alpheus T. Mason's biography, *Harlan Fiske Stone: Pillar of the Law* (New York: Viking/Penguin, 1956), is still the finest.

The Manuscript Reading Room at the Library of Congress Madison Building houses the public papers for several justices on the Hughes Court, including Chief Justice Charles Evans Hughes and Associate Justices Harlan Fiske Stone, George Sutherland, and Willis Van Devanter. The Hughes papers contain general correspondence from citizens and a few notes on cases. Memos among Justice Stone, Chief Justice Hughes, and Justice Cardozo can be found in the Stone papers. Court memos are missing from the Sutherland papers, but they contain several letters from citizens praising the justice for his dissent in the *Blaisdell* case. The same types of letters were found in the papers of Willis Van Devanter. The Brandeis papers are housed at the University of Louisville Law Library. The collection is divided into ten topical series. Series II, *Supreme Court, 1907–1938*, contains material for Brandeis's years on the bench.

The decades-old debate about FDR, the New Deal, and the Supreme Court shows no signs of abating. Good entries include Jeff Shesol, *Supreme Power: Franklin Roosevelt vs. the Supreme Court* (New York: W. W. Norton, 2010); Peter Irons, *The New Deal Lawyers* (Princeton, N.J.: Princeton University Press, 1993); Joseph P. Lash, *Dealers and Dreamers: A New Look at the New Deal* (New York: Doubleday, 1988); William Lasser, Benjamin v. Cohen: *Architect of the New Deal* (New Haven, Conn.: Yale University Press, 2002); Marian McKenna, *Franklin Roosevelt and the Great Constitutional War* (New York: Fordham University Press, 2002); Stephen K. Shaw, William D. Pederson, and Frank J. Williams, eds., *Franklin D. Roosevelt and the Transformation of the Supreme Court* (Armonk, N.Y.: M. E. Sharpe, 2004); and Burt Solomon, *FDR v. the Constitution* (New York: Walker and Company, 2009).

Barry Cushman challenges the traditional view of the Four Horsemen as staunch advocates of laissez-faire constitutionalism in "The Secret Lives of the Four Horsemen," *Virginia Law Review* 83 (1997): 559–84. An early perspective on Justice Sutherland's jurisprudence is found in Harold M. Stephens, "Mr. Justice Sutherland," *American Bar Association Journal* 31 (1945): 446–53. For a sympathetic treatment of Sutherland's natural-rights jurisprudence, see Hadley Arkes, *The Return of George Sutherland: Restoring a Jurisprudence of Natural Rights* (Princeton, N.J.: Princeton University Press, 1994).

Traditional interpretations insist that external factors forced a sudden revolution in constitutional jurisprudence in 1937, while revisionist works argue that change was much more gradual and a product of internal forces. William E. Leuchtenburg's *The Supreme Court Reborn: The Constitutional Revolution in the Age of Roosevelt* (New York: Oxford University Press, 1995), defends the traditional emphasis. For a revisionist interpretation that highlights the 1934

Nebbia v. New York decision, see Barry Cushman, *Rethinking the New Deal Court: The Structure of a Constitutional Revolution* (New York: Oxford University Press, 1998). See also G. Edward White, *The Constitution and the New Deal* (Cambridge, Mass.: Harvard University Press, 2002). White's thesis is critiqued by David E. Kyvig, "Straight Ahead or Sharp Turn? The Court and the Constitution in 1937," *Reviews in American History* 29 (2001): 559–66. A forum in the *American Historical Review* neatly summarizes the historical debate over the Constitutional Revolution of 1937. See, especially, all in *American Historical Review* 110 (2005), Alan Brinkley, "The Debate over the Revolution of 1937: Introduction," 1046–51; Laura Kalman, "The Constitution, the Supreme Court, and the New Deal," 1052–79; William E. Leuchtenburg, "Comment on Laura Kalman's Article," 1081–93; and G. Edward White, "Constitutional Change and the New Deal: The Internalist/Externalist Debate," 1094–115.

The brief revitalization of the Contract Clause in the 1970s is examined in Bernard Schwartz, "Old Wine in Old Bottles? The Renaissance of the Contract Clause," *Supreme Court Review* 1979 (1979): 95–121. For the libertarian critique of *Blaisdell*, see Robert A. Levy and William Mellor, *The Dirty Dozen: How Twelve Supreme Court Cases Radically Expanded Government and Eroded Freedom* (New York: Penguin, 2008). Charles A. Bieneman criticizes the decision from an original-intent and textualist perspective in "Legal Interpretation and a Constitutional Case: *Home Building and Loan Association v. Blaisdell*," *Michigan Law Review* 90 (1992): 2534–64. See also Richard A. Epstein, "Toward a Revitalization of the Contract Clause," *University of Chicago Law Review* 51 (1984): 735–38.

For the recent subprime mortgage crisis of the Great Recession and the state and federal government response, see Christopher Rosenbleeth, "Legislative and Other Responses to the Subprime Crisis," *Real Estate Finance Journal*, Spring 2008, 1–5, and Edward V. Murphy, "Economic Analysis of a Mortgage Foreclosure Moratorium," *CRS Report for Congress*, September 12, 2008. Marcus Stanley, policy director of Americans for Financial Reform, takes a critical look at the Obama administration's mortgage-modification program in "Designed to Fail," *American Prospect*, June 2011, A10–A13. For an analysis of the roots of the subprime crisis from a critic of the Court's Contract Clause jurisprudence, see Richard A. Epstein, "Why Constitutions Matter: Examining the Legal Root of the Financial Crisis," *National Review*, May 4, 2009, 39. Economist David C. Wheelock, vice president of the St. Louis Federal Reserve Bank, looks back to the 1930s mortgage crisis for guidance on the subprime mortgage crisis in "The Federal Response to Home Mortgage Distress: Lessons from the Great Depression," *Federal Reserve Bank of St. Louis Review* 90 (May/June 2008): 133–48.

For Minnesota's handling of the subprime mortgage crisis, consult "2010

Foreclosures in Minnesota: A Report Based on County Sheriff's Sale Data," Minnesota Home Ownership Center (Minneapolis), February 9, 2011, and Jeff Crump, "Addressing the Housing Crisis in Minnesota: State Legislative Responses," in eds. Christopher Niedt and Marc Silver, *Forging a New Housing Policy: Opportunity in the Wake of Crisis* (Hempstead, N.Y.: National Center for Suburban Studies, Hofstra University, 2010).

INDEX

AAA. *See* Agricultural Adjustment
  Administration
ACLU. *See* American Civil Liberties
  Union
ACORN, 179
Adams v. Spillyards (1933), 93
"Adaptable Constitution, The" (*St.
  Paul Pioneer Press*), 145
Adkins v. Children's Hospital (1923), 44,
  164, 168
Agricultural Adjustment Act (1938),
  77–78
Agricultural Adjustment Act (1933),
  55, 77, 78, 80, 83, 163
Agricultural Adjustment
  Administration (AAA), 2, 58, 77,
  80, 83
Agricultural crisis, 8, 50, 85
Agricultural Marketing Act (1929), 51
Agricultural policy, 50, 77–78
*A. L. A. Schechter Poultry Corp. v.
  United States* (1935), 160
Albares, Mabel, 156
Allgeyer v. Louisiana (1897), 40
Allied Financial Inc., 186
Allied Structural Steel Co. v. Spannaus
  (1978), 172–173
Allison, Herbert, 184
Alston, Lee, 83
American Bar Association, 175
  Committee on American
    Citizenship, 154
American Civil Liberties Union
  (ACLU), 175, 177
American Prospect, 183

American Securitization Forum, 181
Americans for Financial Reform, 183
Anderson, Ellen, 181
Anti-Federalists, 19, 21, 24, 26
Antistatism, 119, 174
Arkansas Supreme Court, 93
Arnold, Thurman, 168
Article I, Section 8 (U.S.
  Constitution), 25
Article I, Section 10 (U.S.
  Constitution), 9, 10–11, 16, 19,
  24, 30, 133, 141
Articles of Confederation, 11, 15, 25

Bachmann, Michele, 8
Bailouts, 178, 183
Baldwin, Mathias, 103, 104, 105, 106,
  194
Bancroft, George, 140
Bank of America, 184, 185
Bank of North Dakota, 51
Bankers' Magazine, 155
Bankruptcy laws, 23, 25, 31
Barnitz v. Beverly (1896), 36, 93, 96,
  125
Barofsky, Neil, on HAMP, 184
Beard, Charles, 11–12, 140
Beck, James, on *Blaisdell*, 155
Bellamy, Edward, 56
Bill of Rights, 10, 19
Black, A. G., 52, 53
Black, Hugo, 169, 170
Black Monday, 151, 160
Blackmun, Harry, 171, 173
Blackstone, Sir William, 17

emergency powers, 45, 101, 171, 176
  distinguished from police powers,
  45
Emmer, Tom, 182
Employers' Liability Act, 110
*Energy Reserves Group v. Kansas Power
  and Light* (1983), 173
Epstein, Richard A., 6, 176
equal protection, 87, 124, 126, 135
Equal Protection Clause, 127–128, 130,
  181
  Contract Clause and, 39
  violation of, 102, 103
Equitable Life Insurance Company,
  66
Eriksson, Leonard, 94, 98–99
Ervin, William S., 94, 126, 144
Ex Parte Milligan (1866), 45, 130

Fannie Mae, 183, 185
Farm Bureau, 60
Farm Credit Administration, 1, 52, 64,
  65, 78, 79
farm crisis, 3, 4, 48, 84, 180
Farm Loan Act (1916), 50, 52
Farm Mortgage Moratorium Act
  (1935), 82, 161
Farm Mortgage Refinancing Act
  (1934), 81
Farm News Letter, 60
"Farm Strike Talk Revived"
  (*Minneapolis Tribune*), 79
Farmer-Labor Association, 57
Farmer-Labor Leader, 76, 146
Farmer-Labor Party (Minnesota),
  4–5, 47, 48, 55, 57, 59, 61, 73, 82,
  84
  agenda of, 85
  communists and, 63, 82
  Democratic Party and, 180
  Minnesota Mortgage Moratorium
  Act and, 144
Farmers' Holiday Association
  (National), 55–56, 58, 69, 77, 196
  anti-capitalistic rhetoric of, 85
  arbitration by, 63–64

communism and, 63
formation of, 55, 193
growth of, 4, 56–57
leadership of, 60, 64
moratoria and, 5, 68, 81
Non-Partisan League and, 57
power of, 80
strikes and, 59–60, 78–79, 194
success of, 61
waning of, 80–81
See also Minnesota Farmer's
  Holiday Association
Farmers' Holiday Movement, 57, 61,
  73
Farmers' National Committee for
  Action, 63
FDR v. The Constitution (Solomon), 121
Federal Farm Loan Act, 52
Federal Farm Loan Board, 50, 51
Federal Farm Mortgage Corporation,
  81
Federal Housing Administration
  (FHA), 182, 185
Federal land banks, 53, 65, 77
Federal Surplus Relief Corporation,
  79
Federal Trade Commission, 160
Federalist Paper No. 7 (Hamilton), 21
Federalist Paper No. 44 (Madison), 20,
  133
Federalist Party, 19
Federalist Society, 175, 176
Federalists, 19, 26, 30
  Constitution and, 23, 24
  Contract Clause and, 27
FHA. *See* Federal Housing
  Administration
Field, Stephen, 39
Fifth Amendment, 38, 150, 161
  due process and, 39, 168
  Takings Clause of, 10, 18, 170, 173,
  187
financial crisis, 14, 49, 101, 140, 141,
  178
First Amendment, 170
First Minneapolis Trust Company, 71